A-LEVEL
AND AS-LEVEL

LAW

Jacqueline Martin and Mary Charman

LONGMAN

© LONGMAN A-LEVEL AND AS-LEVEL REVISE GUIDES

Series editors:
Geoff Black and Stuart Wall

Titles available:
Accounting
Art and Design
Biology*
Business Studies
Chemistry*
Computer Science
Economics*
English
French
Geography*
German
Government and Politics
Law
Mathematics*
Modern History
Physics*
Psychology
Sociology*

*New Editions

Addison Wesley Longman Limited
Edinburgh Gate, Harlow,
Essex CM20 2JE, England
and Associated Companies throughout the world.

© Longman 1996

First published 1996

ISBN 0 582 28701 4 PPR

British Library Cataloguing-in-Publication Data
A catalogue record for this title is available from the British Library

Set in 10/12 pt Century Old Style by 34QQ

Printed in Great Britain by Henry Ling Ltd., at the Dorset Press,
Dorchester, Dorset

CONTENTS

EDITORS' PREFACE

Longman A-level Revise Guides, written by experienced examiners and teachers, aim to give you the best possible foundation for success in your course. Each book in the series encourages thorough study and a full understanding of the concepts involved, and is designed as a subject companion and study aid to be used throughout the course.

Many candidates at A-level fail to achieve the grades which their ability deserves, owing to such problems as the lack of a structured revision strategy, or unsound examination technique. This series aims to remedy such deficiencies, by encouraging a realistic and disciplined approach in preparing for and taking exams.

The largely self-contained nature of the chapters gives the book a flexibility which you can use to your advantage. After starting with the background to the A- and AS-level courses and with details of the syllabus coverage, you can read all other chapters selectively, in any order appropriate to the stage you have reached in your course.

Geoff Black and Stuart Wall

ACKNOWLEDGEMENTS

We are indebted to the following examination boards for permission to reproduce their questions.

Associated Examining Board
Northern Examinations and Assessment Board
University of Oxford Delegacy of Local Examinations
University of London Examinations and Assessment Council
Welsh Joint Education Committee

The answers given are not the only possible answers and are entirely our responsibility. We would like to thank our students for allowing us to use their answers. The law stated is as we believe it to be in January 1996.

EXAMINATION BOARDS

Associated Examining Board (AEB)
Stag Hill House
Guildford
Surrey GU2 5XJ

Northern Examinations and Assessment Board (NEAB)
Devas Street
Manchester M15 6EX

University of Oxford Delegacy of Local Examinations (UODLE)
Ewert House
Ewert Place
Summertown
Oxford OX2 7BZ

University of Cambridge Local Examinations Syndicate (UCLES)
Syndicate Buildings
1 Hills Road
Cambridge CB1 2EU

University of London Examinations and Assessment Council (ULEAC)
Stewart House
32 Russell Square
London WC1B 5DN

Welsh Joint Education Committee (WJEC)
245 Western Avenue
Cardiff CF5 2YX

THE SYLLABUSES AND EXAMINATIONS

GETTING STARTED

Who is this book for?

This revise guide is intended as a useful aid for students taking an examination course in Law at A-level or AS-level. The book offers a systematic review of the major topics covered by the various syllabuses and gives guidance on how to study law for examinations. There are a large number of real examination questions together with answers which vary in format. There are model answers provided by the authors, answers written by A-level students accompanied by an examiner's comments and some outline answers so that students can both compare their own essay plans with and practice writing a full essay from such outlines.

How should this book be used?

It is intended that you will find this guide useful throughout your course.

- From the start of the course it will help to identify key issues in each topic.
- Throughout the course it will be an aid in analysing and understanding each new area of law.
- At the end of the course it will provide a framework for revision notes and help you to understand what the examiners are looking for in response to questions.

ESSENTIAL PRINCIPLES

STUDYING LAW

Law has become an increasingly popular subject at A-level, both for 16–18 year olds and for adults returning to study. Many candidates find it both an interesting subject and a useful preparation for higher education, other training, professional qualifications or work.

One of the main objects in studying law is to promote logical thinking and the ability to apply the law to factual situations. This means that when studying a topic the first stage is to make sure that you understand the key concepts and principles: the next stage is to learn to apply the law and explain to the examiners how it will operate in a given situation. As well as applying the law, the approach at A-level requires you to develop an analytical and critical viewpoint of both the institutions in the legal system and the actual law itself.

An important point to remember is that law is developing all the time; it is not a static subject. This means that it is necessary to be aware of changes and keep up to date with developments. Some of the changes may be in response to public opinion and in such areas there will be much public debate so it is worthwhile reading a quality newspaper on a regular basis. There are also law journals and other publications which can help to keep you informed on both the main proposals for reform and important changes to the law. A list of suggested further reading material is given at the end of this chapter.

TOPICS AND SYLLABUSES

Law is a vast subject and the various A-level syllabuses obviously do not cover all areas, but concentrate on the more common sections of law and/or those which are likely to be of most interest and relevance to the average 16–18 year old. Although the syllabuses vary in their content, the first paper usually includes similar common elements of the English legal system. The examination boards then usually offer a choice of topics for the second section of the examination. It is important to be clear exactly which topics are included in the course you are following. Where necessary, copies of syllabuses can be obtained by writing to the relevant examination board.

This book covers all or some of the knowledge and skills necessary to follow the following syllabuses:

A-LEVEL	AS-LEVEL
AEB	AEB
NEAB	UODLE
UODLE	UCLES
ULEAC	ULEAC
WJEC	

The table in figure 1.1 shows which syllabuses offer which topics and gives the chapter number in this book where that topic can be found.

Although the topics are divided up into chapters for ease of study, it is important to realise that many topics may be linked together in an examination question. Some of the questions included at the end of various chapters have been chosen to illustrate this and to remind students of the need to refer to different topics.

METHODS OF ASSESSMENT

The main method of assessment is by examination at the end of a one or two year course, although there are moves to bring in some modular syllabuses. Coursework is not generally offered, the exception being ULEAC, where coursework can account for 20% of the assessment. Since examinations feature so prominently, it is sensible to be aware of the types of questions that may be asked.

TYPES OF QUESTION

Each board sets a variety of types of question which are designed to test different skills.

Essay questions

All boards set some essay questions as part of the method of assessment. These will require a thorough knowledge of the topic involved *and* the ability to use the material to answer the actual question. One of the commonest failings of examination candidates is that they tend to regard an essay question as the opportunity to write all they know on the given topic. This is not what the examiners are looking for; they want the candidate to select material and use it to make points which are pertinent to the particular question.

TOPIC	CHAPTER NUMBER	AEB A	AEB AS	NEAB A	UODLE A	UODLE AS	UCLES AS	ULEAC A	ULEAC AS	WJEC A
Jurisprudence	2	✓	✓					✓	✓	✓
Sources of law 1	3	✓	✓	✓	✓	✓	✓	✓	✓	✓
Sources of law 2	4	✓	✓	✓	✓	✓	✓	✓	✓	✓
Civil disputes	5	✓	✓	✓	✓	✓	✓	✓	✓	✓
Criminal cases	6	✓	✓	✓	✓	✓	✓	✓	✓	✓
Legal personnel	7	✓	✓	✓	✓	✓	✓	✓	✓	✓
Legal aid and advice	8	✓	✓	✓	✓	✓		✓		✓
Lay people in the legal system	9	✓	✓	✓	✓	✓	✓	✓	✓	✓
• General principles of criminal law	10	✓	✓	✓	✓		✓	✓	✓	
• Defences in criminal law	11	✓	✓	✓	✓		✓	✓	✓	
• Offences against the person	12	✓	✓	✓	✓		(✓)	✓	✓	
• Offences against property	13			✓	✓		(✓)	✓	✓	
Sentencing	14	✓	✓	✓	✓	✓	✓	✓	✓	✓
• Formation of a contract	15	✓	✓	✓	✓			✓	✓	
• Contents of a contract	16			✓	✓			✓	✓	
• Vitiating factors	17	✓	✓	✓	✓			✓	✓	
• The ending of a contract	18	✓	✓	✓	✓			✓	✓	
• General principles of tort	19	✓	✓	✓*	✓					
• Negligence and occupiers' liability	20	✓	✓	✓*	✓					
• Other torts	21	✓	✓	✓*	✓		(✓)			
• Consumer law	22	(✓)			(✓)			✓	✓	✓
• Employment law	23							✓	✓	✓
• Rights and freedoms	24						✓	✓	✓	✓

(✓) – syllabus involves only part of chapter
* – from 1997
• – OPTIONS – none of the boards requires all to be studied candidates choose options

Figure 1.1 Analysis of examination syllabuses by topic and chapter

Problem style questions

These are also set by all the boards. Such questions present candidates with a set of fictitious happenings and require them to apply their knowledge and understanding of the law to the given situation. An important aspect of answering such questions is to identify all the relevant points of law; there are no marks for bringing in totally irrelevant material.

Structured questions

These are used by some, but not all, of the boards. Such questions tend to be broken down into a series of components which may test different skills and/or different areas of knowledge. Usually the mark for each component is provided and this indicates the suitable length of the answer.

Stimulus and data response questions

These only feature in a few of the examinations. In these the candidates are presented with some source material and expected to use that material in answering the question or series of questions. However, the source material will not provide all the answers; candidates are also expected to draw on their own knowledge.

MARKING SCHEMES AND OBJECTIVES

Most examination boards publish marking schemes to previous years' questions. These can be obtained from the relevant board on the payment of a small sum and are useful in showing what type of material the examiners expect in an answer. In addition, most boards also publish a report on the previous years' examination, highlighting common mistakes and problems. These reports are automatically sent out to all centres which entered candidates in the previous year.

The examination boards also specify the skills which they are looking for by setting out assessment objectives at the front of any syllabus. These vary slightly from board to board but the overall pattern is that boards expect the following skills:

- **Knowledge and understanding** of legal rules, institutions, processes and methods.
- **Analysis** of problems.

- **Evaluation** of the rules and institutions.
- **Application** of legal rules to given situations.
- **The ability to communicate** relevant material effectively in a logical and structured way. Note that all examination boards also take into account the use of grammar, punctuation and spelling.

TIPS FOR REVISION

The assessment objectives set out above mean that candidates will have to learn and remember essential facts about both the institutions and the actual legal rules. So it is good policy to make sure that you make clear notes on each topic throughout the course. Since legal rules are applied and developed in cases, it is necessary to support answers with relevant case authority. This does involve learning a fair number of cases by heart and many candidates find this daunting and difficult. Here are three suggested strategies which may help:

- try learning essential cases at the end of each topic as you progress through the course; do not leave all the learning until the weeks just before the examination;
- keep a separate notebook for jotting down all the case names; group these cases under headings, e.g. 'contract-offers' or 'murder-duress'; note the essential point of law decided by the case and include a very brief note of the facts of the case;
- make up mnemonics to help remember a series of cases on one topic; by doing this you may find that remembering one case will act as a memory jerker for the other cases.

In the examination do not panic if you forget a few case names; you certainly do not need a perfect answer to pass and one missing case name will not prevent you from gaining an A grade.

FURTHER READING

There are some general textbooks which cover wide areas of the various A-level syllabuses. These are good starting points and the following are widely used:

- Denham, P 1994 *A Modern Introduction to Law*, London: Hodder and Stoughton.
- Hogan, B, P Seago and G Bennett 1992 *A level Law*, London: Butterworths.
- Dugdale, AM *et al* 1992 *A level Law*, London: Sweet and Maxwell.

Students should take care to use the most recent edition of these books. However, it is also sensible to read more widely, especially on the option papers, as the general textbooks are unlikely to cover every topic in enough depth. The examination boards provide reading lists, but remember that some of these books are aimed more at teachers than students, so that it is worthwhile consulting your tutor for specific titles.

Updating

For all textbooks it is important to use the most recent edition. In addition the following are suggested as useful in keeping up to date on legal changes:

- *Student Law Review*, published three times a year by Cavendish Publishing.
- *Law Update*, published annually by HLT Publications.

CHAPTER 2

JURISPRUDENCE

RULES

LAW AND MORALS

NATURAL LAW AND POSITIVISM

JUSTICE

GETTING STARTED

Jurisprudence is about the theory behind the making of the law. It examines various views of well-known writers and legal theorists, and poses questions, often not completely answered, on the philosophy of law.

The main themes of examination questions on this topic are:

- the purpose served by the law;
- rules and the formation of law;
- enforcement of law;
- the relationship with morality.

ESSENTIAL PRINCIPLES

RULES

Law in its most general sense is based on rules, and these are as old as mankind itself. Whenever people have lived together in any kind of community, there has been some kind of code of behaviour, although this would obviously not take the form of the law as we know it today. Such a code may be little more than an unspoken understanding that on the whole people do not kill others, take their possessions, etc. As society has become more developed and complex, rules have grown accordingly, and are found in most of our institutions. Consider, for example, how many rules, mostly unwritten, are obeyed when a person belongs to a school, takes part in a football match, goes to the cinema, etc.

❝So why have rules?❞

These rules provide a basic standard of behaviour to others, and broadly define the norm for the group. Within the larger framework of society, such rules help to prevent a state of anarchy, which would arise if everyone did whatever they wanted and there was total confusion and conflict.

RULES DEFINED

❝Broad definition❞

Twining and Miers define rules as 'a general norm mandating or guiding conduct'. This broad definition includes precepts, such as the 'respect for sanctity of human life' which arose in the case of *Airedale NHS Trust v Bland (1993),* a difficult case where judges had to decide whether treatment of Tony Bland should cease. It would also include conventions, which are less rigid than our normal concept of laws, and include, for instance, the monarch's agreement to Bills which have passed through the House of Commons and House of Lords.

❝Distinction between rules and practices❞

On the other hand, Professor Hart argues that rules should be distinguished from mere habits and practices. There should be some sense of obligation attached to rules, as opposed to something which arises out of routine or convenience.

❝Why obey?❞

Such rules may change from time to time, and only operate because there is general agreement to them. That is not to say that everybody considers them to be ideal, but that the broad consensus of opinion is that they are reasonable given the circumstances. People obey rules generally for a variety of reasons:

- out of a sense of moral obligation (more about morality later);
- because they see that the rule is reasonable;
- because of a penalty of some kind which may be imposed for not obeying.

Some rules are negative in nature and some are positive, but many could be expressed in either form. For example, a notice in a library could state that reference books *must* be kept within the reference room, creating a positive duty. Another notice may state that reference books *must not* be taken out of the reference room, which is a prohibition. These would clearly amount to the same thing in practice.

LAW AND MORALS

Some rules form the law of a country merely to enable things to run smoothly, and are largely administrative in nature, such as the requirement to tax a motor vehicle. This does not involve moral judgements, it is simply a matter of raising money to pay for such things as building and maintaining roads. However, we have seen that some rules arise out of a sense of moral duty, and many of these rules also form the laws of a country.

❝Law and religion❞

Many laws are directly in line with the religious ideas prevalent in that country, e.g. the law relating to murder and theft, and these will be broadly similar whether based on, for example, the Christian principles of the Bible or the Muslim principles of the Koran. Most people would be in agreement on the moral wrong of many of these major crimes, but with other less fundamental issues there may be some conflict, particularly from country to country, as to what really is right or wrong. Examples include the law relating to marriage and divorce, consumer protection and drinking alcohol. Clearly there is a lot of overlap between morality and legal rules, but they do not always coincide completely. Some things may be considered to be morally wrong, such as lying, or not keeping a promise, when there may be no legal wrong involved. On the other hand, the law may be greatly concerned with morality, as was seen in the *Bland* case (above), and in legislation concerning issues such as abortion or the scientific use of a foetus.

❝Law as a reflection of society❞

Where society's views on a subject like this changes over a period of time, then the law should eventually change to reflect those views. Examples include the law relating to homosexuality and to Sunday trading. The Abortion Act 1967, now modified by the Human

Fertilisation and Embryology Act 1990, is a result of the law changing to reflect changes in moral views of society. However, there is not always a direct correlation between the number of people who subscribe to a view and the law on that particular matter. There have been, at some times, according to poll surveys, a slight majority of the population in favour of the death sentence in certain circumstances. However, here the law has taken a paternalistic approach, actually leading society's views. The law in such circumstances can only go so far, because if it oversteps a certain boundary anarchy would result.

SO, WHICH RULES FORM THE LAW?

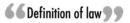 **Definition of law**

The rules which form the law are generally the most formal rules. They are normally written in statutes (Acts of Parliament) or in case judgments. Sir John Salmond defined law as 'the body of principles recognised and applied by the state in the administration of justice'. This encompasses the mass of law created by statute, through Parliament, and also the law either decided by judges or interpreted by them. It covers wide areas of law, from dealing with behaviour thought to be outside acceptable boundaries, i.e. crime, to settling of disputes between individuals. It also deals with relationships, e.g. in marriage, ownership of property, commerce and employment, and many other aspects of life. This inevitably involves a degree of paternalism, or the laying down of laws by some for the general good of society or of groups within it.

NATURAL LAW AND POSITIVISM

Natural law is based on the coincidence of law and morality. It looks for its justification from some divine source and is concerned with what ought to be taking place. Some believers of this principle, such as St Thomas Aquinas, would even suggest that there could be occasions when breaking the law would be justified, if the law did not coincide with morality.

On the other hand, positivists believe that if law is made through the correct procedures, then it **is** the law to be obeyed, even if it is not liked. It is up to the individual whether to obey or not, and to consider the consequences of disobedience.

 **Some leading views**

Many leading jurists have put forward in their writings views on how law is formulated. A few will be discussed, but others should be read and considered.

- **Jeremy Bentham** went further than this on the conflicting roles of law and religion, but in a different direction, away from natural law. He felt that law which conflicted with divine law was not law at all or at least need not be obeyed. His theory was a utility theory, in that he said that the law should be rational and codified. He felt that the role of the judge should be inquisitorial, rather than forming the law.

- **Professor H L A Hart** continued this theme by separating morals and law as two distinct concepts. He felt that a legal system should be based on logical ideas, producing 'correct' decisions from rules.

- **Hans Kelsen** followed a scientific approach to the theory of law. He felt that law was the 'norm' of the human conduct, and that force should be used to make people conform to it.

- **Emile Durkheim** felt society to be held together by social structures, with law as an integral part of the structure.

- **Karl Marx** viewed law as oppressive and an expression of the domination of one class by another. It was a product of a capitalist society.

- **Max Weber** was a positivist who saw law as an imposition of some kind of order from leaders of the country, with defined consequences for those who chose to disobey.

- **Professor L L Fuller** is a modern follower of the natural law school. In his work *The Morality of Law* he talks of an 'inner morality' with various features. This has led to the Hart–Fuller debate on morality, Hart following positivist view, Fuller following natural law theories.

- **Lord Devlin** follows the Fuller line, stating that the law is based on morality and to some extent religion.

- **John Stuart Mill** wrote in his *Essay on Liberty* of the 'harm principle' as the only valid reason for interfering with freedom. His view was that what was good for someone should not form the basis of law. The only reason for interfering with a person's liberty is to prevent harm to others. Of course 'harm' can be interpreted widely. The Wolfenden Committee followed this theme in 1957, with the view that there is an area of private morality which is not the concern of the law. This resulted in the recommendation that homosexuality between consenting adult males in private should not longer be an offence, but that activities in public, which may affect others, such as soliciting and running a brothel, ought to be illegal.

■ **Stephen J** criticised Mill in that it could be very difficult to divide acts which harmed only an individual from acts which harmed others. He advocated that the 'grosser forms of vice' should be punishable in their own right. This is in line with Lord Devlin's view that the law should tolerate what the reasonable man would tolerate, and ban what would disgust the reasonable man.

It is argued that however much Parliament rules along the lines of clinically formulated principles, neither they nor the judges can avoid having to make decisions which involve moral judgments. The question to be considered is whether morality does largely form the law, and whether it should do so.

Examples of legal debates very much centred on morality include:

66 Examples of judgements concerning morality 99

■ the Wolfenden Committee Report of 1957 on homosexual offences, and the case of *R v Brown (1992)*;

■ *Shaw v DPP (1961)*, the famous ladies' directory case involving advertisement of prostitution and the alleged conspiracy 'to corrupt public morals';

■ *R v R (a husband) (1991)* involving rape within marriage;

■ The *Bland* case (above) and *Re J (a minor)(medical treatment) (1992)* concerning the discontinuing of life support equipment;

■ *Gillick v West Norfolk and Wisbech AHA (1985)* and *Re J (a minor)(inherent jurisdiction: consent to treatment)(1992)* regarding the need for parental consent for treatment.

JUSTICE

The main purpose of a modern system of law, then, is to create an orderly society, and to provide a remedy for a person who has suffered a wrong. This is the aim of justice in society. Justice should be seen in all aspects of society, but is most closely linked with the law. This is clearly seen in the model of the 'scales of justice' on the top of the Old Bailey (the Central Criminal Court in London). The whole question of the process of law, including a trial in court, the procedure before and during it, and the consequences, must be seen to be fair. Recently there have been a number of examples of difficulties in this area, some of the most notorious being the Guildford Four and the Birmingham Six.

THE RULE OF LAW

66 No-one is above the law 99

The concept known as the 'rule of law' is that no-one is above the law, not even the government itself, ministers or public bodies. Remember the saying, 'be you ever so high, the law is above you'. This is in accordance with the principles of justice outlined above. Dicey in the nineteenth century stressed the 'absolute supremacy of regular law', with all classes of persons being equal before the law. In some ways the law acts to ensure this equality, e.g. by protecting certain vulnerable groups through legislation, such as the Sex Discrimination Act 1975 and the Race Relations Act 1976. On the other hand, it may not be possible to ensure total equality, and the law actually gives some people special status for the purposes of enforcement, e.g. the police.

66 Equality before the law 99

Where there is a written constitution, such as in the USA, this supremacy of law can be seen very clearly, but even without one there is control over such bodies, in the form of scrutiny by the courts. This has been increasingly true since the European Convention on Human Rights. Not even a government body can act in a totally arbitrary way, but must be consistent, although the main body of government has more freedom than other agencies. If, however, a minister or local authority acts outside its powers it is subject to judicial review, and can be declared to be acting *ultra vires*, or beyond its powers, the action being declared void.

66 Ultra vires 99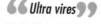

A consequence of the rule of law is a set of safeguards against such things as the power to arrest and detain a person. Police need to function to protect society, but must be subject to limits, so that individual liberty is in turn protected. Powers given to a person or body of people, then, must be subject to a system of checks and limitations. The possible consequences of acting above the law were identified as:

■ an excess of power;

■ acting unlawfully;

■ acting beyond jurisdiction.

in the case of *Anisminic v Foreign Compensation Commission (1969)*.

An example of a limitation being *implied* into a given power is found in the case of *Congreve v Home Office (1976)* where the Home Secretary was given power to revoke licences but not allowed to use this power except for 'good cause'. He was not therefore allowed to revoke the licences of those who had bought them early to avoid an increased fee.

NATURAL JUSTICE

In order to bring about the general aim of justice, or basic fairness, two main rules have been developed:

- *nemo judex in res sua* – no-one should judge his own cause;
- *audi alteram partem* – there is a right to be heard for both sides

"The rule against bias"

The first rule against bias prevents a person with an interest in the subject matter being involved in a decision making process regarding it. It was said in *R v Sussex Justices, ex parte McCarthy (1924)* that 'justice should not only be done, but should … be seen to be done'.

"The right to a fair hearing"

The second rule of a right to a fair hearing is illustrated in the case of *Ridge v Baldwin (1964)* where it was held that a police officer should be given an opportunity to present his defence before being dismissed.

See further on this the following cases:

- *Council of Civil Service Unions v Minister for the Civil Service (1985)* – the GCHQ case, where a ban was placed on the joining of unions. It was said that a requirement of natural justice was 'a duty to act fairly'.
- *R v Secretary of State for the Home Department, ex parte Khan (1985)* concerning the discretion of the Secretary of State over the adoption of a child from Pakistan.
- *R v Lord Chancellor, ex parte The Law Society (1993)* about a challenge to the legal aid provisions.
- *Bromley v Greater London Council (1983)* regarding the levying of extra rates to cover the provision of low cost transport in the borough.

EXAMINATION QUESTIONS

1 What is the relationship between law and morality? (ULEAC)
2 Consider whether societies could exist without law. (ULEAC)
3 a) Explain and illustrate the distinction between legal and moral rules. (*10 marks*)
   b) Consider how far moral rules influence the development of legal rules. (*15 marks*)
        (AEB)
4 What is the Rule of Law? What role does it play in the criminal justice system? (WJEC)

ANSWERS TO QUESTIONS

OUTLINE ANSWERS TO SELECTED QUESTIONS

Question 1

Introduce the idea of rules forming the law and discuss the meaning of morality.

- Discuss whether the law should be based on morals, or whether morals should form the law.
- Look at the various views of morality and law from jurists.
- Discuss the principles of justice and the rules of natural justice.

Question 3

a) Explain that rules are very old, probably as old as society, not necessarily written down, but merely carried out as a moral code. Develop the theme of rules forming a framework of behaviour to prevent anarchy.

- Define rules; you can use the definition by Twining and Miers.
- Distinguish rules from habits and practices (Professor Hart's theory).
- Examine why people obey rules.

This leads into the second part of the question.

b) Some obedience to rules comes merely from the fact that they are part of the law and therefore there is a penalty for disobedience. In other cases people obey the law because it has been developed from morals and therefore it is seen as just.

- Law often stems from religion, which is based largely on moral values. Give examples.
- Law generally reflects society's views and these are largely moral judgements. Again, give examples.
- Law is sometimes paternalistic, in that parliament will make a moral judgement as to what is good for the rest of society in creating a statute.

However, law does not always fit morals exactly.

- There will not normally be a total agreement among the population as to what is morally just, or among politicians, so the law will reflect the moral codes of some people but not others.
- Where the law concerns administrative procedures morals may not be involved to a great extent, e.g. in the payment of television licences.
- Consider briefly some of the natural law and positivist theories on breaking the law.

STUDENT'S ANSWER WITH TUTOR'S COMMENTS

Question 4

66 Good introduction 99

The rule of law means that everyone is equal before the law. Even people in authority and the people who rule the country have to obey the law on the whole, e.g. some members of the royal family have been prosecuted for speeding. This is fair, because why should they do something that is dangerous which the rest of society cannot do and which might harm the people that they rule? The rule of law comes from the saying 'be you ever so high, the law is above you'.

66 Does not come from the saying, but is in accordance with it 99

Some law is not quite as equal as others, e.g. a barrister cannot be sued in court and a policeman has powers to catch criminals that we do not have, so everyone is not quite as equal as it seems. But the majority of people have equal status, and those that have special powers are like that on the whole to protect others.

Some laws are made just to protect other people and make sure that they are equal. For example the law of minors' contracts are to protect minors who might be treated unfairly by adults. The Race Discrimination Act tries to stop people being prejudiced against people of other races. It cannot do this completely but at least it can try to stop them being openly prejudiced in public. The Sex Discrimination Act is the same in stopping people discriminating against people just because they are men or women.

66 Good – some examples 99

In European law there is a lot more protection, so that it is part of English law now, e.g. people who do the same work must get the same pay.

If the government and local authorities are unfair to people they can be sometimes taken to court under judicial review. If they have acted outside their powers they will be declared ultra vires. Then what they are doing is stopped. An example is *Congreve v Home Office*. In this case the Home Secretary tried to stop people getting new television licences just to save money but he was not allowed to do this because he was not supposed to do that, so he was acting outside his powers, so it was *ultra vires*.

66 Explains *ultra vires* 99

Natural justice supports the rule of law. This is where there are two rules. Both sides must get a fair hearing, so a person cannot be sentenced without getting a chance to tell his side of the story. The other rule is that no one should judge his own cause, so a case should be heard in an unbiased way. In *Ridge v Baldwin* it was unfair and against natural justice because a policeman was sacked without being able to tell his side of the story.

66 Rather an abrupt ending 99

So people all have to act fairly, whoever they are. Nobody is above the law and everybody is supposed at least to be equally protected by the law.

Tutor's Comments

The answer covers the basic concepts quite well, but is a little brief. It would be much better if more examples were included from cases (see the examples in the chapter). It also needs a slightly fuller and more substantial conclusion to avoid the rather abrupt ending. The answer would just about reach grade C.

CHAPTER 3

SOURCES OF LAW I

GETTING STARTED

Sources of law refers to where the law comes from and how it is made. These are important topics on all syllabuses and it is necessary to have a clear understanding of each and their interrelationship. An understanding of sources of law will also help students with other areas of the syllabus, as law is constantly changing through different processes outlined in this chapter and the next chapter. In the early years of legal history key sources of law were custom and the decisions of judges; judicial precedent has remained a major factor in our sources of law but today other sources such as statute law, delegated legislation and European law have also become important. This chapter concentrates on judicial law making in all its aspects, that is in accepting customs as part of the law, using past cases to decide new cases and developing new principles of law.

The most important topic in this chapter is judicial precedent and within judicial precedent there are several concepts to grasp, the main ones being:

- the hierarchy of the courts;
- *ratio decidendi* and *obiter dicta*;
- binding and persuasive precedent.

Knowledge of these is essential but students must be aware that questions will require them to use that knowledge; simply reciting facts is not sufficient. Another point to remember is that, since precedent is the reliance on decisions in past cases, answers should contain references to cases when explaining points. An understanding of judicial precedent will also help students to understand how the substantive law in a particular field has developed.

ESSENTIAL PRINCIPLES

COMMON LAW

The basis of English law is unwritten. It was developed by the judges over the centuries and, historically, customs are believed to have been very important in forming the basis of English law. In the seventeenth century Lord Justice Coke described custom as 'one of the main triangles of the laws of England'. Customs have long since ceased to be of any major significance in forming new law. However, the common law is still developing today through decisions of the judges in cases.

The phrase 'common law' has more than one meaning:

1   When referring to it as a source it is used to describe the law which was developed by judges from general customs during the centuries immediately after the Norman Conquest and which has continued to be developed by the judges since.

2   It is also used to distinguish laws which have never been enacted by Parliament. So today we can speak of murder as a common law crime, since murder has never been defined in an Act of Parliament. This contrasts with the statutory law of theft which is set out in the Theft Act 1968.

3   It is used to distinguish between rules that were developed by the common law courts and the rules of equity which were developed by the Chancery courts.

JUDICIAL PRECEDENT

The decisions of the judges create law for future judges to follow. The English system of precedent is based on the Latin maxim *stare decisis et non quieta movere* which loosely translated means 'stand by what has been decided and do not unsettle the established'. This maxim upholds the idea of fairness and provides certainty in the law. In England and Wales our courts operate a very rigid doctrine of judicial precedent so that:

■ every court is bound to follow any decision made by a court above it in the hierarchy; and

■ appellate courts are in general bound by their own past decisions.

Precedent looks at the judgment given by the court at the end of the case in order to discover the legal reason for the decision. This legal reason or principle of law is the *ratio decidendi* of the case and it is this that forms a precedent for the future. The remainder of the judgment is known as *obiter dicta* or 'other things said'. It is not always easy to pinpoint the *ratio decidendi* in a judgment.

BINDING PRECEDENT

This is a precedent which must be followed by a court even if the judge in the later case does not agree with the legal principle. However, a decision is only a binding precedent if it was decided by a court which binds the court hearing the later case and the facts of the second case are sufficiently similar to the original case.

PERSUASIVE PRECEDENT

This is not binding on any court but the court may be persuaded to follow it. Persuasive precedent comes from a number of sources including:

■ decisions of the Judicial Committee of the Privy Council;

■ decisions of courts in other countries, especially Commonwealth countries such as Canada and Australia;

■ *obiter dicta*, particularly where the comment was made in a House of Lords decision.

THE HIERARCHY OF THE COURTS

The European Court of Justice

Since 1973 the highest court affecting our legal system is the European Court of Justice and a decision made by this court is binding on all other courts. The European Court is not bound by its own past decisions.

The House of Lords

Next in the hierarchy is the House of Lords and its decisions bind all other courts in the English legal system. The debate about the House of Lords is the extent to which it should follow its own past decisions. The critical date in this argument is 1966 as before then the House of Lords held that it was bound by its own past decisions *(London Street Tramways v London County Council (1898))*.

"1966 Practice Statement"

In 1966 the Lord Chancellor issued a Practice Statement announcing a change to this rule. The Practice Statement said:

> 'Their Lordships regard the use of precedent as an indispensable foundation upon which to decide what is the law and its application to individual cases. It provides at least some degree of certainty upon which individuals can rely in the conduct of their affairs, as well as a basis for orderly development of legal rules. Their Lordships nevertheless recognise that the rigid adherence to precedent may lead to injustice in a particular case and also unduly restrict the proper development of the law. They, therefore, propose to modify their present practice and while treating former decisions of this House as normally binding, to depart from a previous decision when it appears right to do so...'

This Practice Statement therefore allows the House of Lords to change the law in later cases if they believe that the earlier case was wrongly decided. However, the House of Lords has been reluctant to use this power since many judges feel that certainty in the law is essential.

"Use of the Practice Direction"

The first case in which it was used was *Conway v Rimmer (1968),* but this only involved a technical point on discovery of documents. The first major use did not occur until 1972 in *British Railways Board v Herrington* which involved the law on the duty of care owed to a child trespasser. *In Miliangos v George Frank (Textiles) Ltd (1976)* the House of Lords used the Practice Statement to overrule a previous judgment that damages could only be awarded in sterling. More recently in *Murphy v Brentwood District Council (1990)* the House of Lords overruled the decision in *Anns v Merton London Borough (1978).*

The Practice Statement stressed that criminal law needs to be certain so it was not surprising that the House of Lords did not rush to overrule any judgments in criminal cases. The first use in a criminal case was in *R v Shivpuri (1986)* which overruled the decision in *Anderton v Ryan (1985)* on attempts to do the impossible.

The Court of Appeal

The next court down in the hierarchy is the Court of Appeal; this has two divisions, Civil and Criminal, and the rules for precedent are not quite the same in these two divisions.

1   The first rule is that both divisions of the Court of Appeal are bound by decisions of the European Court of Justice and the House of Lords. This is true even though there have been attempts in the past to argue that the Court of Appeal should not be bound by the House of Lords. Lord Denning refused to follow earlier House of Lords' decisions in *Broome v Cassell & Co. Ltd (1971)* and again in the cases of *Schorsch Meier GmbH v Henning (1975)* and *Miliangos v George Frank (Textiles) Ltd (1976).* The House of Lords pointed out that the Court of Appeal had no right to ignore or overrule decisions of the House of Lords. The main argument in favour of the Court of Appeal being able to ignore House of Lords' decisions is that very few cases reach the House of Lords so that if there is an error in the law it may take years before a suitable case is appealed all the way to the House of Lords.

"The rule in Young's case"

2   The second rule is that the Court of Appeal is bound by its own previous decisions with some small exceptions. This rule comes from the case of *Young v Bristol Aeroplane Co. Ltd (1944)* and the only exceptions allowed by that case are:

   ■ where there are conflicting decisions in past Court of Appeal cases, the court can choose which one it will follow and which it will reject;

   ■ where there is a decision of the House of Lords which effectively overrules a Court of Appeal decision the Court of Appeal must follow the the decision of the House of Lords;

   ■ where the decision was made *per incuriam,* that is carelessly or by mistake.

The Criminal Division can also refuse to follow a past decision of its own if the law has been 'misapplied or misunderstood'. This extra exception arises because in criminal cases people's liberty is involved.

The Civil Division of the Court of Appeal under Lord Denning tried to challenge the rule in *Young's* case claiming that as they had made the earlier decision they could change it. As Lord Denning said: 'It was a self-imposed limitation and we who imposed it can also remove it.' However, in *Davis v Johnson (1976)* when the Court of Appeal refused to follow a decision made only days earlier regarding the interpretation of the Domestic Violence Act 1976, the case went to the House of Lords on appeal. There the Law Lords ruled that the Court of Appeal had to follow its own previous decisions and said that they 'expressly, unequivocally and unanimously reaffirmed the rule in *Young v Bristol Aeroplane*'.

Divisional Courts

The three divisional courts (Queen's Bench, Chancery and Family) are bound by decisions of the European Court of Justice, the House of Lords and the Court of Appeal. In addition the divisional courts are bound by their own past decisions, although they operate similar exceptions to those in the Court of Appeal.

The High Court

This is bound by decisions of all the courts above and in turn it binds the lower courts. High Court judges do not have to follow each others' decisions but will usually do so.

DISTINGUISHING

This is a device which can be used by any court to avoid following a past decision which would otherwise be binding. It means that the judge finds that the material facts of the case he is deciding are sufficiently different for him to draw a distinction between the present case and the previous precedent. He is not then bound by the previous case. Two cases demonstrating this process are *Balfour v Balfour (1919)* and *Merritt v Merritt (1971)*. Both cases involved wives claiming against their husbands for breach of contract. In the earlier case it was decided that the claim could not succeed because there was no intention to create legal relations; it was merely a domestic arrangement between a husband and wife. The second case was successful because the court held that the facts of the two cases were sufficiently different in that although the parties were married they were separated when they made the agreement and it was made in writing. It was not just a domestic arrangement but meant as a legally enforceable contract.

OVERRULING

This is where a court in a later case states that the legal rule decided in an earlier case is wrong. Overruling can only occur:

- when a higher court overrules a decision made by a lower court; or
- when the European Court of Justice overrules a past decision it has made; or
- when the House of Lords uses its power under the Practice Statement to overrule a past decision of its own.

REVERSING

This is where a court higher up in the hierarchy overturns the decision of a lower court on appeal in the same case.

THE ROLE OF PRECEDENT IN LAW MAKING

Judges have used precedent to create new law and to extend old principles. In the law of negligence most of the development has been as a result of judicial decisions, starting with *Donoghue v Stevenson (1932)* and continuing with cases on liability for nervous shock (*McLoughlin v O'Brian (1982), Alcock v Chief Constable of South Yorkshire Police (1991)*) and cases on liability for economic loss (*Hedley Byrne & Co Ltd v Heller and Partners Ltd (1964), Caparo Industries plc v Dickman (1990)*). In the criminal law the judges have effectively created new crimes as in *Shaw v DPP (1962)* creating an offence of conspiracy to corrupt public morals and *R v R (1991)* deciding that a husband could be guilty of raping his wife.

However, precedent is subordinate to statute law, delegated legislation and European regulations, so that case decisions cease to have effect if there is another law on the point.

ADVANTAGES AND DISADVANTAGES OF PRECEDENT

The advantages are:

- **certainty** – following past decisions allows people to know what the law is and how it is likely to be applied in their case; it also means that lawyers can advise clients;
- **consistency and fairness** – it is seen as just and fair that similar cases should be decided in a similar way;

- **precision** – since each principle of law is set out in an actual case the law becomes very precise;
- **flexibility** – there is room for the law to change with the use of the Practice Statement and distinguishing.

The disadvantages are:

- **rigidity** – because lower courts have to follow decisions of higher courts and the Court of Appeal has to follow its own past decisions the law can be too inflexible and bad decisions made in the past may be perpetuated;
- **complexity** – since there are nearly half a million reported cases it is not easy to find all the relevant case law even with computerised data bases; further, the judgments are often very long and it is difficult to extract the *ratio decidendi*;
- **illogical distinctions** – the use of distinguishing to avoid past decisions can lead to 'hair-splitting' and some areas of the law have become very complex;
- **slowness of growth** – it is necessary to wait for suitable cases to come before the courts in order to have a decision on areas of the law that are known to be in need of reform.

EQUITY

THE HISTORICAL DEVELOPMENT

The early common law became very rigid, particularly after the Provisions of Oxford 1258 restricted the issue of writs for new types of action. People who could not obtain justice in the common law courts appealed directly to the King for him to intervene and grant them their rights. Most of these cases were referred to the King's Chancellor, who became known as the keeper of the King's conscience. The Chancellor based his decisions on principles of natural justice and fairness, rather than on the strict following of previous precedents. Eventually a Court of Chancery came into being under the control of the Chancellor which operated these rules of fairness or equity. Equity was not a complete system of law; it merely filled the gaps in the common law.

CONFLICT BETWEEN EQUITY AND COMMON LAW

This overlapping of the two systems led to conflict. The common law courts would make an order in favour of one party and the Court of Chancery an order in favour of the other party. This conflict was finally resolved in the *Earl of Oxford's case (1616)* when the King ruled that equity should prevail. This rule was subsequently enacted in the Judicature Act 1873 s. 25.

PROBLEMS

1   Equity was initially very uncertain as each successive Chancellor had his own ideas of fairness and justice. This caused John Seldon, a seventeenth-century jurist, to say that equity varied with the length of the Chancellor's foot.

2   Litigants who wanted both an equitable remedy and the common law remedy of damages were obliged to take to separate actions.

3   By the nineteenth century the Chancery courts had become rigid in their approach to cases and also slow.

THE JUDICATURE ACTS

In 1873 and 1875 the court structure was completely reformed with the common law courts and the court of Chancery being merged into one single system. However, equitable principles were still clearly recognised as being distinct from common law rules since the Judicature Act 1873 s. 25 stated: 'where there is any conflict or variance between the rules of equity and the common law … the rules of equity shall prevail.' The key point was that all courts could now use equitable rules where suitable and all courts could grant both common law and equitable remedies.

EQUITABLE MAXIMS

Many of the rules on which equity is based are expressed in a series of sayings. The most important of these maxims are:

- **equity looks to the intention and not the form** – *Berry v Berry (1929)* where a deed was held to have been altered by a simple contract;

- **equity will not suffer a wrong to be without a remedy** – this allows equity to create new remedies such as Anton Pillar orders and Mareva injunctions;
- **he who comes to equity must come with clean hands** – an equitable remedy will not be granted to a plaintiff who has not acted fairly;
- **delay defeats equity** – *Leaf v International Galleries (1950).*

EQUITABLE REMEDIES

These are discretionary, the court does not have to grant them even if the plaintiff wins the case. The most important remedies are:

- **injunctions –** court orders to do or refrain from doing something;
- **specific performance** – an order that a contract should be carried out as agreed;
- **rescission** – where the parties are returned as far as possible to their precontractual position;
- **rectification** – where the court will order that a document be altered to reflect the parties' intention.

THE RELEVANCE OF EQUITY TODAY

Equitable rights, interests and remedies remain important in the law today. Concepts such as mortgages and trusts are founded on the idea that one person can own a legal interest in property while another owns the equitable interest. Equitable remedies are still important and used in a variety of circumstances, ranging from injunctions in cases of domestic violence and trespass to rectification in contract cases. The courts are prepared to expand these remedies though the principle that they are discretionary still remains. New areas of law have been developed and are still developing, such as equitable estoppel.

EXAMINATION QUESTIONS

1   'Precedent is an excuse for a judge to follow unthinkingly and mechanically what previous judges in a different social climate have decided.'
Is this necessarily true?   (UODLE)

2   The doctrine of precedent depends on three things: the hierarchy of the courts, the written records of cases and the approach of the judges. Discuss the relative importance of these three things.   (NEAB)

3   'It is not open to the Court of Appeal to give gratuitous advice to judges of first instance to ignore decisions of the House of Lords.' (Lord Hailsham in *Cassell v Broome (1972)*)
Discuss the system of judicial precedent in the light of this quotation.   (UODLE)

4   'The contribution of Equity to the development of English Law was of the utmost importance but it was exhausted a very long time ago.' Examine the validity of this statement.
                                                                                  (AEB)

5   To what extent have the principles of common law and equity merged during the course of the twentieth century?   (WJEC)

ANSWERS TO QUESTIONS

STUDENT'S ANSWER WITH TUTOR'S COMMENTS

Question 1

> Centuries ago when the English legal system was being evolved into how we know it today the doctrine of precedent came about. It involved King Henry II's own judges going about the country and discovering the popular or common law. As time went by it

❝This introduction is too long and too general❞

became inevitable that judges would look back to earlier cases and make their decisions accordingly. This means that an individual can be certain of the law in the conduct of their daily lives because one could not do anything without that certainty.

Stare decisis is a Latin phrase meaning stand by the decision and is the basic principle of justice. It is fair because in similar cases similar decisions are made. The formal structure of binding authority which exists today required two foundations, one a clear hierarchy of the courts – from the House of Lords down and two, good law reports. The legal system was reformed in the Judicature Acts of 1873 and 1875 into what we have today.

The basic doctrine is that the binding nature of a decision works down the court system, i.e. every court is bound to follow the decision of the court above and appellate courts are in general bound by their own past decisions. At the end of each case the judge makes a speech called a judgment which consists of two parts, one the *ratio decidendi* which means the reason for deciding and two, the *obiter dicta* which means other things said. *Ratio decidendi* sets the precedent on a principle of law. *Obiter dicta* is not binding precedent, it is simply other things said, but might be persuasive precedent where a judge has put a hypothetical case and explained what the law might be in that situation.

❝A reasonable summary but not linking it to the question❞

This can be explained by the case of *R v Howe* where the House of Lords ruled that duress was not available as a defence to murder. This was the *ratio* of the case. However the House of Lords also said that duress would not be available as defence to a charge of attempted murder. This was an *obiter* statement. Then in *R v Gotts* where the charge was attempted murder, the Court of Appeal looked at the *obiter dicta* of the House of Lords in *R v Howe* and decided to follow it.

There are many instances where the judges create the the law. One such case was *Donoghue v Stevenson (1932)* where the plaintiff was drinking a bottle of ginger beer and found a decomposing snail in it. She sued the manufacturer claiming negligence and it was held that she was owed a duty of care and awarded damages. The principles of negligence were all made by judges over the years since then. In *Donoghue v Stevenson* the judges were not following earlier cases but thinking about and developing the law.

❝Good use of a case to illustrate a point directly aimed at the question❞

In 1966 the then Lord Chancellor issued the Practice Statement which allowed the House of Lords to change the law and not follow its own past decisions (pre 1966 it had to) where it appears right to do so. They were reluctant to use the facility to start with but now show more willingness to use it. The first time it was used was in *BR v Herrington* where Herrington, a small boy, got through a gap in the fence and fell on to the live rail of the railway and was badly burnt. It was held that a duty of care was owed to child trespassers. This changed the ruling from an earlier case in 1929 when it was held there was no duty of care in such cases. This change in the law probably reflects society's changing attitude towards protecting children.

❝Good use of material❞

The Practice Statement does allow flexibility and the case of Herrington shows that judges do not always follow 'unthinkingly and mechanically' earlier cases. However only the House of Lords can use the Practice Statement and it could be argued that because the lower courts have to follow binding precedents the judges there are following 'unthinkingly and mechanically'.

This would be true if it were not for another rule of precedent called distinguishing. This allows a judge to refuse to follow a previous decision on the basis that the facts in the present case are not sufficiently similar to the earlier case. Some judges will use distinguishing as a device to avoid following past decisions with which they do not agree.

❝Could use case examples to illustrate this point❞

This means that judges do not necessarily follow past decisions and certainly that they do not do so without thinking about it.

Tutor's Comments

This essay starts weakly with a long and very general introduction, but it then gets into the question well. There is a nice brief resume of the key ideas in precedent although this is not linked closely enough to the question. The answer then continues to improve with some very good use of material and a real attempt at evaluating when judges do not follow precedent. Overall the strong ending would probably just bring this answer up to a grade B.

TUTOR'S ANSWER

Question 3

The remark made by Lord Hailsham in *Cassell v Broome (1972)* was as a result of the Court of Appeal, especially Lord Denning, having challenged the hierarchical system of precedent that maintains certainty and predictability in the law.

Precedent means that a previous decision of a court may be binding on a future court in a similar case. It is dependent upon the hierarchy of the court system, good law reporting and the identification of the *ratio decidendi* of a case. The hierarchy puts the House of Lords at the top so that its decisions bind all lower courts and normally also bind the House of Lords itself. Below the House of Lords is the Court of Appeal which is bound by the House of Lords and by its own past decisions; it binds all courts below. Next come the Divisional Courts which are bound by the House of Lords, the Court of Appeal and their own past decisions and in turn bind all lower courts. The High Court is bound by the courts above but the decisions of High Court judges are persuasive rather than binding on one another. The Crown Court, County Court and Magistrates' Court are bound by all the courts above.

Precedent creates the certainty and predictability that the law requires, especially civil law, to enable lawyers to advise their clients on the probable outcome of their case. Civil law deals with such things as contracts, wills, mortgages and so it is of paramount importance that this certainty and predictability are maintained. However, a system of this kind does have inherent weaknesses, the main one being inflexibility which may result in bad law being followed for many years before being overruled. It was this inflexibility that so frustrated the Court of Appeal.

The rigidity of the system was slightly relaxed by the Practice Statement made by Lord Gardiner in 1966. This statement was issued in order to give the House of Lords, and that House only, the possibility of avoiding the binding nature of judicial precedent. Lord Gardiner stated that, although certainty in the law is of the utmost importance, if there was an injustice as a result the House of Lords could deviate from its past decisions but must be mindful of the retrospective effect this might have.

This practice statement has not been applied frequently by the House of Lords. It was not until 1972 in *BRB v Herrington* that it was first applied with any note. This decision overruled an earlier decision of the House of Lords in respect of the duty of care owed to a child trespasser, thus allowing the law to develop along with social changes.

The Court of Appeal do not have the advantage of the Practice Statement. Their only means of flexibility is very narrow and is based on the exceptions highlighted in *Young v Bristol Aeroplane (1944)*. Those exceptions mean that the Court of Appeal (Civil Division) need not follow its own past decisions first where a decision was made in error of law (*per incuriam*), or if there are two conflicting decisions of the Court of Appeal and finally if a subsequent decision of the House of Lords overruled a previous decision of the Court of Appeal. The Court of Appeal (Criminal Division) has a further flexibility in that they need not follow a past decision if the liberty of someone is at stake (*R v Gould (1968)*) since liberty is felt to be more important than certainty.

Whilst Lord Denning was in the Court of Appeal he continually tried to widen that court's flexibility. In *The Discipline of Law* he clearly states that certainty is important but it should not be followed blindly where the interests of justice dictate otherwise. In 1978 in *Davis v Johnson* the Court of Appeal once again came up against the House of Lords on this issue. The case involved the granting of an injunction under the Domestic Violence Act 1976. Two previous decisions were ignored and the Court of Appeal granted the injunction. The case went to the House of Lords who, whilst agreeing in principle to the issue of the injunction, made it absolutely clear that the Court of Appeal could not overrule a previous decision of their own. Only the House of Lords had this power.

Lord Denning also challenged the rigidity of *stare decisis* in *Schorsch Meier v Henning (1974)* when the Court of Appeal refused to follow the House of Lords' decision in *Havana Railways*. The *Havana* case decided that damages could only be awarded in sterling, but Lord Denning held that damages could be given in any relevant currency. The same issue arose in *Miliangos v George Frank Textiles (1976)* and once again the Court of Appeal ignored the House of Lords decision. This time the case was appealed to the House of Lords (*Schorsch Meier* had not been) and the House of Lords said it was not for any inferior court to review the Lords' decisions; only the House of Lords itself could do that.

As has been stated earlier, judicial precedent maintains certainty and predictability, which are essential to judge made laws. Similar cases are treated in a similar fashion; the law is the result of concrete situations, not theoretical ones. As Professor Kiralfy said, judicial precedent is forged on the anvil of reality. But the disadvantage of this system is the length of time it may take a case to reach the House of Lords; in fact it may never reach there, since the House of Lords hears only about 100 appeals each year. The Court of Appeal hears 8,000 appeals and that is why, at times, they become frustrated with the system that allows bad law to remain caught up in it. Although not every court in the system should be able to ignore precedents there is a strong argument for allowing the Court of Appeal more freedom.

OUTLINE ANSWER

Question 4

The quotation that you are asked to examine contains two aspects; first that the contribution of equity was 'of the utmost importance' and secondly that the contribution was 'exhausted a very long time ago'. Both these aspects must be covered for a full discussion.

Start by examining the historical contribution of equity and comment on its importance; this should include:

- filling in the gaps of the common law;
- developing new concepts such as trusts;
- developing a range of remedies – injunctions, specific performance, rescission and rectification.

Then look at more recent developments:

- the development of two new equitable remedies – Anton Piller orders and Mareva injunctions;
- the continuing development of new concepts such as equitable estoppel (*Hightrees* case).

Discuss whether these challenge the statement that the contribution was exhausted a long time ago by showing that equity is still contributing to the development of English law.

A review sheet for this chapter can be found on p. 205.

SOURCES OF LAW 2

ACTS OF PARLIAMENT

DELEGATED LEGISLATION

STATUTORY INTERPRETATION

EUROPEAN LAW

LAW REFORM

GETTING STARTED

In the last chapter we looked at so-called unwritten sources of law, but during the twentieth century written sources of law have become increasingly important. Statutory law enacted by Parliament, delegated legislation in the form of statutory instruments, and, since, 1973 European Law have produced a mass of law. This chapter looks at the key factors in each of these.

In addition, there is another facet to these written laws in that there is sometimes the need for clarification of the meaning of the words; this involves the courts (and judges) in the process of statutory interpretation.

Law reform is another issue as, even with the amount of law being passed, there are areas of law which are not satisfactory and where there is a clear need for reform. Reform bodies, such as the Law Commission have been set up to review the law and put forward proposals for changes.

All these topics can feature on examination papers, and candidates are expected to show critical awareness, as well as knowledge. So make sure you have a firm understanding of each topic and all the problems involved. In particular, examination questions tend to concentrate on:

- **Acts of Parliament** – a critical view of the legislative process;
- **delegated legislation** – the 'undemocratic' aspect and the need for controls;
- **statutory interpretation** – the differing approaches;
- **European law** – its affect on English law;
- **law reform** – the effectiveness of the work of the Law Commission and other methods of law reform.

ESSENTIAL PRINCIPLES

ACTS OF PARLIAMENT

These usually have to be passed by both Houses of Parliament through a long and complex process. Before an Act is passed it is known as a Bill. A Bill may start in either the House of Commons or the House of Lords (with the exception of finance Bills which must start in the House of Commons) and must go through the following stages:

1 **First Reading** – this is a formal procedure under which the name and main aims of the Bill are read out and usually no discussion takes place;

2 **Second Reading** – this is the main debate; MPs will debate the principles behind the Bill and at the end of this a vote is taken; obviously there must be a majority in favour for the Bill to progress any further;

3 **Committee Stage** – a detailed examination clause by clause undertaken by a committee of between 20 and 50 MPs; for finance Bills the whole House will sit in committee;

4 **Report Stage** – the committee report back to the House and suggested amendments are voted on;

5 **Third Reading** – if at least six MPs request it, there will be a further debate on the Bill as a whole; in any event there is a final vote on it;

6 **The House of Lords** – if the Bill started life in the House of Commons it is now passed to the House of Lords where it goes through the same five stages outlined above; (finance Bills bypass the House of Lords); if it started in the House of Lords then it passes to the House of Commons;

7 **Royal Assent** – the monarch formally gives approval to the Bill and it then becomes an Act of Parliament; though this does not mean it is actually in force as law; some Acts depend on goverment ministers bringing them into force by a commencement order; this has caused problems with uncertainty as it is difficult to discover which sections have been brought into force.

This legislative process is subject to criticism and in 1994 the Rippon Commission's report underlined five principles:

1 laws are made for the benefit of the citizens and all citizens should therefore be involved as fully and openly as possible in the legislative process;

2 statute law should be as certain and intelligible as possible;

3 statute law had to be rooted in the authority of Parliament and thoroughly exposed to democratic scrutiny;

4 statute law had to be as accessible as possible;

5 getting the law right was as important as getting it passed quickly.

PARLIAMENTARY SOVEREIGNTY

Parliamentary law is sovereign over other forms of law in England and Wales. By this we mean that an Act of Parliament can completely supersede any custom, judicial precedent, delegated legislation or previous Act of Parliament. (Note that European law has undermined the sovereignty of Parliament – this is dealt with in the section on European law later in this chapter.) The reason that Parliamentary law is generally sovereign is based on the idea of democratic law making. The people vote for their member of Parliament so, in theory, that MP is voting on their behalf. Criticisms are that:

■ MPs usually vote on party lines rather than how their particular constituents wish;

■ Parliamentary elections only have to take place once every five years;

■ much of the drafting of Parliamentary law is done by civil servants who are not elected;

■ the House of Lords is not an elected body.

On this last point it should be noted that it is possible to bypass the House of Lords under the procedure in the Parliament Acts 1911 and 1949, though this procedure has only ever been used four times.

ACCESSIBILITY

There are some major problems:

1　It is difficult to discover which Acts and /or which sections have been brought into force.

2　Many statutes are amended by later statutes so that it is necessary to read the two together to make sense of provisions.

3　Codification and/or consolidation could usefully be used to make the law more accessible.

4　The language used in Acts is not always easily understood; in fact about 75% of cases heard by the House of Lords in its judicial capacity each year involve disputes over the interpretation of Acts.

DELEGATED LEGISLATION

WHAT IS IT?

Delegated legislation is law made by some person or body other than Parliament, but with the authority of Parliament. That authority is usually laid down in a 'parent' Act of Parliament known as an **enabling Act**. This creates the framework of the law and then delegates power to others to make more detailed law in the area. Examples of enabling Acts include the Legal Aid Act 1988 which gave the Lord Chancellor wide powers to alter various aspects of the legal aid schemes, and the Local Government Act 1972 which gives local authorities power to make law.

WHY DO WE NEED IT?

1　Because of the increasing volume of legislation, Parliament does not have time to consider and debate every small detail.

2　In an emergency Parliament may not be able to pass law quickly enough.

3　Parliament may not have the necessary technical expertise or knowledge required, e.g. building regulations need expert knowledge, while local parking regulations need local knowledge.

4　Delegated legislation can be amended or revoked easily when necessary so that the law can be kept up to date.

5　It can be used to implement or phase in Acts of Parliament gradually; this occurred with the Courts and Legal Services Act 1990 and also with the Criminal Justice and Public Order Act 1994.

WHO MAKES IT?

1　**The Queen and the Privy Council** have the authority to make Orders in Council under the Emergency Powers Act 1920; this authority is usually only exercised in times of emergency when Parliament is not sitting.

2　**Ministers and government departments** are given authority to make statutory instruments for areas under their particular responsibility, e.g. the Lord Chancellor being given power regarding the legal aid schemes or the Department of the Environment being able to deal with anti-pollution legislation.

3　**Local authorities** can make bylaws for their own area, e.g. Kent County Council can pass laws affecting the whole county while a district or town council can make laws for its district or town.

4　**Public corporations** can pass bylaws for matters within their jurisdiction, e.g. the smoking ban on the London underground system was enacted in this way.

CONTROL OF DELEGATED LEGISLATION

Since there are so many people with the power to make delegated legislation it is important that some check is kept on them. Control is exercised by:

1　Parliament;

2　the courts.

In addition, sometimes there may be a public enquiry before a law is passed on an especially sensitive matter, such as planning laws which may affect the environment. However, Parliament and the courts hold the important methods of control and it is necessary to have more detailed knowledge of these.

Control by Parliament

Since 1973 there has existed a Select Committee on Statutory Instruments, usually called the Scrutiny Committee. This committee reviews all Statutory Instruments (SIs) and where necessary can refer them to the House of Commons for further consideration.

❝Scrutiny Committee❞

The review is technical rather than a look at policy and the main grounds for referring a Statutory Instrument are:

- **it imposes a tax or charge** – this is because only an elected body has such a right;
- **it makes some unusual or unexpected use of the powers** given in the enabling legislation or it has gone beyond the powers given under the enabling legislation;
- **it is unclear** or defective in some way.

Apart from this Scrutiny Committee, there is no general provision that Statutory Instruments have to be laid before Parliament although such a provision is sometimes made in specific enabling Acts. All SIs are, however, subject to either affirmative or negative resolutions. An **affirmative resolution** means that such SIs do not become law unless specifically approved by Parliament; a **negative resolution** means that the relevant SIs, once enacted, are law and will remain so unless rejected by Parliament within 40 days. In effect, Parliamentary checks on delegated legislation are rather limited and it is possible to argue that there is not enough control on what many see as undemocratic law making by civil servants.

Control by the courts

The courts can question the validity of delegated legislation using the judicial review procedure, although it must be noted that the courts cannot challenge an Act of Parliament. Delegated legislation can be challenged on the ground that it is *ultra vires*, i.e. it goes beyond the powers that Parliament intended.

“Ultra vires”

This is illustrated by *R v Home Secretary, ex p Fire Brigades Union (1995)* where changes made by the Home Secretary to the Criminal Injuries Compensation Scheme were held to have gone beyond the power given to him in the Criminal Justice Act 1988.

It also possible for the courts to hold that delegated legislation is *ultra vires* because the correct procedure has not been followed (*Aylesbury Mushroom case (1972)*).

STATUTORY INTERPRETATION

Both statutes and delegated legislation need to be interpreted, as even the simplest statement may be capable of bearing different meanings. So far as Acts of Parliament are concerned, Parliament has provided some assistance to interpretation with the Interpretation Act 1978 which lays down some general rules, and in addition some Acts will have an interpretation section which attempts to define certain words in the Act. These provisions, of course, do not solve all the problems and it has been left to the courts to develop approaches to interpretation. The courts have evolved:

- **three main canons of construction**, which tend to be referred to as the three 'rules' of interpretation; these are the **literal rule**, the **golden rule** and the **mischief rule**;
- **rules of language**, e.g. the *ejusdem generis* rule; and
- **presumptions.**

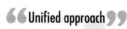
“Unified approach”

Sir Rupert Cross held that there was a unified approach to interpretation and that the various rules should not be considered in isolation. Under this a judge should start by considering the grammatical and ordinary meaning of the words; if this would produce a result which is contrary to the purpose of the Act, the judge may then apply any secondary meaning which the words are capable of bearing or he may read in words which he considers to be necessarily implied by the words which are already in the statute and he has a limited power to add to, alter or ignore words in order to prevent a provision from being unintelligible, absurd or totally unreasonable, unworkable or totally irreconcilable with the rest of the statute.

THE THREE RULES

These have been developed through case law and take such different lines that it has been said that 'the mischief rule, the golden rule and the literal rule are devices which allow the courts to interpret a statute however they like'. It is therefore necessary to understand the three rules but also to realise that they are being superseded by two conflicting approaches – the literal approach and the purposive approach.

1 **The literal rule** – under this the court gives words their plain, ordinary or literal meaning, regardless of whether the result is sensible or not. On some occasions the rule has been applied so strictly that the object of the statute may have been defeated as in *Whiteley v Chappell (1868)* where it was an offence to personate 'any person entitled to vote' at an election. The defendant was acquitted because he had impersonated a dead person and the court considered that a dead person was not 'entitled to vote'.

2 **The golden rule** – this has two applications. In its narrow sense it states that if the words of a statute are ambiguous, then the court should adopt the interpretation which avoids an absurd result. In *R v Allen (1872)* the Offences against the Person Act 1861 made it an offence to 'marry' whilst one's original spouse was still alive. Since the legal meaning of 'marry' was impossible, the more general meaning of going through a cere- mony of marriage was given to the word. However, the rule is also used, even though the meaning of the words is clear, to avoid repugnant situations (*Re Sigsworth (1935)*).

3 **The mischief rule** – this dates back to *Heydon's case (1584)* where the court held that four things were to be considered: what was the common law before the passing of the Act? what was the mischief not covered in that common law? what remedy had Parliament proposed? and the true reason for that remedy. In modern times this rule has been applied in a number of cases including *Smith v Hughes (1960)* (prostitutes inside a building tapping on a window to attract clients were convicted of soliciting in a public place) and *Royal College of Nursing v DHSS (1981)* where a three to two majority in the House of Lords held that an abortion technique whereby nurses perform much of the task was not illegal even though the Abortion Act 1967 provided that a pregnancy could only be 'terminated by a registered medical practitioner' i.e. by a doctor.

LITERAL VERSUS PURPOSIVE APPROACH

Today it is generally recognised that these rules have developed into these two approaches. Some judges favour the literal approach, reasoning that Parliament's words are the only evi- dence of what the law is meant to be. Lord Scarman expressed this idea when he said: 'If Parliament says one thing but means another, it is not … for the courts to correct it.'

Judges who adopt the purposive approach claim that they are following Parliament's inten- tion even though that intention does not appear in the plain words of the Act. This is summed up by Lord Denning's speech in the case of *Magor and St Mellons v Newport Corporation (1950)* where he said: 'We sit here to find out the intention of Parliament and carry it out and we do this better by filling in the gaps and making sense of the enactment.' This view was crit- icised by another judge in the same case, Lord Simonds, who said: 'If a gap is disclosed the remedy lies in an amending act.'

Critics of the literal approach include Professor Michael Zander who believes that it is an irresponsible approach as it is mechanical and 'divorced from the realities of the use of lan- guage'. Critics of the purposive approach point out that except by using the words it is difficult, if not impossible, to find the intention of Parliament.

RULES OF LANGUAGE

In order to help discover the meaning, the courts have also developed rules which apply in certain linguistic situations. These are:

- *ejusdem generis* – general words which follow a list of words are limited to the same kind of item (*Powell v Kempton Park Racecourse (1899)*);
- *expressio unius exclusio alterius* – the express mention of one thing excludes others;
- *noscitur a socciis* – a word is known by the company it keeps (*Inland Revenue Commissioners v Frere (1965)*).

PRESUMPTIONS

The courts will also presume certain points unless the Act being interpreted specifically states otherwise. The main presumptions are:

- that there has been no change to the common law;
- that the crown is not bound;
- that *mens rea* is required in criminal cases;
- that Parliament did not intend to oust the jurisdiction of the courts;
- that a statute does not have retrospective effect.

INTERNAL AND EXTERNAL AIDS TO INTERPRETATION

Internal aids refers to matters contained within the statute which may help in explaining the words in question. These aids include the long title, the short title and the preamble of the Act, other sections, especially an interpretation section, headings and schedules.

External aids are matters outside the Act which may be helpful; these include dictionaries, the historical setting, previous statutes and past cases; documents such as international treaties which led to the passing of the Act are also used. The two more contentious topics are Law Reform Reports and Hansard. In the *Black Clawson* case the judges in the House of Lords decided that reports by such bodies as the Law Commission could be used to discover the mischief that Parliament was trying to correct but not to find Parliament's intention.

" Use of Hansard "

Since *Pepper v Hart (1992)* it has been accepted that Hansard, the record of debates in Parliament, can be consulted but only (1) where the legislation is ambiguous or obscure or leads to an absurdity and (2) there is a clear statement by the minister who introduced the Bill, which will resolve the ambiguity.

EUROPEAN LAW

Since the United Kingdom joined what was then the European Economic Community on 1 January 1973, European law has had an increasing significance as a source of law. The institutions of the European Union are:

- **the Council of Ministers** which is composed of one ministerial representative from each member state and is responsible for formulating policy along with the Commission;
- **the Commission** which is responsible for issuing regulations and directives; there are 17 Commissioners who form the EU's executive body and are supposed to act independently of their national origin;
- **the Assembly** (otherwise known as the European Parliament); Parliament's main function is to discuss proposals put forward by the Commission, but it has no direct law making authority; the members of the European Parliament are directly elected by the people of the member states in elections which take place once every five years;
- **the European Court of Justice** which sits in Luxembourg and has judges taken from each member state. Its function (Article 164 of the Treaty of Rome) is to 'ensure that in the interpretation and application of the treaty the law is observed'. The main way it does this is when cases are referred to it under Article 177.

TREATIES

So far as our law is concerned all treaties signed by our head of government become part of English law automatically. This is as a result of the European Communities Act 1972 s. 2(1) and by virtue of this citizens of the United Kingdom are entitled to rely on the rights in the Treaty of Rome and other treaties even though those rights may not have been specifically enacted in English law. This is well illustrated by the case of *Macarthys Ltd v Smith (1981)* in which Wendy Smith was able to claim that the company which employed her was in breach of Article 119 of the Treaty of Rome over equal pay for men and women, even though there was no breach of domestic English law.

REGULATIONS

Under Article 189 of the Treaty of Rome the European Commission has the power to issue regulations which are 'binding in every respect and directly applicable in each Member State'. Such regulations do not have to be adopted in any way by the individual states as Article 189 makes it clear that they automatically become law in each member country. This has the advantage that laws are uniform across all the member states.

DIRECTIVES

Also under Article 189 of the Treaty of Rome the European Commission has the power to issue directives. These, however, differ from regulations in that they 'bind any Member State to which they are addressed as to the result to be achieved, while leaving to domestic agencies a competence as to form and means'. When a directive is issued a time limit is given within which it must be implemented by the member states and each state then uses its own law making system to incorporate the directive as part of its law.

Direct applicability

In the case of *Van Duyn v The Home Office (1975)* the European Court of Justice held that where:

a)   the purpose of a directive was to grant rights to individuals; and

b)   that directive was sufficiently clear;

it would be directly enforceable by an individual against the member state even though that state had not implemented the directive by the set date.

Vertical effect

In *Marshall v Southampton etc Area Health Authority (1986)* Miss Marshall was able to succeed in an action for unfair dismissal when she was required to retire at the age of 62 when men doing the same work did not have to retire until age 65. She relied on the Equal Treatment Directive 76/207 even though this directive had not been fully implemented in the United Kingdom. She was able to succeed because her employers were 'an arm of the state' and the directive had vertical effect, allowing her to take action against them. The rationale behind this decision is that a member state cannot take advantage of its own failure to comply with European law.

Horizontal effect

Directives which have not been implemented do not, however, give an individual any rights against other people. So in *Duke v GEC Reliance (1988)*, Mrs Duke was unable to rely on the Equal Treatment Directive 76/207 as her employer was a private company. Thus it is said that directives do not have horizontal effect. This has been confirmed by an Italian case, *Paola Faccini Dori v Recreb Srl (1994)*, in which the Italian government failed to implement Directive 85/447 in respect of consumer rights to cancel certain contracts. Dori could not rely on the directive in order to claim a right of cancellation against a private trader. In such cases it may be possible to take an action to claim damages against the member state which has failed to implement the European directive. This was decided in *Francovitch v Italy (1991)*.

CONFLICT BETWEEN EUROPEAN LAW AND NATIONAL LAW

European law takes precedence over national law. This was first established in *van Gend en Loos (1963)* which involved a conflict of Dutch law and European law on customs duty. In *Costa v ENEL (1964)* the European Court of Justice said:

> '…the Member States have limited their sovereign rights, albeit within limited fields, and have thus created a body of law which binds both their nationals and themselves.'

This conflict was seen clearly in the *Factortame case (1991)* when the European Court of Justice decided that Britain could not enforce the Merchant Shipping Act 1988 which had been passed to protect British fishermen and by only allowing vessels to register if 75% of directors and shareholders were British nationals. It was held that this contravened the Treaty of Rome.

LAW REFORM

The government has established various bodies whose task is to put forward proposals for law reform. There are three permanent bodies; these are:

1   **The Law Commission** which was set up in 1965 by the Law Commissions Act. It is the only full time law reform body and has a chairman and four commissioners with support staff. The Law Commission has a duty to keep the law under review with the aim of developing and reforming it through codification, consolidation, the simplification and modernisation of the law and the repeal of obsolete acts. The Commission may be asked by the Lord Chancellor to consider an area of law or it may itself select areas it believes are in need of reform. When it was first formed in 1965 an ambitious programme was announced aimed at codifying family law, contract law, landlord and tenant laws and the law of evidence but was gradually abandoned. The Law Commission has been successful in dealing with smaller areas of law. Its proposals are laid before Parliament each year and some important Acts of Parliament have subsequently been passed. These include the Unfair Contract Terms Act 1977, the Criminal Attempts Act 1981 and the Supply of Goods and Services Act 1982. However, in the late 1980s very few of its proposals were enacted, often due to lack of Parliamentary time. In 1994 a special procedure, known as the Jellicoe procedure, which uses the Special Public Bills Committee of the House of Lords to introduce non-controversial Bills, helped to speed up the introduction of reforms suggested by the Law Commission.

2   **The Law Reform Committee** which is part-time and considers only civil law areas. These are usually rather narrow and technical points but its proposals have led to the Occupiers' Liability Act 1957 and the Latent Damage Act 1986.

3   **The Criminal Law Revision Committee**, another part-time body which recommends changes to the criminal law. The main achievement has been the virtual codification of theft and related offences in the Theft Act 1968, although another Theft Act had to be passed in 1978 to overcome problems under s. 16 of the original act.

ROYAL COMMISSIONS

Apart from these three full-time bodies there are also temporary committees or Royal Commissions set up to investigate and report on one specific area of law. These are dissolved after they have completed their task. Some of these have led to important changes in the law e.g. the Phillips Commission (The Royal Commission on Police Procedure) reported in 1981 and many of its recommendations were given effect by the Police and Criminal Evidence Act 1984. However, the government does not always act on recommendations as was seen with the Pearson Commission on Personal Injury Cases which reported in 1978. More recently the Runciman Commission (the Royal Commission on Criminal Justice) reported in 1993, but the government has been selective in deciding which recommendations to implement.

OTHER METHODS OF LAW REFORM

The impetus for reform can also come from other bodies. These include:

- **the government** which in each session of Parliament sets out its agenda for law reform; often this involves more politically motivated areas;
- **individual MPs** who can introduce private members' Bills;
- **the judiciary** – as seen in Chapter 3 the judges do make law through deciding cases such as *R v R (1991)* which created the offence of marital rape;
- **pressure groups** – where a subject has a particularly high profile, Parliament may bow to public opinion and alter the law; this occurred with the changing of the law on the age of consent for homosexuals.

EXAMINATION QUESTIONS

1   Give a critical account of the legislative process. (AEB)

2   'Delegated legislation is an increasingly important source of law, but one which can lead to abuse of the principle of democratic law making.' Critically evaluate this statement (UODLE)

3   'The decision in *Pepper v Hart (1993)* so changes the approach to statutory interpretation that the old rules have become less important.' Discuss (WJEC)

4   'A judge must not alter the material of which a statute is woven but he can and should iron out the creases.' Discuss (UODLE)

5   a)   Explain the sources of European Community law.
    b)   Discuss the significance for English law of United Kingdom membership of the European Community. (AEB)

6   a)   Explain and illustrate the work of the official law reform agencies.
    b)   Discuss the contribution made by other bodies to the reform of the law. (NEAB)

ANSWERS TO QUESTIONS

OUTLINE ANSWERS TO SELECTED QUESTIONS

Question 1

Note the wording 'critical account'. It is necessary to give an account of the stages an Act of Parliament goes through but there must also be critical comment. A purely narrative account of how an Act of Parliament is enacted will not gain many marks. The answer should contain the type of comments made earlier in this chapter such as:

- MPs usually vote on party lines rather than how their particular constituents wish;
- much of the drafting of Parliamentary law is done by civil servants who are not elected;
- the House of Lords is not an elected body;

■ the rare use of the Parliament Acts 1911 and 1949 to bypass the House of Lords;

some Acts are passed too quickly and are not clear enough; (the Dangerous Dogs Act was a good example of this).

Question 2

The command 'critically evaluate this statement' means just that! Start by looking at the statement; there are two points it makes and these need to be discussed:

1 delegated legislation is 'increasingly important'; and
2 it can 'lead to abuse of the principle of democratic law making'.

On the first point demonstrate knowledge of the increase in delegated legislation by comments on the number of areas it is used in and, especially, the number of statutory instruments passed each year.

On the second point, which is the main focus of the question, you need to discuss why delegated legislation is considered to be 'undemocratic' and whether Parliament exercises enough control. You should include enabling acts; the Scrutiny Committee; affirmative and negative resolutions; the control exercised by the courts.

Finally, a sophisticated answer will point out that there is a difference between delegated legislation passed by local authorities, which are democratically elected and the other forms of delegated legislation.

STUDENT'S ANSWER WITH TUTOR'S COMMENTS

Question 4

Statutory interpretation is not easy for judges. Indeed many of the cases going up to the House of Lords each year are to do with interpretation. To help this Parliament has provided the Interpretation Act 1978 which states, amongst other things, that unless stated otherwise he also means she and singular includes plural. There are also interpretation sections in some Acts of Parliament. Judges have also developed their own three rules which are the literal rule, the golden rule and the mischief rule. Most judges in cases adopt either the literal rule and apply the plainest meaning to the words or the purposive approach of taking a wider view of what Parliament intended. The latter view is what the author of this quote has taken.

> 66 A nice brief summary of the facts, not wasting time on unnecessary details 99

The greatest problem with the literal rule is that many words have more than one meaning. To adhere rigidly to literal interpretation can lead to absurd results as seen in two cases. In *Whiteley v Chappell* the defendant was charged under an Act which made it an offence to impersonate another voter at an election. The voter he was impersonating was dead and as a dead person cannot vote the court said the defendant could not be guilty.

In the *Berriman* case a railway worker was killed while he was oiling points. An Act of Parliament designed to protect railway workers said that compensation was to be given if a person was killed or injured laying or repairing the line. The court decided Berriman was maintaining the railway and so his family received no compensation. This was a particularly hard decision.

The golden rule is sometimes used to avoid an absurd outcome or a repugnant situation. In *R v Allen* a charge of bigamy under the Offences against the Person Act 1861 made it an offence to marry while the original spouse was still living. It was impossible to marry while still married to someone else so the words were read as 'go through a ceremony of marriage'. To take the strict literal view would mean that nobody could ever be guilty of bigamy. This seems a sensible ironing out of the creases without seriously altering the Act. In *Re Sigsworth* a man had murdered his mother. Under the inheritance laws he was entitled to inherit his mother's estate. The court decided in a repugnant situation like this he should not be able to inherit as a result of his act of murder. The words in this case had been clear but the court made its own decision.

The mischief rule dates back to 1584 and *Heydon's case*. The court here decided what the law was before the Act, what the gap in the law was and what remedy has Parliament provided to get rid of the mischief. This can be seen in *Smith v Hughes (1960)* where a law made it an offence to solicit in a public place. Two women prostitutes were enticing men in through the window of a house. The court decided this did come under the Act although under the literal rule it would not have been classed as a public place. In using the mischief rule the

Needs developing

Good use of case to support argument

courts claim to be applying the intention of Parliament. It is impossible to discover what the intention of Parliament was; it is not the intention of those debating the issue because they will have conflicting views.

Those who take the literal view say that it is not up to the courts to tamper with Acts and read their own words into them. In *Re Sigsworth*, although it is obvious why the court decided the way it did, they have rewritten the law. The words of the Act were completely clear. It has been argued that when a gap in the law is uncovered, it should be a new Act of Parliament which remedies the situation, not the judiciary.

Sometimes judges interpret statutes to achieve the outcome which they want. This could be possibly said about the the case of the *Royal College of Nursing v DHSS (1981)*. This concerned the interpretation of the Abortion Act 1967 which said that a termination had to be carried out by a doctor. It was common procedure to induce labour with a doctor carrying out the first part and a nurse performing the second part. In the House of Lords three judges took the purposive view and decided that the practice was lawful, i.e. that the law before the Act was not satisfactory with illegal abortions taking place and the Act was to ensure that abortions were carried out in hospital. The other two judges taking the literal view decided that it was unlawful because the Act said the termination had to be carried out by a registered medical practitioner and with a nurse conducting part of the procedure this was not being done.

In general the purposive approach seems to be a better one to avoid absurd judgments like *Whiteley* and *Berriman* but care must be taken to avoid going too far the other way and actually 'altering the material' of the Act. In *Coltman v Bibby Tankers*, for example, the Act only mentioned aircraft and vehicles not ships. The House of Lords said that there was liability under the Act for death resulting from a ship sinking. Surely if Parliament had intended ships to be included in the Act they would have mentioned them. This appears to be an example of altering the material and not just ironing out the creases

Tutor's Comments

A clear summary of the main points of statutory interpretation with good use of case examples. The answer does not just limit itself to the 'three rules' but goes on to explore the purposive approach. However, more comment could have been included on the difficulty of finding Parliament's intention, especially with a reference to the decision in *Pepper v Hart*. There are good links made between the material and the quotation and a punchy conclusion and the answer would merit a grade B.

A review sheet for this chapter can be found on p. 206.

CIVIL DISPUTES

CIVIL CASES

CIVIL COURTS

TRIBUNALS

ARBITRATION

ALTERNATIVE DISPUTE RESOLUTION (ADR)

GETTING STARTED

It is important to be able to identify civil issues and to be able to distinguish between civil and criminal cases. Do not confuse civil cases with criminal cases. The type of case, the terminology, the court structure and procedure are different for civil and criminal cases.

In civil matters whenever individuals and/or businesses have a dispute most parties concerned will want that dispute resolved fairly, quickly and cheaply. In order to promote these aims there is a structure of courts designed to deal with civil cases but the courts are criticised for being too slow and too costly. As a result there has been a growth in other methods of dispute resolution as well as pressure on the civil justice system to introduce reforms.

The main themes of questions set on this topic are:

- the court structure and method of dealing with cases;
- the problems associated with taking cases in civil courts;
- comparison of different methods of dispute resolution;
- the effectiveness of the different methods.

It is also important to realise that questions asking about civil disputes may look at the wider setting and require extra information; in particular this might involve linking civil legal aid (see Chapter 8) with taking cases to court, or having knowledge about the use of juries in civil cases (see Chapter 9).

This chapter will remind you about the nature of civil cases, explain the court system and then concentrate on different methods of dispute resolution.

ESSENTIAL PRINCIPLES

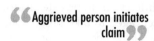

CIVIL CASES

❝Broad definition❞

Civil claims will arise when an individual or a business believes that their rights have been infringed in some way. This is necessarily a broad definition as civil cases cover a wide range.

This is because there are different areas of civil law; these include:

- contract
- tort
- family law
- employment law
- company law.

Also the types of dispute that can arise are equally varied. A claim may be for a few pounds or for several million; money may not be the point at issue, another remedy such as an injunction may be sought or the court may be asked to order the winding up of a company or grant a decree of divorce.

In most civil matters people regard a court case as a last resort. When a dispute arises it is likely that some form of negotiation will take place, e.g. writing letters setting out one's complaint. Many cases will be resolved at this stage by the other party agreeing to pay a sum in compensation or take some other desired action. If the other party will not settle the claim, then the aggrieved person must decide whether it is worth pursuing the matter further. In civil cases it is always the aggrieved person who initiates any claim.

❝Aggrieved person initiates claim❞

Another point to realise is that as the dispute is a private one between the parties involved, they can settle their own dispute at any time, even after court proceedings have been started. In fact fewer than 5% of all cases started in the civil courts actually get as far as a court hearing.

CIVIL COURTS

The party starting a court case is usually called the **plaintiff** and the other party is the **defendant**. (Note that in family law cases the terms are petitioner and respondent.)

A court where a case is started is called a **court of first instance**; for civil cases these are:

- the County Court; and
- the High Court.

In addition the Magistrates' Court hears some civil cases, especially family matters.

STARTING A CASE

For most cases the plaintiff may start proceedings in any County Court or the High Court, *except:*

- personal injury cases for less than £50,000 must be started in a County Court;
- defamation actions must be started in the High Court.

In order to commence proceedings in the County Court the plaintiff pays a fee and applies for a summons which must be filled in giving the name and address of the plaintiff and the defendant and details of the claim. This is then sent by post to the defendant. To start a case in the High Court the plaintiff applies for a writ to be issued, again on payment of a fee. The plaintiff must then arrange for the writ to be personally served on the defendant within four months of the writ being issued.

However, starting a case in one court does not mean the actual trial will be there. The intention of allowing most cases to start in either court is to make it easier for the plaintiff to have access to justice.

TRIAL

The main rules here are that:

- claims worth less than £3,000 are usually tried in the Small Claims Court;
- claims worth less than £25,000 are normally tried in the County Court;
- claims for between £25,000 and £50,000 are generally tried in the court in which the proceedings were started;
- claims for £50,000 or more are tried in the High Court.

However, cases can be transferred from the High Court to the County Court or vice versa after considering the following:

- the value of the claim/counter claim;
- any other importance of the case, e.g. a question of general public interest;
- the complexity of the facts, legal issues, remedies or procedures involved;
- whether transfer is likely to result in a speedier trial of the case.

THE COUNTY COURT

There are nearly 300 County Courts in England and Wales and they deal with the majority of civil cases. They deal with a wide variety of matters as since July 1991 they can deal with all contract and tort cases, landlord and tenant disputes, and some equity cases such actions concerning an alleged breach of trust where the value of the trust fund is not more than £30,000. In addition some County Courts can deal with divorce and all the connected issues, bankruptcy and insolvency matters and some even have admiralty jusridiction. In 1994 over 2½ million cases were started in County Courts.

For claims of £3,000 or less the County Court provides a relatively cheap and quick method of disposal in the Small Claims Court.

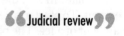 **Small Claims Court**

The procedure is known as arbitration, though this is quite different from private arbitration which is dealt with later in this chapter. Litigants are encouraged to take proceedings without using lawyers and there are simple leaflets setting out all the necessary procedure which are available from the court or from Citizens' Advice Bureaux. The advantages of the small claims procedure are:

- heard by a district judge in private;
- dealt with in a less formal way than in the main County Court;
- costs are kept low;
- litigants are encouraged to take their own case by the fact that the winner cannot claim the costs of using a lawyer from the losing party.

Claims of up to £5,000 can also be dealt with by this method if the parties agree.

Other cases are heard by a circuit judge in court with a more formal procedure.

HIGH COURT

There are three divisions, each of which specialises in hearing certain types of case.

Queen's Bench Division

This deals mainly with contract and tort cases; examples of contract cases are failure to pay for goods or disputes over the quality of work done; examples of tort cases include personal injuries caused by negligence, trespass to land and defamation actions. Usually cases are tried by a single judge but there is a right to jury trial for fraud, libel, slander, malicious prosecution or false imprisonment cases.

Judicial review

This division also has important supervisory functions under the judicial review procedure; this is carried out by the Queen's Bench Divisional Court which also hears appeals by way of case stated from the Magistrates' Court (see Chapter 6). The remedy of judicial review is concerned with whether a decision making process has been carried out legally as distinct from the merits of the decision in question. The Queen's Bench Divisional Court has supervisory powers over inferior courts and tribunals, and the actions and decisions of public bodies and government ministers. The court can make what are called 'prerogative orders'. These are:

- mandamus, which is a command to perform a duty;
- prohibition, which is an order to prevent an inferior court from hearing a case which it has no power to deal with;
- *certiorari*, which removes the decision to the Queen's Bench Division so that its legality can be inquired into and the decision quashed if it is found to be invalid.

In 1995 judicial review was used successfully to challenge the Home Secretary's changes to the Criminal Injuries Compensation Scheme.

Chancery Division

The main business of this division involves disputes concerned with such matters as insolvency, mortgages, trusts and patents; there is also a special Companies Court in the division which deals mainly with winding up companies.

Family Division

This has jurisdiction to hear all cases relating to children under the Children Act 1989 and to other matters regarding the family.

PROBLEMS WITH COURT CASES

- **cost** – can be more than the amount of the claim;
- **delay** – can take five years from the incident to a trial in the High Court;
- **complexity** – the procedure is confusing for the litigant in person.

There have been several reviews of the civil justice system including:

- **Pearson Commission** 1978 on personal injury claims which suggested removing personal injury claims from the courts by the creation of a no-fault compensation fund; the recommendations were not implemented.
- **Civil Justice Review** 1988 which looked at several aspects and led to reforms in the Courts and Legal Services Act 1990: these included:
  - flexible access between High Court and County Court;
  - increased limit of County Court from £5,000 to £50,000;
  - increased small claims limit to £1,000.
- **Lord Justice Woolf's** Interim Report 1995 which proposed:
  - extending small claims up to £3,000;
  - a new fast track for straightforward cases up to £10,000;
  - a new multi-track for cases over £10,000 with capping of costs;
  - encouraging the use of ADR;
  - giving judges more responsibility for managing cases;
  - more use of information technology;
  - simpler documents and procedures.

The final report is due in mid-1996 and it is clear that at least some of the recommendations will be implemented as the small claims limit was increased to £3,000 in January 1996. Because of the problems with taking a case to court there has been a growth in alternative ways of resolving disputes.

APPEALS

In most cases if either party is not satisfied with the decision it is possible to appeal. The general rules on appeals are:

1   From a decision of the small claims court there is usually *no appeal*.
2   From a decision in the County Court the appeal usually goes to the Court of Appeal (Civil Division).
3   From a decision in the High Court the appeal usually goes to the Court of Appeal (Civil Division) *but* there is an alternative of a 'leap-frog' appeal direct to the House of Lords under the Administration of Justice Act 1969. A leap-frog appeal is very rare (about three each year) since it must involve a point of law of general public importance which is either concerned with the interpretation of a statute or where there is a binding precedent of the Court of Appeal or the House of Lords which the trial judge must follow. In addition the House of Lords has to give leave to appeal.
4   From a decision of the Court of Appeal there is a further appeal to the House of Lords but only if the House of Lords give leave to appeal.
5   If a point of European law is involved the case may be referred to the European Court of Justice under Article 177 of the Treaty of Rome. Such a referral can be made by any English court.

The main appeal routes are shown in a diagram form in Figure 5.1.

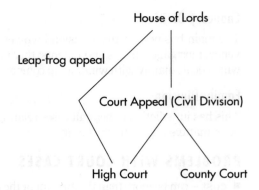

Figure 5.1 Civil appeal routes

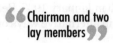

TRIBUNALS

Administrative tribunals are statutory creations designed to help enforce rights which have been granted through social and welfare legislation. Such tribunals have been set up as the welfare state has developed and new developments will often result in the creation of a new tribunal; for example following the Child Support Act 1993 the Child Support Appeals Tribunal was created. Tribunals operate alongside the court system and have become an important and integral part of the legal system. There are now over 2,000 tribunals covering such diverse areas as:

- social security
- rent tribunals
- immigration
- mental health review
- industrial tribunals.

Industrial tribunals were first set up in 1964 under the Industrial Training Act 1964 with a very limited role, but have become increasingly important and are now regulated by the Employment Protection (Consolidation) Act 1978 and cover many aspects including:

- unfair dismissal
- redundancy
- sexual discrimination
- racial discrimination.

COMPOSITION AND PROCEDURE

❝Chairman and two lay members❞

Most tribunals have a legally qualified chairman and two lay members who have expertise in the particular field of the tribunal. For example the lay members of an industrial injuries tribunal would be medically qualified while those on a tribunal hearing an unfair dismissal claim would be representatives of organisations for employers and employees respectively.

The procedure for each type of tribunal tends to vary but there are common elements in that the system is designed to encourage individuals to bring their own cases and not use lawyers; there are no formal rules of evidence and procedure but the rules of natural justice apply. This means that both parties must be given an equal chance to state their side.

CONTROL OF TRIBUNALS

❝Council on tribunals❞

Following the Franks Committee Report in 1957 the Council on Tribunals was set up in 1958 to supervise and keep under review the working of tribunals. It has fifteen members who visit tribunals and observe their work at first hand. The Council also receives complaints about tribunals and issues an annual report. The main problem is that the Council has very little power; it can only make recommendations.

The Queen's Bench Divisional Court hears applications for judicial review against tribunal decisions and can use its prerogative powers, for example, where there has been a breach of natural justice.

Finally, there is an appeal system against the decisions of some tribunals. In particular there is a right of appeal from industrial tribunals to the Employment Appeals Tribunal and from there to the Court of Appeal. There is also a Social Security Appeals Tribunal to hear appeals in this area.

ADVANTAGES OF TRIBUNALS

1 Cheaper than the courts.
2 Speedier than the courts.
3 Simple procedure; more informal hearing than in court; most cases heard in private; NB Industrial tribunals are open to public and tend to be more formal.
4 Flexible; not bound by strict rules of evidence or by precedent.
5 Experts involved in decision making.

DISADVANTAGES OF TRIBUNALS

1 Legal aid is not available for most tribunals; this may put an applicant at a disadvantage if the other side (often an employer or government department) uses a lawyer.
2 Some tribunals do not have to give reasons for their decisions.
3 There is no right of appeal from some tribunals (although an application for judicial review may be made).
4 Not following precedent can make it difficult to predict the outcome.

DOMESTIC TRIBUNALS

These are effectively 'in-house' tribunals set up by private bodies usually for their own internal disciplinary control. They must keep to the rules of natural justice and their decisions are subject to judicial review. In addition for many professional disciplinary tribunals there is an appeal route to the Judicial Committee of the Privy Council in cases where the tribunal has decided to strike off a member from the professional register.

ARBITRATION

Arbitration arises from:

1 an agreement to arbitrate (private arbitration);
2 statutory intervention (e.g. ACAS must be informed in industrial tribunal cases);
3 through the courts in small claims cases and the Commercial Court of the Queen's Bench Division.

 Definition

This section will concentrate on private arbitration.

This is the voluntary submission by the parties of their dispute to the judgment of some person other than a judge.

An agreement to go to arbitration can be made at any time, even before a dispute arises by the inclusion of a *Scott v Avery* clause in a contract. This is a clause where the parties in their original contract agree that in the event of a dispute arising between them, they will have that dispute settled by arbitration. Under the Arbitration Act 1950 the court will normally refuse to hear a case where there is such an arbitration agreement in a contract though it should be noted that in consumer claims if the dispute is for an amount which can be dealt with in the small claims court, the individual has the right to have the case heard in the Small Claims Court. An agreement to go to arbitration can also be made after the dispute arises. Arbitration is becoming increasingly popular in commercial cases.

The arbitrator

The agreement to go to arbitration will either name an arbitrator or provide a method of choosing one. Often in commercial contracts it is provided that the president of the appropriate trade organisation will appoint the arbitrator. There is also the Institute of Arbitrators which provides trained arbitrators for major disputes. In many cases the arbitrator will be someone who has expertise in the particular field involved in the dispute. The decision made by the arbitrator is called an award and can be enforced through the courts if necessary.

ADVANTAGES OF ARBITRATION

1 Parties may chose their own arbitrator.
2 Questions of quality can be decided by an expert in the particular field.
3 Hearing time and place can be arranged to suit parties.
4 Informal and private.
5 Quicker and cheaper than going to court.
6 Award is normally final.

DISADVANTAGES OF ARBITRATION

1 Legal aid not available – this may disadvantage an individual in a case against a business.

2 Legal points are not suitable for decision by a non-lawyer.

3 When a professional arbitrator is used, his fees may be expensive.

4 There is no right of appeal if new evidence becomes available.

ALTERNATIVE DISPUTE RESOLUTION (ADR)

This is any method of resolving a dispute without resorting to using the courts. The most common methods of ADR are:

■ **mediation** – this is where a neutral mediator helps the parties to reach a compromise solution.

■ **formalised settlement conference** (commonly called a 'mini-trial') – this is where each side presents its case to a panel composed of an executive from each party often assisted by a neutral party; this panel of three will then come to a decision.

■ **private arbitration** as described in the previous section.

The advantages of mediation and mini-trials are that the decision need not be a strictly legal one. It is more likely to be based on commercial realism and may include agreements about the conduct of future business between the parties. In 1991 the Centre for Dispute Resolution was set up in London and many important companies are members including almost all of the big London law firms. Businesses say that using the centre to resolve disputes has saved several thousands of pounds in court costs.

EXAMINATION QUESTIONS

1 Consider whether recent changes in the civil court system are sufficient to answer the criticisms made of negligence actions in personal injury cases. (ULEAC)

2 a) What role do tribunals play in our legal system?

   b) Are the methods of supervising tribunals and reviewing their decisions adequate? (UODLE)

3 Harriet has been injured in a road traffic accident caused by Angela's negligence and wishes to claim damages for her pain and suffering.

   a) Advise Harriet as to where and how she should start civil proceedings against Angela.

   b) If she is dissatisfied with the result of her case, what appeals are open to her?

   c) To what extent have the changes in jurisdiction under the Courts and Legal Services Act 1990 improved the court as a forum for personal injury disputes? (UODLE)

4 'We aim at a Rolls-Royce system of civil justice, but most people would prefer an affordable mini.' Are the courts the most effective way of dealing with civil claims? (UODLE)

ANSWERS TO QUESTIONS

OUTLINE ANSWER

Question 2

Part a) The key word in this part of the question is *role*. This requires you to:

■ explain why tribunals were established;

■ give some details of the work of the most important types of tribunal, especially industrial tribunals and social security tribunals;

■ compare them with the courts.

Part b) Explain what methods of supervising tribunals exist and examine the adequacy of each. This should include:

- the Council on Tribunals – limitations – can only report and make recommendations;
- judicial review in the Queen's Bench Divisional Court – need to show that the tribunal has acted *ultra vires* and the narrowness of this;
- the existence of appeals systems for some tribunals, especially for industrial tribunals, as an effective way of correcting errors;
- the ombudsman who can investigate but has no real powers.

TUTOR'S ANSWER

Question 3

Part a) This is a civil claim for personal injury and therefore the amount that Harriet wishes to claim will affect where and how she should start proceedings. If the claim is for less than £50,000 Harriet must start the case in the County Court. This has been the rule since 1991 following regulations made under the Courts and Legal Services Act 1990. However, there is no geographical limitation on starting a case and Harriet may choose the most convenient County Court for her; probably the nearest court to her home address. She should be warned that if Angela defends the case the court may decide to transfer it to her local court for hearing. In order to commence proceedings in a County Court Harriet will need to pay a court fee and obtain a summons in which she sets out her claim. The court will then post this to Angela. If the claim is for less than £3,000 will not normally be heard in the Small Claims Court as it is a personal injuries case and such cases were excluded when the limit was raised to £3,000.

If the claim is for £50,000 or more then the case can be started in either the County Court or the Queen's Bench Division of the High Court. Again, Harriet can choose the most convenient County Court or she can use the nearest District Registry of the High Court. The method of starting the case in the High Court is that Harriet must obtain a writ from the court and must arrange for it to be served on Angela personally within four months of the writ being issued.

Part b) If the case is heard in the Small Claims Court then there is no appeal. If the case is tried in the County Court, then Harriet can appeal to the Court of Appeal (Civil Division). This appeal is as of right unless Harriet was awarded less than £5,000 in damages by the County Court when she will need to obtain leave to appeal. There is the possibility of a further appeal from the Court of Appeal to the House of Lords but for this it is always necessary to obtain leave to appeal.

If the hearing took place in the Queen's Bench Divison of the High Court then Harriet can either appeal to the Court of Appeal (Civil Division) as of right and from there to the House of Lords or she may be able to use the leap-frog procedure under the Administration of Justice Act 1969 and appeal direct to the House of Lords. This route can only be used if the case involves a point of law of general public importance which is either concerned with the interpretation of a statute or is one where the trial judge is bound by a previous decision of the Court of Appeal or the House of Lords. In addition the House of Lords must give leave to appeal.

Finally, there is the possibility of having the case referred to the European Court of Justice under Article 177 of the Treaty of Rome. However, it seems unlikely that a point of European law will be involved in Harriet's case.

Part c) The main problems involved in using the courts as a forum for solving personal injury disputes are cost and delay. The Courts and Legal Services Act 1990 made several changes which were aimed at improving access to the courts in civil cases. The main change was the increasing of the County Court limit from £5,000 to £50,000. This means that many more personal injury cases can now be dealt with in the County Court, which should mean a faster and cheaper hearing. County Court costs are lower than those in the High Court and, in addition, solicitors have rights of audience there so that there is no need to use a barrister or a solicitor with special rights of advocacy.

Another reform was that the geographical restriction on which County Court could be used was removed to make it easier for plaintiffs to commence proceedings. However, cases may be transferred to the defendant's nearest court once a defence is filed so that the plaintiff may still be faced with a long journey to court and all the attendant inconvenience.

The Courts and Legal Services Act 1990 also allowed solicitors to obtain certificates of advocacy to enable them to conduct cases in the High Court. This means that plaintiffs may be able to have the same lawyer representing them right through a case, whereas previously a barrister had to be briefed for any case going to the High Court.

There are, however, problems which still remain. Delay is a major problem; it has been estimated that on average it takes five years from the accident causing the injuries for a case to get to trial in the High Court. Cost is another major problem; and the Courts and Legal Services Act 1990 allows a conditional fees agreement in personal injury cases, so that non-legally aided plaintiffs have some protection from cost in the event of losing their case. This, however, will not protect them from having to pay the costs of the other party.

Finally, the reforms do little to solve fear of using courts and the trauma of having to give evidence and be subject to cross examination.

STUDENT'S ANSWER WITH TUTOR'S COMMENTS

Question 4

The courts can be a very effective way of settling civil claims if they are for small amounts as the Small Claims Court offers a fast and cheap service for claims of up to £3,000. However, the public still have a reluctance to go to court if at all possible.

"A good start showing breadth of knowledge"

The further up the system you go after this the longer and costlier it becomes, and with the reduction in the number of people eligible for legal aid it is really taking away their ability to seek redress through the courts.

The County Court can hear claims up to £50,000 and beyond this amount the claim will usually be heard in the High Court increasing both costs and the length of time the case will last. Where a person cannot get legal aid, an 'affordable mini' would be better than being denied justice at all. This is particularly true in defamation cases where no matter how poor the plaintiff is, legal aid is not available.

"This needs to be developed"

The problems with cases in civil courts have led to a growth of Alternative Dispute Resolution procedures. This can be by the parties agreeing to be bound by the decision of an independent third party or by asking for a third party to act as a mediator.

"Good point"

One way the courts could be made more effective would be to adopt a more European approach in that most evidence be supplied in writing and only a short speech made by the advocate in court. This should speed up and cheapen cases and might encourage more people to bring actions.

"Good link with quotation, but the information on tribunals is too brief"

In some cases tribunals are effective at settling disputes. This has the advantage of involving people who have specialist knowledge of a subject in the decision making process as the panel usually consists of a legally qualified chairman and two lay specialists. There are an increasing number of tribunals and this should bring justice to the people. Tribunals have always been considered the 'affordable mini' running alongside the Rolls-Royce of the courts. However, tribunals are becoming expensive since, particularly for industrial disputes, professional advocates are increasingly used.

Another way a person could seek justice without resorting to court is through an ombudsman. This is free but, compared to the courts, a bit toothless as the powers of ombudsmen are limited.

"Weak conclusion"

All in all the courts are probably the best way because they can make a judgment and have the power to enforce it with bailiffs etc.

Tutor's Comments

A short but reasonably successful attempt at considering the most effective way of dealing with civil claims. Rather thin on detail, especially of alternatives to court proceedings; references to the Civil Justice Review or Lord Justice Woolf's proposals could have been incorporated in the argument.

Overall just worth a C grade.

A review sheet for this chapter can be found on p. 207.

CRIMINAL CASES

GETTING STARTED

This chapter encompasses the whole criminal justice process. There are many important areas included. The sections on police powers, law enforcement and bail can feature in civil liberties questions as well as being part of the criminal justice system.

When looking at the court structure and the procedure for criminal cases remember that the personnel of the court should also be considered, particularly the role of lay people in the criminal justice system with the use of lay magistrates and juries. These are dealt with in Chapter 9.

Some key definitions in this topic are:

- **arrestable offence** – which is one for which the sentence is fixed by law *or* one which carries a maximum sentence of at least five years' imprisonment *or* any offence which Parliament has made an arrestable offence;

- **serious arrestable offence** – which include murder, manslaughter, rape, kidnapping and terrorist offences;

- **summary offences** – these are the least serious offences and are always tried in the Magistrates' Court; they include nearly all driving offences, common assault and criminal damage which has caused less than £5,000 damage;

- **triable either way offences** – these can be regarded as the middle range of crimes; they include a wide variety of offences such as theft and assault causing actual bodily harm; in such cases the magistrates must decide whether they are prepared to hear the case and, if so, the defendant must then be given the choice of venue for the trial;

- **indictable offences** – these are the more serious crimes and include murder, manslaughter and rape; such offences must be tried at the Crown Court.

POLICE POWERS OF ARREST AND DETENTION

BAIL

CROWN PROSECUTION SERVICE

MAGISTRATES' COURTS

CROWN COURTS

APPEALS

POLICE POWERS OF ARREST AND DETENTION

ESSENTIAL PRINCIPLES

It is necessary to obtain a balance between protecting individual liberty and preventing /detecting crime. Parliament has tried to regulate this area of the law and the main police powers are set out in the Police and Criminal Evidence Act 1984 (PACE), though some of the provisions have been altered by the Criminal Justice and Public Order Act 1994. PACE also provides for extra detail on the procedures for searching, detaining, questioning and identifying suspects to be issued in Codes of Practice. These codes were revised in 1995.

POWERS TO STOP AND SEARCH

Section 1 of PACE gives the police the right to stop and search people and vehicles in a public place but only if there are reasonable grounds for suspecting that the person is in possession of (or the vehicle contains) stolen goods or prohibited articles such as offensive weapons. Since the power is very wide there are safeguards in that the police officer must give his name and station and the reason for the search. Only outer clothing of coat, jacket and gloves can be requested to be removed if the search is in public. A written report has to be made as soon as possible after the search.

The Prevention of Terrorism Act 1989 also gives powers to stop and search where there is reasonable suspicion of involvement in terrorism.

SEARCHING PREMISES

The police can enter premises without the occupier's permission to make a search if:

■ a warrant has been issued by a magistrate; or
■ it is necessary in order to arrest a person named in an arrest warrant; or
■ to arrest someone for an arrestable offence; or
■ to recapture an escaped prisoner.

POWERS OF ARREST

The police may make an arrest when authorised to do so by a warrant naming the person to be arrested and there is a right of arrest for breach of the peace. Apart from this, PACE gives general rights of arrest in certain circumstances involving arrestable offences.

Section 24 of PACE allows an arrest without a warrant in the following circumstances:

■ where the suspect has committed or is in the act of committing an arrestable offence;
■ where an arrestable offence has been committed or is being committed and there are reasonable grounds for suspecting the person arrested (even if it turns out later that he did not commit the offence);

(The above rights of arrest are given to private citizens as well as the police.)

■ where there are reasonable grounds for suspecting that an arrestable offence has been committed (even if it turns out later that no offence was committed) and there are reasonable grounds for suspecting the person arrested;
■ where the suspect is about to commit an arrestable offence;
■ where there are reasonable grounds for suspecting that the person arrested was about to commit an arrestable offence.

Section 25 of PACE allows the police to arrest for any offence where:

■ the suspect's name and address cannot be discovered;
■ there are reasonable grounds for believing that the name and address given by the suspect are false;
■ there are reasonable grounds for believing that the suspect will cause injury to himself or others or will cause damage to property;
■ the arrest is reasonably believed to be necessary to protect a child or other vulnerable person.

POWERS OF DETENTION

Once a person has been arrested and taken to a police station there are very strict limits on how long they may be held there. These limits are longer if the offence being investigated is a serious arrestable offence (e.g. murder, manslaughter, rape). There are also rules about the treatment of people in detention. Initially the detainee must be told his rights by the custody officer. These rights include:

- having someone informed of his arrest;
- being told that independent legal advice is available free and being allowed to consult privately with a solicitor;
- being allowed to consult the Code of Practice.

The first two may be delayed for up to 36 hours in the case of a serious arrestable offence. The detention must also be reviewed by the custody officer initially not later than six hours after the detention and then at intervals of not less than nine hours. For most offences the police may only detain a person for a maximum of 24 hours and must then either charge them with an offence or release them. For serious arrestable offences the police may detain for an initial period of 36 hours and may then apply to the Magistrates' Court for permission to detain the person for up to a maximum of 96 hours. The detainee has the right to be represented and oppose such an application. The Prevention of Terrorism Act 1989 allows for detention of 48 hours and up to another five days with the Home Secretary's permission.

While a person remains in custody under powers of detention the custody officer must keep a record of all events that occur, such as interviews or visits to the cell by police officers.

INTERVIEWING

Loss of right to silence

Any detained person may be questioned by the police; such interviews may be recorded. Before the interview starts the detainee should be cautioned, pointing out that the suspect does not have to say anything but that he may harm his defence if he does not mention something which he then later relies on in court. He must also be told that anything he does say may be given in evidence. There has been considerable dispute about this so-called loss of the right to silence. The change in the law brought about by the Criminal Justice and Public Order Act 1994 does not mean that the defendant can be forced to speak; he can still remain silent. However, at any trial which follows the judge may comment on the defendant's failure to mention a crucial matter and this failure can form part of the evidence against him. It is argued that this alters the basic premise of criminal trials that the prosecution must prove the defendant's guilt. However, a defendant's silence is not enough for a conviction on its own; there must be prosecution evidence as well.

FINGER PRINTS AND BODY SAMPLES

Whilst a person is detained the police may take fingerprints and non-intimate body samples such as hair and saliva without the person's consent. Intimate samples can only be taken if the offence being investigated is a recordable offence and must be taken by a registered medical practitioner or a nurse. Although a sample will only be taken where there is reasonable ground for suspecting involvement in a particular recordable offence, the sample may then be checked against information held on other crimes. Any samples taken must be destroyed if the suspect is not charged or is later found not guilty.

BAIL

At any point after being arrested by the police a person can be bailed either by the police pending further inquiries or when charged to appear at court or by a court at any stage during the criminal proceedings. Bail means release from custody on condition that the person returns at a set date to either a police station or a court.

THE BAIL ACT 1976

This is the key Act and starts with the assumption that an accused person should be granted bail, though this right has been withdrawn for certain cases (see below). Section 4 gives a general right to bail but the court need not grant a defendant bail if the court is satisfied that there are substantial grounds for believing that the defendant, if released on bail, would:

a) fail to surrender to custody;
b) commit an offence while on bail;
c) interfere with witnesses or otherwise obstruct the course of justice.

The court can also refuse bail if it satisfied that the defendant should be kept in custody for his own protection. In deciding whether to grant bail, the court shall have regard to:

a)   the nature and seriousness of the offence (and the probable method of dealing with it);

b)   the character, antecedents, associations and community ties of the defendant;

c)   the defendant's record as respects the fulfilment of his obligations under previous grants of bail in criminal proceedings;

d)   the strength of the evidence against him.

If a defendant is charged with an offence which is *not* punishable by imprisonment, bail can only be refused if the defendant has previously failed to surrender to bail *and* there are grounds for believing that he will not surrender on this occasion.

Conditions can be imposed on the grant of bail, such as:

a)   where the accused must reside, possibly at a bail hostel;

b)   the surrender of his passport;

c)   reporting to a police station (daily or weekly);

d)   sureties can be demanded; these are people who are prepared to promise to pay a set sum of money if the defendant fails to attend.

AMENDMENTS TO THE BAIL ACT 1976

The Criminal Justice Act 1988 s. 153 has amended the Bail Act in that it requires a court to give reasons for granting bail where the offence charged is murder, manslaughter or rape. **The Criminal Justice and Public Order Act 1994** s. 25 also amends the Bail Act so that a court *cannot* grant bail if the charge is murder, attempted murder, manslaughter, rape or attempted rape and the defendant has served a custodial sentence for such an offence previously. Also under s. 26 the presumption in favour of bail is removed where it appears that the defendant has committed an offence triable either way or an indictable offence while already on bail for another offence. However, the court can still decide to grant bail. It is argued that too many people are refused bail as nearly a quarter of the prison population is comprised of those remanded in custody. Many of these, if found guilty, are subsequently given non-custodial sentences.

> **"Too many are refused bail"**

RENEWED APPLICATIONS AND APPEALS

Normally only one further application can be made to the magistrates unless there is a change of circumstance. The defendant can appeal against a refusal to grant bail (except where s. 25 applies). Such an appeal is to a judge in chambers in the Queen's Bench Division of the High Court. A defendant who has been committed for trial to the Crown Court can also apply there for bail.

THE BAIL AMENDMENT ACT 1993

This gives the prosecution the right to appeal to a judge at the Crown Court against the granting of bail provided:

- the offence charged carries a maximum sentence of at least five years' imprisonment or is the offence of taking a conveyance without consent;

- the prosecution objected to bail; and

- the prosecution give immediate verbal notice of the intention to appeal, followed by a written notice to the magistrates within two hours.

CROWN PROSECUTION SERVICE

The Crown Prosecution Service (CPS) was established under the Prosecution of Offences Act 1985 and began operating in 1986. Before this, prosecutions were normally conducted by the police, but it was thought that the investigation of crime should be separated from the prosecution of cases. The CPS is headed by the Director of Public Prosecutions (DPP), who is accountable to the Attorney-General, and each area has a Chief Crown Prosecutor.

From the beginning, there have been problems:

- insufficient staff; though this has now largely been overcome;

- lack of coordination between police and local crown prosecutors;

- a belief that the CPS discontinues too many cases.

This last point can be supported by statistics which show that each year the CPS discontinue over 150,000 cases. The peak was in 1992 with over 190,000 cases. As a result there have been instances where private prosecutions have been brought for serious crimes. For example, in 1995 there was a successful prosecution in a rape case which the CPS had refused to prosecute.

In order to overcome some of this criticism, the DPP has issued a code showing the factors taken into account when deciding whether to go ahead with a prosecution. The factors include the strength of the evidence and whether the public interest would be served by continuing the case.

MAGISTRATES' COURTS

There are over 700 Magistrates' Courts in England and Wales. They have jurisdiction over a variety of matters involving criminal cases in their location:

1 **To exercise criminal jurisdiction** – i.e. actually try criminal cases. This accounts for 97% of all criminal trials. The categories of offence that the magistrates try are all summary offences and the majority of triable either way offences.

2 **To act as examining magistrates** – this is in committal proceedings where the magistrates take a preliminary look at the evidence and if there is a *prima facie* case send the case for trial to the Crown Court. This is the preliminary stage for any triable either way offence that is going to the Crown Court and all indictable offences. Under the Criminal Procedure and Investigations Bill 1996 committal proceedings are to be phased out and transfer proceedings used instead.

3 **Work connected to criminal cases** – e.g. issuing warrants for arrest and deciding bail applications.

4 **Youth court work** – trying criminal cases where the defendant is aged 10–17 inclusive. This court has a specially trained panel of magistrates under 65 and the panel must have a mix of sexes.

CHOOSING TRIAL BY JURY

Only about one in twenty triable either way offences actually go to the Crown Court for trial and of these two-thirds are by the magistrates' direction and one-third at the defendant's election. This suggests that the vast majority of defendants prefer trial at the Magistrates' Court, even though many of these will plead guilty. It is thought that the magistrates send cases to the Crown Court unnecessarily, as a study by Hedderman and Moxon (1992) showed that only 38% of defendants sent to the Crown Court by magistrates received a higher sentence than could have been given by the magistrates.

Implications of choosing jury trial

- Longer to wait plus the need for committal proceedings.
- More expensive, but more likely to get legal aid.
- Only a barrister or solicitor with advocacy certificate has rights of audience at the Crown Court.
- Trial by one's peers at the Crown Court.
- Better chance of an acquittal: 20% found not guilty at Magistrates' Court; 60% acquitted at the Crown Court (includes cases discharged by judge without a trial).
- Risk of a higher sentence if found guilty in the Crown Court.

Committals for sentence

Magistrates can also commit a defendant charged with a triable either way offence for sentence to the Crown Court if at the end of a case, having heard the defendant's past record, they feel that their powers are insufficient.

CROWN COURT

Following the Beeching Commission Report 1969, the Courts Act 1971 set up the Crown Court to replace the previous system of Assizes and Quarter Sessions which was out of date and unable to cope with the growing number of criminal cases. The Crown Court sits at over 90 centres throughout England and Wales.

CROWN COURT PROCEEDINGS

Although the defendant will have been sent for trial charged with specific crimes, the indictment can be drawn up for any offence that the depositions reveal. In more complicated cases the indictment may be for several counts. It is normal for a defendant appearing at the Crown Court to be represented.

Procedure

A plea and directions hearing is the first stage at the Crown Court. At this hearing the defendant is arraigned, i.e. his identity is established and he is asked how he pleads to all the counts on the indictment.

If the plea is *guilty* the judge will proceed to sentence if it is possible. However, there may be a need for reports.

If the plea is *not guilty* then the prosecution and defence will be expected to inform the court of the issues in the case and the number of witnesses. Also, whether it will be necessary to use a video link etc. All this allows the court to plan their lists but defence lawyers feel it prevents justified 'fishing trips' through the prosecution evidence.

At the trial

Where the defendant pleads not guilty the order of events at the trial is:

1 the jury is sworn in (for further information on juries see Chapter 9);
2 prosecution opening speech;
3 prosecution evidence;
4 if a weak case, defence may submit no case to go to the jury and the judge can direct an acquittal;
5 defence opening speech (provided calling witness other than the defendant);
6 defence evidence, including defendant if he wishes to give evidence (he does not have to but the judge may comment on this fact in his summing up to the jury);
7 prosecution closing speech;
8 defence closing speech;
9 summing up by the judge to the jury;
10 jury retire to consider verdict;
11 jury's verdict;
12 if guilty judge then passes sentences; if not guilty the accused is discharged and cannot be tried for that offence again (autrefois acquit).

APPEALS

APPEALS FROM THE MAGISTRATES' COURT

There are two quite different appeal routes from a decision in the Magistrates' Court.

Appeal to the Crown Court

This is available only to the defence. An appeal can be made against sentence and/or conviction. The case will be reheard at the Crown Court by a judge and between two and four magistrates. Normally, the decision by the Crown Court is final; it is unusual for there to be any further appeal, though technically it is possible for an appeal to be made to the Queen's Bench Divisional Court on a point of law as below.

Appeal to the Queen's Bench Divisional Court

66 Case stated appeals 99

This is available to the prosecution or the defence. It is an appeal on a point of law by way of case stated. This means that the magistrates set out their findings of fact and those are accepted as accurate so that the appeal concentrates on how the law applies to those facts. Following a decision by the Queen's Bench Divisional Court both the prosecution and the defence may appeal to the House of Lords. It is necessary to have the case certified as involving a point of law of general public importance and to have leave to appeal.

Figure 6.1 shows this appeal system in diagram form.

APPEALS FROM THE CROWN COURT

Appeals by the defence

At the end of a trial, when a defendant has been found guilty, his lawyer should advise him on the possibility of an appeal. This can be done verbally at the court or in writing within fourteen days of the trial. The intention is to make sure that each defendant has advice within the time

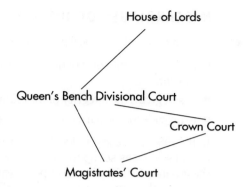

Figure 6.1

limits. Notice of appeal must be filed at the Court of Appeal (Criminal Division) within six weeks of conviction.

An appeal can be:

1 against conviction on a point of law;
2 against conviction on a point of fact;
3 against conviction on a point of mixed law and fact;
4 against sentence.

Leave to appeal is necessary in all cases except where the appeal is on law alone. Leave can be given by the trial judge but usually the application is considered by a single judge of the Court of Appeal in private. Even if he refuses leave it is possible to apply to a full Court of Appeal for leave. It is difficult to get leave to appeal as about 75% of applications are refused. Even when a defendant gets leave to appeal that does not mean automatic success. In 1994, 38% of appeals against conviction were allowed and 68% against sentence.

Appeals by the prosecution

Against an acquittal

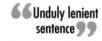

"Unduly lenient sentence"

The prosecution has no right of appeal against a finding of not guilty by a jury, but under s. 36 of the Criminal Justice Act 1972 the Attorney-General can refer a point of law for the Court of Appeal to rule on. The decision by the Court of Appeal does not affect the acquittal but it creates a precedent for any future case involving the same point of law.

Against sentence

The Attorney-General can appeal against an unduly lenient sentence under s. 36 of the Criminal Justice Act 1988. This power has been used successfully in a number of cases, including *R v W (1993)* where a boy of 15 had been given a supervision order for three years for raping a girl (and his parents ordered to pay £500 compensation to the girl). His sentence was increased to a two years' custodial sentence.

Appeals to the House of Lords

In theory both the prosecution and the defence may appeal from the Court of Appeal to the House of Lords. In practice very few appeals are made. It is necessary to have the case certified as involving a point of law of general public importance and to get leave to appeal, either from the House of Lords or from the Court of Appeal (Criminal Appeal Act 1968 s. 33).

Figure 6.2 shows the appeal routes from the Crown Court in a diagram form.

Figure 6.2

MISCARRIAGES OF JUSTICE

❝Functions of an appeal process❞

The functions of an appeal process are:

- to check that the court of first instance reached the correct result and to put matters right if it did not;
- to safeguard the integrity of the criminal justice system;
- to provide for the harmonious development of the law.

In the 1980s and early 1990s there were a number of miscarriages of justice and the Runciman Commission was set up to consider the whole system. The Criminal Appeal Act 1995 makes the grounds for allowing an appeal clearer; the Court of Appeal will allow any appeal where it considers the conviction unsafe and will dismiss it in any other case.

Review body

One of the key recommendations by the Runciman Commission was that an independent review body should be set up to consider possible miscarriages of justice. Previously, the Home Secretary had the power to review cases and refer them to the Court of Appeal, but cases such as the Birmingham Six and Judith Ward left people feeling that the Home Secretary was not sufficiently independent of the government. The Criminal Appeal Act 1995 finally enacted the Runciman recommendation and established the **Criminal Cases Review Commission**. Members of the Commission will be appointed by the Queen and at least one-third will be legally qualified and at least two-thirds will have relevant experience of the criminal justice system. They will have about 60 support staff, treble the number previously used in the Home Office for such work. The Commission will have the power to investigate possible miscarriages of justice (including summary offences) and to refer cases back to the courts on the grounds of conviction and/or sentence.

EXAMINATION QUESTIONS

1   Following an attack on an elderly woman in a Cardiff street, the police set up a road block and question motorists leaving the area. Micky, a 16-year-old school student, attempts to ride past the road block on his bicycle. He is stopped by PC Rod, who thinks Micky matches an eye-witnesses's description of the attacker. When asked for his name and address, Micky does not answer. He is taken to a police station and questioned for seven hours by detectives. Micky replies to every question by asking to be allowed to telephone his mother. The police take Micky's fingerprints and a sample of his blood. After this, Micky is placed in a cell, where he spends the night. Next morning PC Rod tells Micky that he will be allowed to see his mother if he admits to having carried out the attack. Micky makes a confession, and is charged with attempted murder. Advise Micky.   (WJEC)

2   'The law relating to bail strikes a fair balance between the unconvicted person's right to remain at liberty while awaiting trial, and the need to protect the public against the commission of further offences.' Discuss   (WJEC)

3   Jeremy, aged 40, is alleged to have stolen £60,000 from his employer, Katherine.

   a)   In what courts may Jeremy be prosecuted? What are the implications if one court is chosen rather than another?

   b)   If he is convicted of theft, to what courts may he appeal, assuming that he takes every opportunity of appealing open to him?

   c)   If he is acquitted, or convicted and given what the prosecution regards as a light sentence, how can the prosecution have the acquittal or sentence appealed against or reviewed?   (UODLE)

4   a)   Explain the criminal appeal system from the Magistrates' Court and the Crown Court.

   b)   To what extent should this appeal system be reformed?   (UODLE)

5   Evaluate the current mechanisms for dealing with alleged miscarriages of criminal justice.   (ULEAC)

ANSWERS TO QUESTIONS

OUTLINE ANSWER

Question 1

As there is a sequence of events in this question, it is advisable to work through the situation in chronological order.

1   Deal with the police powers to set up a road block and stop Micky under s. 4 of PACE.

2   Next discuss the police taking Micky to a police station; this involves the police powers of arrest under s. 24 of PACE – the attack on the elderly woman is an arrestable offence and the police officer thinks Micky matches an eye-witnesses's description of the attacker so there are reasonable grounds for suspecting him; also note that Micky refused to give his name and address so that s. 25 of PACE can also apply.

3   Now deal with events at the police station – note that Micky is 16 so that he is entitled to have an appropriate adult present – explain the Code of Practice and the rights of detained persons to have someone informed of his arrest and to consult a solicitor. Since this is a serious arrestable offence these rights can be withheld for up to 36 hours. Go through each event at the police station:

   ■ length of questioning;
   ■ the taking of fingerprints and blood;
   ■ the night in the cells:
   ■ PC Rod telling Micky that he will be allowed to see his mother if he makes an admission.

Discuss whether these matters make the signed confession inadmissible as evidence.

TUTOR'S ANSWER

Question 2

The granting of bail is an important factor in upholding civil rights, but at the same time it is true that there is a need to balance these rights against the protection of the public. The rules on bail are primarily derived from the Bail Act 1976. This Act laid down the presumption that bail should be granted; this was the first time that this right to bail had been enacted and it led to an increase in the granting of bail. The Act, however, did give the court some discretion in that bail need not be granted if there are substantial grounds for believing that the defendant, if released on bail would do one of the following: fail to turn up for the next hearing of the case; commit an offence while on bail; interfere with witnesses or otherwise obstruct the course of justice. Thus it can be seen that one of the reasons for refusing bail is to protect the public from the commission of further offences.

During the 1980s and early 1990s there was concern over the number of offences committed by those already on bail for an earlier offence. This led to gradual changes in the law. The first amendment being under s.153 of the Criminal Justice Act 1988 which requires a court to give reasons for the granting of bail where the offence is murder, manslaughter or rape. Clearly this provision was designed to ensure the balance between the unconvicted person's right to be at liberty and the need to protect the public from the possible repetition of such serious offences.

The Bail Amendment Act 1993 allows the prosecution to appeal against the granting of bail for offences carrying maximum penalties of five years' imprisonment or more. Again this is a sensible way of ensuring the balance, since it allows further consideration of any risks posed by the defendant without taking away the presumption of the right to bail.

However the Criminal Justice and Public Order Act 1994 has made more drastic changes. Firstly defendants who are charged with murder, attempted murder, manslaughter, rape or attempted rape no longer have the right to bail if they have previously served a custodial sentence for a similar offence. They will automatically be remanded in custody. This development upsets the balance between the defendant's right and public protection and means that some defendants will spend many months on remand in custody, only to be found not guilty. The second alteration brought in by the Criminal Justice and Public Order Act 1994 is that the presumption in favour of bail is taken away from defendants who are alleged to have committed a triable either way offence or an indictable offence while on bail for another offence. This is less controversial since such defendants can still be granted bail where the court thinks it suitable.

However it must be remembered that the defendant has not been found guilty of either of the offences; he is still unconvicted and the Act is a restriction on his right to liberty. It can be argued that the public were adequately protected by the previous rules of the Bail Act 1976, since one of the reasons in that Act for refusing bail was a belief that the defendant would commit further offences.

Even before the changes made by the Criminal Justice and Public Order Act 1994, there were some worrying statistics about the number of defendants who were remanded in custody. Such remand prisoners account for about a quarter of the total prison population. Further, about 14% of untried prisoners are found not guilty, either by being acquitted after trial or by the prosecution discontinuing the case against them. There is also the fact that another third, although pleading or being found guilty, will not receive a custodial sentence. Clearly there is a substantial number of remand prisoners who should have been granted bail and the changes to the law made in the Criminal Justice and Public Order Act 1994 are likely to exacerbate the situation. Although it is necessary to protect the public, it appears that the law no longer strikes a fair balance.

STUDENT'S ANSWER WITH TUTOR'S COMMENTS

Question 4

> **66** Good start showing understanding **99**

a) The appeal routes from the Magistrates' Court and the Crown Court are different. From the Magistrates' Court there are two separate appeal routes; the first is to the Crown Court and the second to the Queen's Bench Divisional Court. An appeal to the Crown Court can be made as of right by the defendant against conviction or sentence or both. Normally the defendant cannot take the appeal any further. The prosecutor has no right to appeal to the Crown Court. The second method of appeal from the Magistrates' Court to the Queen's Bench Divisional Court is open to both the defence and the prosecution. This type of appeal must involve a point of law and it is called an appeal by way of case stated. From the Queen's Bench Divisional Court the losing side may appeal to the House of Lords, but only if there is a point of law of general public importance and leave to appeal is granted.

If a case is tried in the Crown Court there is only one appeal route and this is to the Court of Appeal (Criminal Division). In most cases the defendant will need leave to appeal. A prosecutor can appeal against a lenient sentence, but cannot appeal if the jury has acquitted the defendant. Where there is a point of law of general public importance in the case, there may be a further appeal to the House of Lords.

> **66** A nice compact accurate answer to part a) **99**

Technically it may be possible to have a case referred to the European Court of Justice under Article 177 of the Treaty of Rome, but this will not often happen as most criminal cases do not involve European law.

b) As there have been miscarriages of justice where defendants have served several years in prison before their convictions were quashed, it is clear that the appeal system does not always work. However it is difficult to know how it could be reformed. Perhaps the Court of Appeal should hear more evidence from witnesses, as appeals at the moment are usually arguments about the law. There are only a very few cases going to the House of Lords, so this seems to be another point for reform and more cases should be allowed to appeal to the House of Lords.

> **66** Rather vague, needs developing **99**

The fact that the prosecutor cannot appeal when a jury acquits is open to criticism as there may be cases where new evidence comes to light showing that the defendant was definitely guilty. The system should be reformed giving the prosecution the right to appeal.

Tutor's Comments

A good part a) showing that the student understands the appeal system. Unfortunately part b) is much weaker and rather brief. The points made are valid but are not sufficiently developed, for example the answer could include more specific points about the difficulty of getting leave to appeal. Another area which could be explored is the creation of the Criminal Cases Review Authority to investigate possible miscarriages of justice. Overall this would achieve a grade C.

A review sheet for this chapter can be found on p. 208.

LEGAL PERSONNEL

GETTING STARTED

This chapter considers the professionals who work in the law; barristers, solicitors and judges. Barristers and solicitors are jointly referred to as the legal profession. Judges are collectively referred to as the judiciary. The Lord Chancellor plays a key role in the legal system. There are several themes that occur in examination questions:

- the respective roles of barristers and solicitors;
- reforms of the two professions, both past and possible future reforms;
- the appointment and composition of the judiciary;
- the independence of the judiciary;
- the role of the Lord Chancellor and/or whether a Ministry of Justice would be more effective.

Some of these are areas which are often in the news and it is worthwhile keeping abreast of any recent criticisms or developments, as it is possible to use such information in examination answers to demonstrate a good understanding of the topics.

As always, do remember to use relevant information from other areas to develop arguments and show a wider understanding of the topic. For example, in discussing the cost of using lawyers it could be useful to refer to the fact that many people are ineligible for legal aid (Chapter 8) or when explaining the functions of the judiciary draw on your knowledge of civil and criminal cases (Chapters 5 and 6).

ESSENTIAL PRINCIPLES

TRAINING

At the moment the normal route of entry to both professions is by obtaining a law degree (those without a law degree have to do an extra year's training and pass the Common Professional Examination) and then going on to a vocational training stage aimed at the particular branch. Barristers have to pass the Bar Vocational Course which emphasises the practical skills of drafting pleadings for use in court and advocacy; solicitors have to pass the Legal Practice Course which includes training in interviewing and business management, e.g. keeping accounts. After this stage both have 'on the job' training; solicitors through a training contract under which they work in a solicitors' firm for two years getting practical experience; barristers as pupils effectively 'work shadowing' another barrister for twelve months. At this stage trainee solicitors and barristers are paid a small salary, but even with this the training is long and expensive.

WORK

Solicitors in private practice may work as a sole practitioner or in a partnership. The number of partners is not limited and some of the biggest firms have over 200 partners as well as assistant solicitors. The work of solicitors is varied and includes:

- interviewing clients;
- negotiating on clients' behalf;
- drafting documents such as leases, contracts and wills;
- doing conveyancing;
- acting as an advocate in court.

Some solicitors may be general practitioners handling a variety of work, but more often a solicitor will specialise in one particular field. Prior to 1985 solicitors had a monopoly on conveyancing but this has been eroded by the Administration of Justice Act 1985 and the Courts and Legal Services Act 1990. Solicitors have increased rights of advocacy following the Courts and Legal Services Act 1990. All solicitors can appear in the County Court and the Magistrates' Court but now those who obtain a certificate of advocacy can appear in the court to which that certificate applies.

"Certificates of advocacy"

Barristers are self employed but usually work from a set of chambers where they can share administrative expenses with other barristers. They will employ a clerk as a practice administrator booking in cases and negotiating fees. The majority of barristers will concentrate on advocacy although there are some who specialise in areas such as tax and company law and who rarely appear in court. Barristers have rights of audience in all courts in England and Wales.

Clients cannot as a general rule go direct to a barrister but must use a solicitor who will then brief a barrister if it becomes necessary. Certain professions including accountants and surveyors can brief a barrister directly without the need for a solicitor as an intermediary.

After at least ten years as a barrister or a solicitor with an advocacy certificate it is possible to apply to the Lord Chancellor to become a Queen's Counsel (QC). The Lord Chancellor's criteria for selecting QCs has been criticised as being too secretive, together with the facts that less than 10% of QCs are women and only a very few are from ethnic minorities. This also has an effect on the composition of the judiciary since senior judges are usually chosen from the ranks of Queen's Counsel.

"Queen's Counsel"

COMPLAINTS AGAINST THE LEGAL PROFESSION

Solicitors are controlled by the Law Society, which has a disciplinary tribunal to hear serious complaints of professional misconduct. This tribunal has the power to order that a solicitor may be struck off the roll and so stop that solicitor from practising. For less serious matters the Solicitors' Complaints Bureau can investigate complaints by the public about delay or overcharging or similar matters. The Bureau has the power to award up to £1,000 compensation. However, the Bureau itself has been criticised for being slow and ineffective; this may be because it has become overloaded with complaints, handling about 25,000 a year.

Barristers can be disciplined by the Senate of the Inns of Court and in extreme cases disbarred from practising. There are also proposals to set up a complaints bureau to investigate complaints by the public of shoddy work.

Legal Services Ombudsman

Under the Courts and Legal Services Act 1990 the post of Legal Services Ombudsman was created to examine complaints against solicitors, barristers and licensed conveyancers where the professions' own regulatory bodies did not provide a satisfactory answer. The Ombudsman deals with over 1,000 complaints each year, the main problems being delay by solicitors and inadequate advice about cost, but is limited in his powers.

FUSION

A major debating point has been whether the two legal professions should be merged into one profession. The changes made by the Courts and Legal Services Act 1990 make this proposition less necessary, but there are still arguments that can be put for and against the idea.

Advantages

1   Reduction in costs for clients – only one lawyer would be needed.

2   Less duplication of work – at the moment when a barrister is briefed copies of all documents and statements have to be sent.

3   More continuity – the client would deal with the same lawyer throughout the case.

4   Later choice of specialisation for students – all law students would follow the same basic training.

Disadvantages

1   Loss of independent bar – this would mean that a solicitor would not be able to seek expert advice except by going to a rival firm.

2   Loss of specialist skills of advocacy.

3   Loss of the objectivity of a second opinion.

4   Possibility that costs would not decrease.

In fact for many smaller cases these arguments are irrelevant as a solicitor can handle the whole case. The increasing of the financial limits in the County Court and the creation of certificates of advocacy for qualifying solicitors means that it is already possible for the same lawyer to take the case from beginning to end, even where the value involved is considerable.

THE JUDICIARY

There are important distinctions between superior judges and inferior judges in the method of appointment and tenure of office, so it is as well to start by understanding which judges are involved.

Superior judges are those in the High Court and above:

- puisne judges in all divisions of the High Court;
- Lords Justices of Appeal in the Court of Appeal;
- Lords of Appeal in Ordinary (the Law Lords) in the House of Lords.

Inferior judges are all other judges:

- circuit judges who sit in both the Crown Court and the County Court;
- recorders who are part-time judges sitting usually in the Crown Court;
- district judges who hear small claims in the County Court;
- stipendiary magistrates who sit in Magistrates' Courts.

To become a judge at any level it is necessary to have qualified as a barrister or solicitor and the relevant qualifications are set out in the Courts and Legal Services Act 1990. This Act made some major changes as it broke the previous monopoly that the bar held on all superior judgeships by basing qualifications on the relevant certificate of advocacy and also providing for promotion from one level to the next.

SUPERIOR JUDGES

Qualifications

High Court judges must either have had the right to practice in the High Court for at least ten years or have been a circuit judge for at least two years. Both these qualifications give solicitors the chance to become High Court judges and the first solicitor so appointed was Sir Michael Sachs in 1993. Academic lawyers can also be appointed as it is no longer necessary actually to have practised.

Judges in the Court of Appeal must have a High Court qualification or be existing High Court judges, while the **Law Lords** are appointed from those who:

- hold high judicial office; or
- have been qualified to appear in the Supreme Court for at least fifteen years; or
- have practised as an advocate in Scotland for at least fifteen years; or
- have practised as a member of the bar in Northern Ireland for at least fifteen years.

Appointment

All appointments are made by the Queen, with High Court judges being nominated for appointment by the Lord Chancellor and the judges in the Court of Appeal and the House of Lords being nominated by the Prime Minister, though presumably after consultation with the Lord Chancellor. In all cases the appointment is by invitation; at this level it is not possible to apply to be a judge. This is a major criticism of the system as it is secretive and relies heavily on information compiled in the Lord Chancellor's Department about senior advocates who might be considered for future appointment.

66 **Secretive system** 99

Tenure of office

Superior judges have security of tenure in that they cannot be dismissed by the Lord Chancellor or the Prime Minister. Since the Act of Settlement 1701 they can only be removed by the monarch following a petition presented to her by both Houses of Parliament. This gives superior judges protection from political whims and allows them to be independent in their judgments. The Lord Chancellor can, however, declare vacant the office of any judge who is through ill-health incapable of carrying out his work and of taking the decision to resign. All superior judges appointed following the Judicial Pensions and Retirement Act 1993 have to retire at the age of 70. Judges appointed before this Act have to retire at 75.

INFERIOR JUDGES

Appointment

These are appointed by the Queen on the advice of the Lord Chancellor. Circuit judges and recorders must hold a ten-year Crown Court or County Court qualification while district judges and stipendiary magistrates need a seven-year general qualification. It is also possible to become a circuit judge by being promoted from any of the lower posts. The normal route to a circuit judgeship is by being first an assistant recorder and then a recorder. Posts are now advertised and applicants who are shortlisted face an interview by a panel which includes a serving judge, a member of the Lord Chancellor's Department and a lay person.

Training

66 **Limited training** 99

Once a lawyer has been appointed as an assistant recorder, they go on a one-week course run by the Judicial Studies Board, then they shadow an experienced judge for a week. After this they will sit to hear cases, though there will be one-day courses available from time to time. A recent initiative in training is to include racial awareness courses. Critics point out that the training is very short and that even though all the people involved are experienced lawyers this does not mean that they have any experience of doing such tasks as summing up to the jury or sentencing.

Retirement and dismissal

The Lord Chancellor has the power to dismiss inferior judges for incapacity or dismissal. All inferior judges now retire at 70.

COMPOSITION OF THE BENCH

One of the main criticisms of the bench is that it is dominated by elderly, white, upper class males. There are very few women judges and even fewer judges from ethnic minorities. With the introduction of a younger retirement age, the average age of judges will reduce slightly, but it is unusual for any judge to be appointed under the age of 40 with superior judges usually being well above this age. Women are rare at the higher levels with only one, Elizabeth Butler-Sloss, in the Court of Appeal and, up to 1995, none in the House of Lords. During the 1990s there has been an increase in the number of women appointed to the High Court and there are now women in all three divisions. However, the total number of women judges in the High Court in 1995 was still only seven out of nearly 100 judges; lower down the ladder there has been a greater increase, e.g. between 1992 and 1995 the percentage of assistant recorders who were female rose from 10% to 16%. Ethnic minorities are very poorly represented at the lower levels although, as with women, there has been an improvement at the level of assistant recorder. There are no judges from ethnic minorities in the higher courts.

Out of touch with society

At the higher levels judges tend to come from the upper levels of society, with many having been educated at public school and nearly all attending Oxbridge. As a result judges are seen as out of touch with society. Occasionally the media report actions or comments which appear to support this view, e.g. where a judge placed a 15 year old rapist on supervision and ordered him to give his victim £500 compensation so that she could have a holiday. At least in this case the Court of Appeal later changed the sentence to two years' detention.

INDEPENDENCE OF THE JUDICIARY

An independent judiciary is seen as important. Our judges can be seen to be independent in the following ways:

1 **Independent from politics** – judges are not allowed to be members of the House of Commons although the Law Lords do sit in the House of Lords but by convention do not take part in political debates.

2 **Independent from the government** – since superior judges cannot be dismissed by the government. However, their appointment has political overtones as the Lord Chancellor, who is a member of the government, is involved in the appointment of judges at all levels and the Prime Minister is responsible for the nomination of the most senior judges.

3 **Financial independence** – judicial salaries are paid out of the consolidated fund so that payment is made without the need for Parliament's authorisation. However, changes can be made to retirement ages and qualifying periods for pensions. The present rates of salary are not attractive to top barristers and it is believed that some have refused appointment as a judge.

4 **Freedom from pressure** – judges have immunity from being sued for actions taken or decisions made in the course of their judicial duties (*Sirros v Moore (1975)*). It is still possible for pressure to be placed on them, as happened in 1993 in the case of Sir John Wood, the High Court judge who chaired the Employment Appeals Tribunal.

THE LORD CHANCELLOR

The Lord Chancellor is the only person who is involved in all three arms of the state. This runs contrary to the theory of separation of powers put forward by Montesquieu in the eighteenth century. This identifies three functions of the state as:

- **legislative** – making law – in our system this is Parliament;
- **executive** – administering the law – the Cabinet;
- **judicial** – applying the law – the judges.

The Lord Chancellor is:

- the speaker of the House of Lords when it is sitting in its legislative capacity;
- a member of the Cabinet: and
- one of the judges in the House of Lords and head of the Chancery Division in the High Court and entitled to act as judge there.

As well as the above roles the Lord Chancellor plays a major part in the appointment of the judiciary and he has important administrative functions controlling the legal aid scheme, being responsible for the work of the Law Commission and the Council on Tribunals and other bodies including the Land Registry and the Public Trustee Office.

The Lord Chancellor is also a political appointment as he is appointed by the Prime Minister and can be dismissed by the Prime Minister. He holds office only while that political party is in power and if there is a change of government there will be a new Lord Chancellor.

A MINISTRY OF JUSTICE?

Under the present system responsibility for various functions of justice is divided between different goverment departments:

- **the Lord Chancellor's Department** has the major share covering appointment of judges, administration of the courts, civil and criminal procedure and legal aid;

- **the Home Secretary and the Home Office** are responsible for criminal law and procedure, penal policy, prisons and the probation service and the police;
- **the Attorney-General** gives legal advice to the government and is also responsible for prosecutions as the Director of Public Prosecutions is answerable to him.

Apart from these major areas there are Parliamentary counsel who draft Bills for proposed new statutory law put forward by the government.

❝ Low priority ❞

This muddled overlapping system means that low priority is given to:

- law reform;
- legal services;
- quality of the statute book.

Another problem is that the Lord Chancellor sits in the House of Lords and is therefore not available for questioning in the House of Commons. Although a junior minister from his department represents him in the Commons, there is still a lack of accountability. Conversely, while the Lord Chancellor is in the Cabinet, the Attorney-General is not.

In order to rationalise the system the Haldane Committee as long ago as 1918 suggested that there should be one department – a Ministry of Justice. This would lead to:

- greater political accountability;
- increased efficiency; and
- more momentum for reform.

However, there are possible disadvantages:

- the loss of the specialist legal knowledge of the Lord Chancellor and other law officers who are all qualified lawyers if the minister became a political figure as in other government departments;
- would it be feasible for the same minister to be responsible for law, prosecutions, the penal system and the police – is this a threat to the liberty of the subject?
- it could erode the independence of the judiciary by leading to a continental system in which judges are civil servants.

EXAMINATION QUESTIONS

1   Does the present system of legal education and training provide the lawyers that this country needs? (UODLE)

2   To what extent is it true that the lines of demarcation between the legal professions have become increasingly blurred? (UODLE)

3   To what extent did the Courts and Legal Services Act 1990 change the legal profession and the provision of legal services? (ULEAC)

4   English judges have increasingly been subjected to criticism in recent years. Examine the background, appointment, status and functions of the judges, explain and assess the validity of these criticisms. (AEB)

5   How true is it to say that the Lord Chancellor's position is in conflict with the principle of judicial independence? (UODLE)

ANSWERS TO QUESTIONS

OUTLINE ANSWERS TO SELECTED QUESTIONS

Question 1

1   Start with a *brief* description of the training of both solicitors and barristers:
- law degree or other degree plus CPE;

- followed by vocational stage – Bar Vocational Course / Legal Practice Course;
- pupillage (barrister) or training contract (solicitor).

2 Next consider the type of lawyers needed, e.g. wide variety, civil, criminal, need for company lawyers as well as those to deal with private individuals' problems, different skills required, negotiating, advocacy.

3 Now comment on both where the training produces the right skills and where there are problems. Such comments could include:

- prospective lawyers have to choose between the bar and becoming a solicitor at an early stage in training before they have enough experience to decide where their strengths lie;
- the training is long and expensive with lack of funding for the vocational stage – this may lead to lawyers coming mainly from financially well-off backgrounds and thus having little or no experience of the problems faced by many of their clients; conversely this may produce lawyers who are well able to deal with business problems;
- should those without a law degree be able to train after only a one-year conversion course?
- both the Bar Vocational Course and the Legal Practice Course have become more practically based, teaching necessary skills such as interviewing, negotiating and advocacy;
- pupillage and the training contract allow 'hands-on' experience;
- would a completely different training scheme, e.g. all train to be solicitors followed by later specialisation, be more effective.

4 Finally draw your points together in a brief conclusion.

Question 4

1 Examine background and status; give some facts and make criticisms:
- only seven women in the High Court and one in the Court of Appeal;
- never has been a woman judge in the House of Lords;
- no ethnic minority judges at the higher levels;
- public school/Oxbridge background, particularly of superior judges.

2 Examine and comment on the system of appointment:
- the necessary qualifications;
- draw distinction between superior and inferior judges;
- inferior judges – beginning to become more open with posts advertised, job interviews and the progression from assistant recorder up the judicial ladder;
- superior judges – by invitation, secretive system.

3 Consider the functions of judges:
- civil actions – decide entire case (with the few exceptions where a jury is used);
- criminal cases – decide points of law and sentence;
- appeal cases and judicial review – points of law.

4 Evaluate the criticisms in the light of the functions:

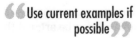
Use current examples if possible

- some criticisms valid – e.g. out of touch with society – use any recent examples that have been publicised;
- imbalance in composition of the bench;
- does this matter in deciding points of law – 75% of cases heard by the House of Lords involve statutory interpretation;
- problems arising from sentencing;
- training can help judges' awareness of problems.

TUTOR'S ANSWER

Question 3

The Courts and Legal Services Act 1990 was a culmination of the process of change in the legal profession that had started gradually. The two legal professions used to be more greatly divided in their work. Solicitors concentrated on what could be regarded as office based work, dealing with leases, conveyancing, wills and probate, and doing the preparatory work in litigation, whereas barristers were traditionally the advocates in court. There has always been a certain overlap in their work though, with solicitors having rights of audience in the lower courts, that is the County Court and the Magistrates' Court, and since the Courts Act 1971 also having the right to appear in the Crown Court when the case was an appeal or committal for sentence from the Magistrates' Court. In addition the Courts Act allowed the Lord Chancellor to authorise the appearance of solicitors in trials in remote Crown Courts such as Bodmin.

The Courts and Legal Services Act 1990 allowed solicitors to obtain certificates of advocacy so that they could practise as an advocate in any court. Solicitors wishing to do this must show that they have relevant experience, attend a short course and pass examinations in evidence; the first certificates of advocacy were granted in 1994.

The Act also allows solicitors with the relevant certificate of advocacy to be eligible for appointment as a circuit judge, a High Court judge or an appeal judge; previously the superior judiciary had been open only to barristers. It also allows for the promotion of circuit judges to the High Court bench. The first such promotion was made in 1993. In time those solicitors with the relevant certificate of advocacy will also filter up to the higher judicial post, although this will take some time, as ten years' experience is needed to be eligible for appointment. This might open up the judiciary and make it less elitist although the effect will be fairly minimal in the foreseeable future as only a small number of solicitors have become advocates in the High Court. In addition the training of both barristers and solicitors is becoming financially restrictive with only those from prosperous homes able to afford it so that candidates for the judiciary will still be likely to come from an elitist section of society.

The Court and Legal Services Act 1990 has set up the Advisory Committee on Legal Education which in its initial report suggested that all law students should follow the same initial training with those who then wished to become advocates going on to extra training.

The monopolies of solicitors have also been affected by the Courts and Legal Services Act. Again these changes followed on from earlier changes made by the Administration of Justice Act 1985 which gave licensed conveyancers the right to do conveyancing. The 1990 Act extended this concept by allowing banks and building societies the right to become licensed conveyancers. The result has been a marked lowering of prices in this area, which is good for the consumer, but has made it difficult for some smaller firms of solicitors to survive. The Act has also abolished solicitors' monopoly on probate and litigation.

Another provision in the Act is the future possibility of multi-disciplinary practices which would allow solicitors to form partnerships with other professions such as accountants. This should mean a 'one-stop' service for certain types of case, including taxation problems and house sales. This would clearly benefit the public but this provision has not yet been implemented.

Contingency fees were introduced by the Act, although it was not until 1995 that they came into operation and then only for personal injury cases, insolvency and human rights. In such cases the client and solicitor agree a fee at the beginning of the case together with an uplift of up to 100% if the case is successful. This allows those who do not qualify for legal aid a greater chance of representation at a reasonable cost and is an important development in the provision of legal services.

Finally, the Act created the post of Legal Services Ombudsman. This allows for an impartial investigation of complaints against lawyers when their own complaints mechanism has not proved satisfactory to the client. However, since the Ombudsman has few powers, this is still not adequate to protect the public from poor legal services.

In all, the Courts and Legal Services Act 1990 made some wide sweeping changes to the legal profession and the provision of legal services but in some areas it can be argued that it has not gone far enough.

A review sheet for this chapter can be found on p. 209.

LEGAL AID AND ADVICE

GETTING STARTED

Access to justice means not only having a good legal system but also being able to afford to use that system. As Mr Justice Darling said: 'The law courts of England are open to all men like the doors of the Ritz hotel.' In other words, the courts are there for anyone to use but cost may prevent many people from seeking justice.

With the development of a welfare state the idea of publicly funded legal aid developed.

It is best to start by understanding the types of aid and advice and their scope before going on to more detail. The government schemes are:

- **Green Form scheme** – this is for advice only and solicitors may do up to two hours of work (three in matrimonial cases); it covers most civil and criminal matters.

- **ABWOR (advice by way of representation)** – this is an extension of the Green Form scheme to give representation for certain cases where full legal aid is not available. Its main use is for family cases in the Magistrates' Court and various matters where an individual's liberty is at risk in some way, e.g. defending applications by the police to extend the period of detention in serious arrestable offences.

- **Duty solicitors** – there are two schemes: (1) a 24-hour rota of solicitors to give advice to anyone arrested and held at a police station; (2) a rota of solicitors who attend Magistrates' Courts to give defendants advice in criminal cases.

- **Civil legal aid** – this gives full representation for plaintiff or defendant in cases in the County Court, High Court and civil appeal courts. It is not available for defamation cases, small claims, undefended divorces or tribunal hearings.

- **Criminal legal aid** – this gives full representation for a defendant on a criminal charge and is also available for criminal appeal cases.

Many of the government funded schemes are means tested so that two figures are considered – the disposable income and the disposable capital. **Disposable income** is the amount left after deducting essential living expenses and other matters such as tax, NI, pension payments and union dues. **Disposable capital** is assets excluding the house in which one lives, ordinary furnishings and workman's tools.

ESSENTIAL PRINCIPLES

HISTORY

The present system of government funded legal aid and advice has its roots in the report by the Rushcliffe Committee in 1945. Its main recommendations were:

1 legal aid should be available in the types of cases where lawyers normally represented private individual clients;

2 it should not be limited to people 'normally classed as poor' but should also include those of moderate means;

3 it should be means tested and there should be an increasing scale of contributions paid by those with income or capital above minimum levels;

4 there should be a merits test to be judged by legal practitioners *not* by a government agency;

5 lawyers acting for legally aided clients should receive 'adequate' pay.

The Legal Aid and Advice Act 1949 implemented these proposals in civil cases and over the next twenty years the scheme was gradually extended. For example the Legal Advice and Assistance Act 1972 set up the Green Form scheme of advice. Finally, the whole scheme was rationalised in the Legal Aid Act 1988.

The Legal Action Group in Strategy for Justice describes the history as being divided into three distinct periods:

1 **Foundation** – 1949 to 1970 encompassing the establishment and gradual evolution of the legal aid scheme.

2 **Expansion** – 1970 to 1986 when there was a massive expansion of all forms of publicly funded legal services.

3 **'Stagflation'** – 1986 onwards when there have been a succession of major challenges to the fundamental structure of publicly funded legal services so that the numbers of people assisted have declined and lawyers fees are well below those from private clients.

PRESENT SYSTEM

The avowed purpose of the 1988 Legal Aid Act is set out in s. 1 as being 'to establish a framework for the provision ... of advice, assistance and representation which is publicly funded with a view to helping persons who might otherwise be unable to obtain advice, assistance or representation on account of their means'.

The framework is supplemented by detailed regulations made under the authority of the Act by the Lord Chancellor. The Act gave him very wide powers and since 1988 he has used these to alter the system radically.

ADVICE AND ASSISTANCE

There are four schemes under the Legal Aid Act 1988.

GREEN FORM SCHEME

This is for advice only and solicitors can usually do only two hours of work for the client. It covers most civil and criminal matters, but does *not* cover:

■ matters involving non-English law;

■ drafting of wills (unless the client is 70 or over or disabled);

■ conveyancing unless under a court order.

There is no merits test, but there is a strict means test which is administered by the solicitor with the help of a key card. In 1995 it was available to those whose disposable income was below £72 per week and whose disposable capital was less than £1,000. (Figures for single person – extra allowances for dependants.) A person on income support, family credit or disability working allowance automatically qualified provided they were not over the capital limit.

Criticisms

Prior to April 1993 the scheme was available to people with a higher income on payment of a contribution. (Under £75 free – up to £145 contribution on a sliding scale.) The Law Society estimated that the cuts in April 1993, which limited the scheme to those below the minimum disposable income, meant that 11.5 million people became ineligible. Payment rates for solicitors, as with all legal aid schemes, are low.

ABWOR

This is an extension of the Green Form scheme to give 'assistance by way of representation' under s. 8 of the 1988 Act. It is available for some cases where full legal aid is not given and these include:

- most civil proceedings in the Magistrates' Court;
- all proceedings under the Children Act 1989;
- hearings by the Mental Health Review Tribunal;
- applications in the Magistrates' Court for a warrant for further detention in cases of serious arrestable offences;
- disciplinary hearings for prisoners.

As with the Green Form scheme it is means tested but the limits are higher and those above the minimum levels but below the maximum can use the scheme on payment of a contribution.

ADVICE AND ASSISTANCE FOR PERSONS IN POLICE STATIONS

This started in 1986 and there is no means or merits test. The service is free. Local solicitors operate a rota scheme so that theoretically there is a 24-hour service. Under the PACE Code of Practice the police must tell a detained person of the scheme. Suspects do not have to use it, they may choose to pay their own solicitor. In 1989 research by Sanders et al (LCD) showed that only about 20% of those held in the ten police stations surveyed received legal advice and often that advice was given over the telephone.

DUTY SOLICITOR AT THE MAGISTRATES' COURT

This was originally voluntary but was put on a statutory base in 1982 and is now covered by the 1988 Act. Local solicitors on a rota basis attend the court to give advice. There is no means or merits test and the defendant is not required to pay any contribution. It is limited to advice although the solicitor may also represent in court in limited circumstances.

Apart from schemes under the Legal Aid Act 1988 there are other schemes available.

CITIZENS' ADVICE BUREAUX

These exist in most towns. They were first set up in 1938 and today there are about 700. They give general advice free to anyone on a variety of issues including legal matters. They can also provide information on which local solicitors do legal aid work or give cheap or free initial interviews. Many also have solicitors who attend once a week or fortnight to give more qualified advice on legal matters.

 **Para-legals**

The Benson Commission in 1979 emphasised the importance of CABx as a first tier legal advice service. Benson recommended that they should be staffed by 'para-legals' and given more government funding. This has not happened and funding is still patchy and they rely heavily on volunteers. However, there is a training system for these volunteers and some become quite expert in certain fields.

One of the biggest problems is attracting enough volunteers in inner cities causing limited hours, even at the CAB at the Royal Courts of Justice.

LAW CENTRES

The first of these opened in North Kensington in 1970. Their aim is to provide free legal advice (and sometimes representation) in areas where there are few solicitors. Law centres play a pioneering role in identifying previously unrecognised areas of need and are orientated to the needs of the particular community they serve. The most common areas of work include housing; welfare rights/debts; employment; planning and environment; children's rights; immigration; discrimination; juvenile crime. The Home Office provides some funding but law centres are largely reliant on local authority funding which is patchy. As a result some have been forced to close.

As a result of cuts to the legal aid programme more help services have developed: these include:

FREE REPRESENTATION UNIT

The bar have set up schemes in different areas aimed at helping those who are ineligible for legal aid. The first started in 1992. More than 2,000 cases per year are handled in this way. This goes beyond advice and allows barristers to represent people in court.

LEGAL INSURANCE

Most motor insurance policies offer cover (for a small amount extra) for help with legal fees in cases arising from road accidents. There are also policies purely for insurance against legal costs.

CONDITIONAL FEES

Under s. 58 of the Courts and Legal Services Act 1990 solicitors are now allowed to come to a conditional fee arrangement. The regulations for this finally came into place in July 1995 but conditional fees can only be used in:

- personal injury cases;
- insolvency cases;
- human rights cases.

Solicitor and client will agree a fee at the beginning of a case and also agree that if the solicitor wins the case he can charge an 'uplift'; this can be of up to 100%. The problem is that the uplift may absorb all the client's damages, although the Law Society has recommended a cap of 25% of damages in its model agreement. Also the agreement does not protect a client from having to pay the other side's cost in the event of losing the case but it is suggested that the plaintiff insure against this.

LEGAL AID IN CIVIL CASES

A legal aid order will entitle the client to full representation throughout all phases of a case. The civil scheme is now run by the Legal Aid Board, the members of which are appointed by the Lord Chancellor. At least two of the members must be solicitors.

It is available in most civil cases but is *not* available for:

- small claims cases;
- defamation cases;
- undefended divorces;
- most tribunal hearings (but it *is* available for the Employment Appeal Tribunal and the Lands Tribunal).

There is a **means test** and a **merits test**.

On the **merits**, the client must show that he has reasonable grounds for taking or defending proceedings (Legal Aid Act 1988 s. 15(2)) but he can be refused if the Board think he would gain only a trivial advantage from the proceedings.

The **means** are assessed by the Department of Social Services. For both disposable income and disposable capital two figures are set each year. If the applicant is below the set minimum figures legal aid is free; if they are above the minimum but below the maximum, legal aid is available on the payment of a contribution based on a sliding scale. Above the maximum figures legal aid is not available.

CONTRIBUTIONS

If the applicant has to pay a contribution it is one thirty-sixth of the excess above the minimum level to be paid each month for the life of the case as well as the excess capital.

STATUTORY CHARGE

"Clawback"

At the end of a case a successful legally aided party will be asked to pay any shortfall in costs out of his damages (s. 16). This statutory charge is also called the **clawback** and can mean that a successful plaintiff gains very little by bringing the case.

CRITICISMS

1. Financial limits are too low, creating a middle income 'poverty trap'. The rates have not kept pace with inflation and it is estimated that sixteen million people have dropped out of eligibility since 1979 (the last major increase).

2   Problems created by the clawback.

3   Low rates of pay mean that many solicitors have pulled out of the scheme as it does not even cover their overheads.

4   Non-availability for certain cases can create injustice, particularly for tribunal hearings and other social areas of law where the other party is either a government department or a business with access to funds. Personal injury cases in the Small Claims Court are also disadvantaged with an insurance company helping the other party. Some of the gaps have been filled by ABWOR and the Lord Chancellor is considering extending some legal aid to tribunal hearings.

5   The cuts in 1993 caused problems.

6   The introduction of franchising means fewer solicitors to undertake legal aid work.

The Lord Chancellor defended the cuts to the system by saying (in 1992) that the legal aid budget cost one billion (double of that four years earlier) and pointed out that every extra pound for legal aid meant a pound less for the NHS, for schools and for social security. In 1994 the total net cost of legal aid was about £1.3 billion.

LEGAL AID IN CRIMINAL CASES

This is governed by Part V of the Legal Aid Act 1988. The Act has provisions for the Legal Aid Board to take over the administration of the scheme but at the moment it is administered by the courts. Legal aid is only available to a defendant; it is *not* available to prosecute.

PROCEDURE

Once a person has been charged with a criminal offence he can apply to the Magistrates' Court where his case will be dealt with (either for trial or committal proceedings). He has to fill in a form setting out what he has been charged with and explaining any special reasons why he should get legal aid. He also has to fill in another form with his financial information. The application is dealt with by the clerk of the court who can grant or refuse aid. There is an appeal against refusal of legal aid for serious offences and for summary cases a further application can always be made to the Magistrates' Court.

MERITS TEST

The basic test is whether it is in the interests of justice for the defendant to be given legal aid (s. 21). Section 21 also says that a defendant must be given aid if:

- the charge is murder; or
- the prosecution is appealing to the House of Lords; or
- there is a bail application by a person in custody.

❝Interests of justice❞

For other cases the criteria set out in s. 22 (formerly the Widgery criteria) apply. The original criteria set out in s. 22 were reformulated by the Lord Chancellor in 1994 so that it is considered to be 'in the interests of justice' to grant legal aid if:

1   the offence is such that if proved it is likely that the court would impose a custodial sentence or lead to loss of the defendant's livelihood or serious damage to their reputation;

2   the determination of the case may involve consideration of a substantial question of law;

3   the accused may be unable to understand the proceedings or state their own case because of inadequate knowledge of English, mental illness or other mental or physical disability;

4   the nature of the defence is such as to involve the tracing and interview of witnesses or expert cross-examination of a witness for the prosecution;

5   it is in the interests of someone other than the defendant that the defendant be represented.

These are only guidelines and other factors may be considered.

❝Variations in refusal rates❞

The decision on the merits is left to the clerk of the court with the result that some clerks grant legal aid more readily than others. In 1988 the national refusal rate was 9%, but some courts had a refusal rate of more than three times that figure. It was suggested that these discrepancies might be because different areas had different types of crime or that solicitors in some areas were more willing to put in applications. However, research by Young and MacNair in the early 1990s showed wide variations in approach. They put forward the same applications to six courts and in each court two clerks considered them. One court granted ten out of the twelve, whilst two courts granted only five out of the twelve.

If there is any doubt whether legal aid should be granted then that doubt should be resolved in the defendant's favour (Legal Aid Act 1988 s. 21(7)).

MEANS TEST

1995 figures – legal aid is granted *free* where:

- disposable income is not more than £48 per week; and
- disposable capital is not more than £3,000.

Above these figures a *contribution* is payable of one-third the excess income while the legal aid order is in force and usually all the excess capital. There are no upper limits.

RICH DEFENDANTS

There have been several recent cases where defendants who appear to be wealthy have been granted legal aid. These include Asil Nadir (Polly Peck), charged with theft and fraud, who received £1 million in legal aid before fleeing to Cyprus where he is said to have business assets worth £25 million and Gordon Foxley who had a house worth £500,000, weekend cottages and luxury cars (*The Times*, 24 October 1994).

In December 1994 the Lord Chancellor issued a consultation paper on this problem seeking views on:

- developing the idea of legal aid as a loan;
- the possibility of refusing legal aid to a defendant who appeared to be leading an affluent lifestyle;
- putting a limit on the amount of equity value of a house which is ignored in assessing capital;
- freezing assets of a defendant to recover legal aid costs from them if a defendant is convicted.

DEVELOPMENTS IN THE 1990s

FRANCHISING

Since 1994 the government has started offering franchises for legal aid to solicitors. This is aimed at providing an 'accessible and quality assured service for clients giving improving value for money to the taxpayer'. In return for minimum quality standards the franchise holders will have delegated to them some of the existing powers of the Legal Aid Board, thus enabling them to grant legal aid instantly in some cases. Franchised firms will receive preferential treatment in payment, especially with payments on account, thus easing the cash flow problem where solicitors used to have to wait until the end of a case to be paid. In 1995 franchisees were given rises in payments for legal aid cases but other lawyers received no increase.

To obtain a franchise firms must meet certain criteria for both legal and business management. These include a wide range of points from the scope of the legal library available to the systems for detailed financial analysis. One problem of franchising is that the number of firms of solicitors doing legal aid work will be reduced, causing problems of access for the public, particularly in country areas.

CAPPING OF FUNDS

In May 1995 the Lord Chancellor in a Green Paper outlined the following proposals:

- cash limits on the budget available;
- bigger role for advice agencies with a reduction in the number of legal aid law firms;
- access to legal aid services only via quality controlled law firms and agencies working under block contracts to fixed budgets;
- a central multi-million pound emergency for high cost cases;
- barristers' fees to be negotiated by other agencies as well as law firms;
- enhance 'no win, no fee' scheme.

At the same time two more positive proposals were made:

- pilot projects to test legal aid for tribunals and mediation services;
- legal aid to be available for 'exceptional' cases for coroners' inquests.

The thirteen areas of the Legal Aid Board would be awarded budgets based on past demand within their region in an NHS-style of funding. This could lead to legal aid being granted in one area, but refused in another because that area has run out of funds.

EXAMINATION QUESTIONS

1   Explain and critically assess the provision of funding for legal advice, assistance and representation in civil matters.   (AEB)

2   Describe and evaluate the system of civil legal aid, including advice and assistance.   (NEAB)

3   To what extent does the legal system provide an adequate service for a poor person charged with a criminal offence?   (UODLE)

4   Brown has been involved in a road traffic accident with Green, as a result of which the police have charged Brown with dangerous driving and Green has started civil proceedings against Brown claimimg damages in excess of £100,000.

   a)   Advise Brown as to how he may obtain legal aid and advice.

      and

   b)   Do you think that such provisions for legal aid and advice are adequate?   (UODLE)

5   'Financial constraints on legal aid and advice schemes have severely limited access to justice.' Discuss   (UODLE)

ANSWERS TO QUESTIONS

OUTLINE ANSWERS TO SELECTED QUESTIONS

Question 2

Note that this question asks *only for the civil system of legal aid*. Do *not* discuss legal aid in criminal cases. Also note that you have to include legal aid, advice and assistance.

■ describe the Green Form scheme for advice and ABWOR for advice by way of representation; explain what these two schemes cover;

■ describe civil legal aid including availability, means and merits tests;

■ evaluate the schemes by looking at the problems, for example low levels on income limits, areas which the schemes do not cover, the clawback, low fees to solicitors leading to poorer service and difficulty with access to justice.

Question 4

In this style of question you must first be clear which areas of law are involved so that you know whether you should write about civil or criminal legal aid or both. Here there are two situations involved:

1   Brown is being charged with dangerous driving – this is clearly a criminal case;

2   Green has started civil proceedings against Brown claiming damages – you are told this is a civil case.

Part a) – it is clear that you need to advise on both the civil and criminal aspect as follows:

■ criminal advice may be obtained via the Green Form scheme or the duty solicitor at the Magistrates' Court;

■ criminal legal aid – Brown must apply to the clerk of the Magistrates' Court involved, giving details of the case and his finances;

■ civil advice may be obtained via the Green Form scheme, but initial advice may come from CABx or a free/cheap interview with a solicitor;

■ civil legal aid – Brown must apply to the legal aid board with details of the case and his finances.

Part b) – comment on the adequacy of the provision, the main points to make are:

■ the granting of criminal legal aid varies from court to court;

- the low income levels required to qualify for the Green Form scheme;
- the cut-off maximum levels are too low in civil legal aid;
- the clawback.

STUDENT'S ANSWER WITH TUTOR'S COMMENTS

Question 5

 **Good introduction setting the scene**

In an ideal world everyone would have equal opportunity to get access to justice, but in practice there are restrictions on such access because of the cost of legal services. The various legal aid schemes have tried to partially address this problem but in today's economic climate stricter financial limits are being imposed.

Originally when the legal aid programme started in 1949, it was meant to provide help for both the poor and those of modest means, and civil legal aid was available to some 80% of the population. Today the financial limits mean that the middle income group are excluded from help and less than 50% will qualify for legal aid.

In order to decide whether someone qualifies for legal aid two figures are assessed, the disposable income and the disposable capital. For each of these there is a minimum amount below which legal aid will be given free. There is also a maximum figure and if the applicant exceeds this figure, then they will not get legal aid. If the applicant's income and capital are between the two figures, they will qualify for legal aid, but only on payment of a contribution.

There are three points that can be made about these limits; first the minimum figures are very low, so that only the very poor will be given legal aid free of charge. However this can be justified as clearly it is the poorest people in society who could not get access to justice in any other way and it is important that they be given this sort of help.

Clear presentation and good quite sophisticated points

Secondly the contribution scheme is a reasonable idea; the problem is that the levels of contribution are really quite high, one-third of any excess income, and even worse this has to be paid for as long as the case lasts. This could mean that a plaintiff claiming for personal injuries might have to pay thousands of pounds by way of contribution, as the case would be likely to last for four or five years. This could severely limit access to justice and may account for the fact that only about one in four accident victims bother to start court cases.

Thirdly, the maximum cut-off point for both income and capital is far too low. These figures have not kept pace with inflation, so that more and more people are being squeezed out of the legal aid scheme and consequently denied access to justice.

Conditional fees have been introduced, whereby the solicitor will charge more if he wins the case, as a small gesture towards helping this group to take cases in court.

Financial restrictions have also affected the Green Form scheme. Until 1993 this scheme had an upper and a lower limit, with a contribution system, but since 1993 it is only available to those on very low income levels, and not available to those who used to be able to pay a contribution. These people can now only get advice from a solicitor by paying the market rate, which might be as much as £300 an hour, and is outside their financial means. Fortunately there are some solicitors who will give a short interview free of charge, but this does not replace the Green Form scheme.

Excellent use of material

Another financial problem with civil legal aid is the clawback, under which a winning plaintiff will have to pay some or, possibly all, of their damages to the Legal Aid Board.

These damages are meant to compensate for injuries etc. and it seems wrong that although legal aid gave them 'access to justice' they are then denied justice by the confiscation of this compensation.

It is true that the cost of legal aid has risen dramatically and that there must be some limitations put on its availability, but it appears that the present system does truly prevent many people from getting access to justice.

Tutor's Comments

This shows a good understanding of the problems and the material is used well to make points supporting the discussion. The presentation is also very clear, but the essay could include a little more detail on the schemes. Overall this is just worth a grade A, because of the high standard of the discussion.

A review sheet for this chapter can be found on p. 209.

CHAPTER 9

LAY PEOPLE IN THE LEGAL SYSTEM

LAY MAGISTRATES

JURIES

JURIES IN CIVIL CASES

OTHER LAY PEOPLE IN THE ADMINISTRATION OF JUSTICE

GETTING STARTED

The English system of justice relies heavily on the use of lay people, that is people who have no legal qualifications. This contrasts with Continental systems of justice where very few lay people take part in legal decision making. The concept of trial by one's peers in the shape of a jury comes from the English common law and today it is often equated with the concept of democracy. Although the main use of lay people is in the Magistrates' Courts and Crown Courts, there are also other areas, such as industrial tribunals where ordinary people are part of the decision making process.

The advantages and disadvantages of the use of lay people are the main themes that occur in examination questions. The starting point is to make sure of the facts; too many candidates in examinations confuse magistrates and juries. Then to be aware of the arguments on both sides, as most questions will require an evaluation. When discussing advantages and disadvantages try to use facts and material in support of your points; do not just list the pros and cons. Even though the material in this book is often given in a list format, this is to help with revision and is not the method of presentation to use in an examination.

Finally, link the topics in this chapter with the work done in the civil and criminal courts (Chapters 5 and 6) to show greater understanding of the system as a whole.

ESSENTIAL PRINCIPLES

There are over 700 Magistrates' Courts in England and Wales. They have jurisdiction over a variety of matters in their location. They rely heavily on the use of lay magistrates who are not qualified lawyers although there are also qualified full-time magistrates called **stipendiary magistrates**.

LAY MAGISTRATES

The main facts about lay magistrates are that they:

- are unqualified;
- must live within fifteen miles of the commission area;
- must be between 21 and 60 on appointment;
- are part-time – must sit at least 26 times per year;
- are unpaid save for expenses.

Some people are not eligible these include:

- people with criminal convictions;
- undischarged bankrupts;
- members of the police or traffic wardens;
- members of the armed forces.

Lay magistrates sit as a bench of two to seven magistrates together, but the usual size bench is three. A single lay magistrate has very limited powers, e.g. he/she can issue warrants for arrest. There are approximately 30,000 magistrates with about 1,500 new magistrates being appointed each year. Another title for lay magistrates is Justice of the Peace (JP) and this office is very old, dating back to the twelfth century at least.

APPOINTMENT

Names are put forward to advisory committees by groups such as the local political parties, trade unions and chambers of commerce. In addition committees can advertise for individuals to put themselves forward and advertisements are placed in local papers, ethnic newspapers and even on buses. The intention is to create a panel that is representative of all aspects of society.

The committees will interview candidates and then submit the names of those they believe are suitable to the Lord Chancellor. The Lord Chancellor has the final decision and will not necessarily appoint all the people whose names are put forward.

Woman now account for 47% of lay magistrates. A major criticism is that most magistrates are Conservatives, even in areas where there is a high Labour vote. Ethnic minorities are under-represented, although appointments are increasing. The lay bench still tends to be 'middle-class, middle-aged and middle-minded'.

> **Middle-class, middle-aged and middle-minded**

DUTIES

Lay magistrates must sit at least 26 times per year. This is one of the problems in attracting working classes as, while employers have to allow time off, they do not have to pay the employee for it. Men aged 35 to 45 are also likely to be involved in careers and promotion chances would be affected by having time off. Lay magistrates are expected to deal with a wide variety of cases. Their main work is trying minor criminal cases, but they also have some civil functions, e.g. hearing applications for licences to sell alcohol and dealing with community debts such as non-payment of the community charge. There is also a youth court to hear cases relating to those under 18 years old. In addition magistrates decide family cases ranging from adoption orders to orders to prevent domestic violence, although they cannot deal with divorce cases.

TRAINING

New magistrates are given about 40 hours of training spread over the first year. This consists of:

- observing court proceedings;
- attending lectures and workshops;
- visiting penal institutions.

The training is not meant to make magistrates proficient in the law, but to give them understanding of their duties. Since over 80% of defendants appearing in the Magistrates' Court plead guilty, a major part of the training is aimed at sentencing.

Since 1980 all magistrates have to attend refresher courses every three years. These are usually weekend courses. Magistrates on the Youth Panel and the Family Panel receive extra training.

THE CLERK

Every bench is assisted by a clerk. The senior clerk in each court has to be qualified as a barrister or solicitor for at least five years. His duty is to guide the magistrates on questions of law, practice and procedure. He is not meant to assist in the decision making and should not normally retire with the magistrates when they go to make their decision. Clerks have been given increased powers to deal with routine matters.

ADVANTAGES OF USING LAY MAGISTRATES

1   The system involves members of the community and provides a wider cross section on the bench than would be possible with the use of professional judges.
2   Lay magistrates have local knowledge.
3   Improved training means that lay magistrates are not complete 'amateurs'.
4   A legally qualified clerk is available to give advice.
5   It is cheap, both for the government and for the defendant.
6   Cases are dealt with relatively quickly.
7   There are few appeals from magistrates' decisions. In 1994 there were 25,000 of which about half were successful.

DISADVANTAGES OF USING LAY MAGISTRATES

1   Lay magistrates tend to be 'middle-class, middle-aged and middle-minded' and will have little in common with the young working class defendants who make up the majority of defendants.
2   Both working class and ethnic groups are under-represented.
3   The training is inadequate for the workload.
4   Lay magistrates tend to be prosecution biased, believing the police too readily. They are likely to convict, with only 20% of defendants being found not guilty after a trial in the Magistrates' Court.
5   Some magistrates may rely too heavily on their clerk.
6   There is inconsistency in sentencing and in the granting of bail. One survey showed that five Magistrates' Courts did not send anyone to prison while at the other end of the scale one court sent nearly one in every five male defendants to prison.
7   The workload is becoming too great and too complicated, especially in the family court.

JURIES

While juries are very important in criminal cases, it must not be forgotten that they are used in other courts as well. They may be used in:

■ some civil cases in the Queen's Bench Division of the High Court and in the County Court;
■ cases in the Coroners' Courts;
■ criminal cases in the Crown Court.

CRIMINAL CASES

The main use of juries today is in the Crown Court, where they decide the guilt or innocence of those tried on indictment. This, however, comprises less than 1% of all criminal trials. A jury in the Crown Court has twelve members.

JURY QUALIFICATIONS

Before 1972 there was a property qualification; this discriminated against women and young people who were less likely to own or rent a property. Following the Morris Committee Report on jury service, which thought that being a juror should be the counterpart of being a citizen, the qualifications for jury service were widened in the Criminal Justice Act 1972.

The present position is in the Juries Act 1974 (as amended). To qualify for jury service a person must be:

- aged between 18 and 70;
- registered to vote on the register of electors;
- ordinarily resident in the United Kingdom, the Channel Islands or the Isle of Man for at least five years since their thirteenth birthday.

However, certain people are not permitted to sit on a jury even though they are within the basic qualifications. These are people who are disqualified or ineligible.

Disqualified

This category includes:

- those who have been sentenced to life imprisonment or detained at Her Majesty's Pleasure;
- those who have received a sentence of five years or more in prison or youth custody;
- anyone who has served any other custodial sentence within the last ten years;
- anyone who has been given a suspended prison sentence within the last ten years;
- anyone who has been placed on probation within the past five years;
- anyone who is currently on bail.

If a disqualified person fails to disclose that disqualification and turns up for jury service, they may be fined up to £5,000.

Ineligible

This category includes:

- those with certain mental disorders;
- those with a religious vocation;
- judges and magistrates;
- others concerned with the administration of justice or who have been so within the last ten years; this is very wide including the more obvious groups such as police, barristers and solicitors, but also including such people as those employed in a forensic science laboratory, and court shorthand writers.

Excusals as of right

Some people are eligible to serve on a jury but may demand to be excused from jury service. These include:

- anyone between 65 and 70 years old;
- anyone who has served on a jury within the past two years;
- members of Parliament;
- those in the armed forces;
- doctors and nurses and people in other essential professions e.g. dentists, chemists and vets.

Discretionary excusals

If people have problems that make it very difficult for them to do their jury service, they may ask to be excused or for their period of service to be put back to a later date. Good reasons for being given a discretionary excusal might be illness or disability that makes it impossible for the person to sit as a juror, or a mother with a small baby. Jury service will be deferred for business appointments that cannot be undertaken by anyone else, examinations or holidays that have been booked.

Lack of capacity

A judge at the court may discharge a person from being a juror for lack of capacity to cope with the trial, e.g. insufficient understanding of English or deafness.

SELECTION OF A JURY

The names are selected at random from the electoral registers for the area which the court covers. At some Crown Courts this is done by a computer, in other Crown Courts it is done manually by a court clerk. More than twelve jurors are summonsed, in bigger courts with more than one court room it may be as many as 150 to allow for disqualifications and excusals. People are expected to attend for two weeks' jury service.

Comments

1 The use of the electors' list as a sampling frame can be criticised; it does not always give a representative sample of the population. This is because not every one registers to vote, especially the young and ethnic minorities. Also it excludes the homeless.

2 The Runciman Commission (1993) recommended that in exceptional cases it should be possible for either the prosecution or the defence to apply for the selection of the jury to contain up to three jurors from ethnic minorities. At the moment there is no power for the judge to empanel a multi-racial jury (*R v Ford (1989)*).

3 The manual selection of jurors can lead to an unbalanced jury as was shown at the Old Bailey in 1993 when out of a panel of twelve jurors nine came from Romford, two of them living within 20 doors of each other in the same street. In this case a fresh jury was called, this time it contained seven members from Ilford! Finally at the third attempt a more mixed jury was obtained.

4 Although some checks are carried out, many disqualified people fail to disclose this fact and sit on juries. One survey of Inner London juries estimated that one in every 24 jurors was disqualified.

CHALLENGING

As the twelve jurors are selected and come into the jury box to be sworn in as jurors, both the prosecution and defence have certain rights to challenge one or more. These are:

1 **To the array** – this means challenging the whole jury on the basis that it has been chosen in an unrepresentative or biased way.

2 **For cause** – this is a challenge to an individual juror pointing out a valid reason why that juror should not serve on the jury, e.g. the juror is disqualified or is related to a witness or defendant.

3 **Prosecution right to stand by jurors** – this puts that juror to the end of the list of potential jurors and they will not be used on the jury unless there are not enough other jurors. The prosecution does not have to give a reason for 'standing by' but the Attorney-General's guidelines issued in 1990 make it clear that this power should be used sparingly.

Peremptory challenge

The defence used to have the right to challenge three jurors without cause, but this was abolished on 1 January 1989 because of abuse of the system, for example in the *Greenham Common case (1985)* the use of peremptory challenges meant that an all female jury was empanelled.

VETTING

There are two types:

1 **Routine police checks** on prospective jurors to eliminate those disqualified. The Court of Appeal approved of this in *R v Mason (1980)* and further said that if in the course of looking at criminal records, convictions were revealed which did not disqualify, there was no reason why these should not be passed on to prosecuting counsel.

2 **Political vetting** where a wider check is made on a juror's background and political affiliations. In *R v Crown Court at Sheffield, ex parte Brownlow (1980)* the Court of Appeal, while holding that they had no power to interfere with the Crown Court judge's order, said that vetting was 'unconstitutional' and a 'serious invasion of privacy' and not sanctioned by the Juries Act 1974.

   Following this case the Attorney-General published guidelines which say that:

   a) vetting should only be used in exceptional cases involving:

       i)   national security where part of the evidence is likely to be given in camera;

       ii) terrorist cases.

   b) vetting can only be carried out with the Attorney-General's express permission.

"Multi-racial juries"

"Attorney-General's guidelines"

THE JURY'S ROLE IN CRIMINAL CASES

"Split function"

The jury is used only at the Crown Court for cases where the defendant pleads not guilty.

The trial is presided over by a judge and the functions split between the judge and jury. The judge decides points of law and the jury decides the facts. At the end of the case the judge will sum up the case to the jury and direct them on any law involved. The jury will then retire to a private room and make the decision on the guilt or innocence of the accused in secret.

VERDICT

Initially the jury must try to come to a unanimous verdict. If after at least two hours the jury have not reached a verdict, a majority verdict will be allowed. These have been possible since 1967, so that where there is a full jury of twelve, the verdict can be ten to two or eleven to one. Majority verdicts were introduced because of the fear of jury 'nobbling' (only one member need be bribed to cause a retrial) and because it was felt that the acquittal rates were too high.

Secrecy

The jury discussion takes place in secret and there can be no inquiry into how the jury reached its verdict. Section 8 of the Contempt of Court Act 1981 makes disclosure of anything that happened in the jury room an offence. The Runciman Commission suggested that this should be amended to allow research into the workings of juries. In particular there should be research into the infuence that jurors with criminal convictions may have on jury verdicts. The judge cannot challenge a jury verdict. This is a long established principle going back to *Bushell's case (1670)*. The jury do not have to give any reasons for their decision.

Directed acquittals

As the judge decides the law, he can rule that there is no prosecution case for the defendant to answer. In this case the judge will direct the jury to find the defendant not guilty.

ADVANTAGES OF JURY TRIAL

1   **Public confidence** – the idea of trial by jury is very old and people prefer it to having a verdict by a single judge. Hence the objection to withdrawing the right to jury trial from cases of 'minor' theft.

2   **Bastion of liberty against the state** – Lord Devlin said juries are 'the lamp that shows that freedom lives'. Several cases have shown the importance of jury equity, e.g. *Ponting's case (1984)* when a civil servant was charged under the old wide-ranging s. 2 of the Official Secrets Act 1911 for leaking information on the sinking of the ship *The General Belgrano* during the Falklands War. The jury refused to convict although the judge ruled there was no defence and subsequently the government amended s. 2.

3   **Mitigates harshness of the law** – e.g. in one case a jury refused to convict a father who shot and injured a lorry driver who had killed his son.

4   **Makes law more open** as points have to be explained and the whole process is public.

5   **Random cross-section** should mean an impartial jury cancelling out each others biases, but problems with selection mean that this is not always so.

6   **No individual is responsible** – the jury dissolves after the end of the case.

7   **A jury is not case hardened** – they sit for only two weeks and are unlikely to try more than three or four cases.

8   **Justice is seen to be done** as the system is open and involves members of the public.

DISADVANTAGES OF JURY TRIALS

1   **Selection** – the jury is not a true cross-selection.

2   **Failure to understand the issues involved** in the trial. This is especially true in fraud trials and the Roskill Committee 1986 suggested that juries should not be used for complex fraud cases. Even in ordinary cases the jury may have difficulty in understanding and some jurors may be illiterate.

3   Some critics say that the lower age of **eighteen is too young** for jury service.

4   **Prejudice** – although jurors have no direct interest they may still be biased e.g. against the police or against ethnic minority defendants. Media coverage may influence them.

5   The **compulsory nature** of jury service is unpopular.

6 **No reasons have to be given** for the verdict, this means that there is no way of knowing whether the jury understood the case and came to the decision for the right reasons.

7 **Jury 'nobbling'** does occur and in some cases juries have had to be provided with police protection.

8 **Slow and expensive** – having to explain each point to the jury means that trials take longer and become more expensive.

ALTERNATIVES TO JURY TRIAL

1 **Trial by a single judge** as already happens in the majority of civil cases and also in the Diplock Courts in Northern Ireland.

2 **A panel of three** (or more) judges as occurs in some Continental countries.

3 **Trial by a judge and two lay assessors**; this has the merit of keeping public involvement.

4 **A mini-jury using six members**; this could be used for less serious criminal cases that at the moment have can have a full jury trial as occurs in some American states.

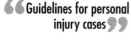
JURIES IN CIVIL CASES

Up to 1854 all common law actions were tried by jury. After 1854 the parties could agree not to use a jury and gradually their use declined. In 1933 the Administration of Justice Act limited the right to use a jury to cases of fraud, defamation, false imprisonment and malicious prosecution. Even for these cases a jury trial can be refused if the case is thought to be unsuitable for jury trial because it involves complicated documents, accounts or scientific evidence.

In other civil cases in the Queen's Bench Division of the High Court the parties can apply to a judge for trial by jury, but it is very rare for such a request to be granted. This follows the case of *Ward v James (1966)* in which the Court of Appeal laid down guidelines for personal injury cases.

❝Guidelines for personal injury cases❞

These were:

1 Normally personal injury cases should be tried by a judge sitting alone; this was because such cases involved assessing compensatory damages which had to have regard to the conventional scales of damages.

2 A jury should be used only in exceptional circumstances.

A High Court jury has twelve members and a County Court jury eight members.

SPECIAL PROBLEMS OF CIVIL JURIES

Damages

Juries in civil cases decide not only the liability of the parties in the case but also decide the amount of damages that will be awarded.

❝Unpredictable awards❞

The amount is therefore totally unpredictable, which makes it difficult for lawyers to advise on settlements. The awards also vary greatly as each jury has its own ideas and does not follow past cases. Judges when deciding awards of damages in personal injury cases look back to past awards and then apply an inflation factor. The jury does not have to give a reason either for its decision or for the amount it awards. A judge always gives a judgment, this makes it easier to see if there are good grounds for an appeal.

Bias

In some cases civil juries may be biased, often against the press. There is the additional problem that many defendants in defamation cases are well known.

DEFAMATION CASES

Juries in defamation cases cause particular problems with very large awards, the highest award to date being £1.5 million. Under s. 8 of the Courts and Legal Services Act 1990 the Court of Appeal, if they feel the damages were excessive or inadequate, can:

a) order a new trial; or

b) substitute such sum as appears proper to the court.

This power was first used in a case brought by the MP Teresa Gorman where the Court of Appeal reduced the damages from £150,000 to £50,000.

Cost

Civil cases are expensive and the use of a jury adds to this as the case is likely to last longer. With the increase in County Court jurisdiction, parties can now agree that their case should be transferred to the County Court. Here a jury of eight may be used and the trial is likely to be less expensive than one in the High Court. Parties may also agree to the case being tried by a judge alone without a jury.

Reforms

The Lord Chancellor has announced proposed reforms to help reduce the cost of libel actions. These include the plaintiff being able to seek a limited sum (probably a maximum of £10,000) in a quick procedure that would be dealt with by a judge. This would allow those who want to clear their name and get immediate compensation at a lower cost to do so. The idea is to stop both 'gold-digger' plaintiffs and the delaying tactics used by some newspapers.

CORONERS' COURTS

Here a jury of seven to eleven members may be used to enquire into deaths or the ownership of treasure trove. A jury is compulsory only in four cases:

1 deaths in prison;

2 deaths in industrial accidents;

3 deaths occurring in circumstances, the continuance or possible recurrence of which is prejudicial to the health and safety of the public, e.g. the *Herald of Free Enterprise* disaster or the *Marchioness* tragedy;

4 deaths occurring in police custody or resulting from an injury caused by a police officer in the execution of his duty.

Since 1977 a coroner is no longer obliged to summon a jury to decide cases involving road accidents or suspected homicide; he has a discretion on the use of a jury in such cases.

OTHER LAY PEOPLE IN THE ADMINISTRATION OF JUSTICE

TRIBUNALS

Most tribunals have a panel of three in which the chairman is legally qualified and the other two members are lay representatives with an expertise in the particular field of that tribunal (see Chapter 5 for further information on tribunals).

Other courts which use lay people include:

■ the Admiralty Court, which is part of the Queen's Bench Division; here the judge often sits with lay nautical assessors who advise the judge on questions of seamanship and navigation;

■ the Patents Court, which is part of the Chancery Division, where the judge may be assisted by scientific advisers;

■ the Restrictive Practices Court, where lay people with knowledge or experience of industry and commerce will help with the decision making.

❝Experts in the field❞ It can be seen that in all these cases the administration of justice is helped by the use of people who are experts in the particular field of the court concerned.

EXAMINATION QUESTIONS

1 'Magistrates' courts are cheap but it is wrong that matters of vital concern to the citizen should be decided by amateurs.' Discuss   (UODLE)

2 Doubts are often expressed about the continued use of juries *and* lay magistrates.

    a) Discuss the selection of juries and lay magistrates and explain the work that they perform.

    b) Examine the reasons for the doubts expressed about their continued use and indicate your own views on the issue.   (AEB)

3 Consider whether the legal system could function without the involvement of lay magistrates.   (ULEAC)

4   Account for the decline in the use of the jury in civil cases. Consider whether this trend is desirable.   (ULEAC)

5   Discuss critically the part played by laymen in the English legal system.   (NEAB)

ANSWERS TO QUESTIONS

OUTLINE ANSWER

Question 4

This question requires you to consider only *civil* juries. As it is only on one section, it means that you need to deal with this area in more detail than a question looking at a wider range of personnel:

1   start with the history of the decline, in particular the Administration of Justice Act 1933 and the case of *Ward v James*;

2   explore the guidelines laid down by *Ward v James* and explain why trial by single judge is thought to be preferable;

3   comment on the various problems associated with using civil juries: cost, bias, unpredictable awards;

4   look at justifications for retaining civil juries – especially where reputation is involved;

5   form a conclusion as to whether the decline is desirable.

TUTOR'S ANSWER

Question 5

The two main uses of laymen are as lay magistrates in the Magistrates' Court and jurors in the Crown Court, although lay people do play a significant role in other areas of the English legal system, particularly tribunals.

The Magistrates' Courts would be unable to function without lay justices as there are only about 85 qualified stipendiary magistrates to the 30,000 lay justices. A bench of a minimum of two lay magistrates has the same powers as a stipendiary magistrate. This means that they can try summary and triable either way criminal cases, decide the guilt or innocence of the defendant and impose sentences of up to 6 months' imprisonment and\or a £5,000 fine on guilty defendants. As well as these functions, magistrates also decide whether to grant bail, issue arrest warrants and search warrants and sit in the Youth Court to hear all but the most serious cases of juvenile crime. Their work load is both wide and heavy; they try about 97% of all criminal cases and on top of these duties in criminal cases, magistrates hear other cases ranging from licensing appplications to family cases.

This wide role is open to criticism as lay magistrates are given only a small amount of training, though Youth Court benches and Family panels are given additional training and there are also refresher courses, usually every three years. Critics also point out that lay magistrates are not representative of their local communities, with an over representation of the white middle classes and the middle aged. As a result of this background, it its thought that many magistrates are too ready to believe police evidence and are prosecution biased. This appears to be borne out by the high conviction rates in Magistrates' Courts; over 80% of defendants who plead not guilty are convicted. The other major criticism is the inconsistencies in the granting of bail and in sentencing between different benches. Recent surveys have revealed wide anomalies, with some Magistrates' Courts not imposing any custodial sentences, whilst others sent 20% of male defendants to prison.

Despite these criticisms there are many points in favour of the use of lay justices. They bring an involvement of local people and provide a wider cross section of society than is possible with the use of professional judges. There is a legally qualified clerk present in court to advise on points of law and the small number of succesful appeals suggests that lay magistrates usually 'get it right'.

The other major use of lay people is in the jury system. Juries are used in both civil and criminal cases, though their use in civil cases is limited to actions for defamation, malicious prosecution, false imprisonment and fraud. The main use is in criminal cases in the Crown Court trying indictable cases and any cases triable either way that have been committed for trial there. The selection of jury members is made from the electoral register of voters, and includes any one aged 18 to 70, though certain people are disqualified or ineligible and others can ask to be excused. The jury's function is to decide whether the defendant is guilty or not guilty; the trial judge will decide points of law and direct the jury on any law that they need to know. If the defendant is found guilty, it is the judge's function to decide the sentence.

The main reason that trial by jury is supported is that it is the sign of a democratic society and both judges and the public have confidence in it. Indeed Lord Devlin said that it is the lamp that shows that freedom lives. A jury will not convict a defendant if they believe that the law is unjust. This was shown in the case of Clive Ponting, a civil servant, who was charged with a breach of the Official Secrets Act when he disclosed information about the sinking of the General Belgrano to a Labour MP. The jury found him not guilty, despite the judge's ruling that there was no defence to the charge. The use of juries makes the law more open and the decision does not rest with one case hardened judge.

However there are many criticisms of the use of juries. The most important of these are that juries do not always understand the points raised by a case; this is particularly true in cases involving fraud and the Roskill Committee recommended that juries should not be used in complex fraud cases. Another criticism is that juries acquit too many defendants, though closer examination of the statistics reveals that almost half of all acquittals occur because the prosecution withdraws the charges or because the judge directs an acquittal. However research by Baldwin and McConville showed that there was reason to believe that juries 'got it wrong' in one third of cases where the defendant was acquitted, and, perhaps more worryingly, that one in every 20 convictions may be wrong. There was a high percentage of ethnic minority defendants in this 'wrong conviction' group and the inference is that in some cases juries are prejudiced. The Runciman Commission suggested that where the defendant was from an ethnic minority group, the trial judge should be able to make sure that the jury panel included three members from ethnic minorities. Juries do not have to give reasons for their verdicts and this means that errors are more difficult to correct.

The use of lay members in tribunals appears more satisfactory as the panel consists of a qualified chairman and two lay representatives with knowledge of the area involved. Perhaps this is the direction for both the lay magistracy and juries in the future. Magistrates' Court benches could be comprised of one qualified lawyer and two lay magistrates, while juries at the Crown Court could deliberate with the judge and give reasons for their decision. In each case the lay representation is kept, and the lay members of the panel would outnumber the professionals, thus ensuring public confidence whilst removing some of the main criticisms that exist at present.

STUDENT'S ANSWER WITH TUTOR'S COMMENTS

Question 1

Without lay magistrates the criminal justice system in this country would collapse. There are around 30,000 magistrates serving in 700 Magistrates' Courts throughout England and Wales. They try all summary offences of which the majority are motoring offences. They also try cases triable either way where they have accepted jurisdiction and the defendant elects to be tried there. Even for serious indictable offences which must be tried at the Crown Court they deal with preliminary matters such as bail and also check that there is a prima facie case to go the Crown Court when required to do so by the defence.

On top of this there is the Youth Court which tries all but the very serious cases involving defendants aged under 18. Magistrates also have civil duties including hearing applications for licences for selling alcohol, collection of community debts like the community charge and family matters such as adoption and maintenance.

To carry out all this work a magistrate has about 40 hours training, although those working in the Youth Court or on the family panel receive extra training. The training includes court procedure, observation of court cases, advice on sentencing and visits to prisons and Young Offenders' Institutions. Magistrates are also required to attend refresher courses every three years.

Lay magistrates are amateurs because they have no legal qualifications. The training they receive is considered by some to be inadequate to carry out their duties effectively. One of the areas of greatest concern has been the inconsistent sentences varying greatly from one area to another. A report by the civil liberties group, Liberty, found that magistrates sent more

66 A good concise run down of the duties of magistrates 99

66 Nice link between training and 'amateur' point in the quotation 99

A sophisticated comparison

than twice as many people to prison in Manchester than in Merseyside. However this is to some extent balanced by the fact that defendants do have an automatic right to appeal to the Crown Court against their conviction or sentence. A defendant tried at the Crown Court would find it difficult to appeal as he would have to get leave to appeal to go to the Court of Appeal. Sentences given by judges at the Crown Court are also open to criticism even though these judges have at least ten years legal experience.

The fact that magistrates have a higher conviction rate than juries in the Crown Court (80% as against 50%), is also a criticism that is levelled at magistrates. Juries though decide their verdict with no legal training whatsoever, so they are even more amateur than lay magistrates and yet are expected to decide cases involving more serious crimes.

Strong positive points balancing the argument

Magistrates sit in benches of three to reach their decisions so at least it is a shared decision, and they also have the help of a clerk on legal points. One of the greatest advantages magistrates have is that ordinary people are involved. They have to live within 15 miles of the area they serve, so they should have good local knowledge and be aware of local social problems such as high unemployment. They are also volunteers and so interested in their duties.

Lay magistrates, though, do not come from a good cross section of the population. In theory anyone aged between 21 and 60 can be appointed and the advisory committees who make recommendations to the Lord Chancellor are supposed to ensure a good mix of sex, age and political support. In practice it appears that the majority of magistrates are supporters of the Conservative party. This is true even in areas where the Labour party is strongly supported. There are also very few young people on the bench. This is worrying because the majority of defendants are likely to be young and they may feel out of touch with a panel of older magistrates. Many young men are excluded because they are following careers and would find it difficult to take the necessary time off work. Young women are likely to have family commitments, though at least about 47% of magistrates are female. This is a much higher proportion than anywhere else in the legal world. A woman has to be included on the bench hearing a youth court or family case.

There is poor representation from ethnic minorities, which is particularly worrying in areas where there is a large ethnic community. Every effort should be made to resolve this problem with advertising aimed at persuading more people from ethnic minorities to put themselves forward.

It is true that lay justices are not legally qualified, but they acquire expertise as they sit to hear cases on a regular basis so it is unfair to describe them as true 'amateurs'. There are many positive points to using lay people in this way and for most cases the system is satisfactory as very few appeals are made from magistrates' decisions. Additional training and the attraction of a wider cross section of magistrates would help to overcome the present criticisms.

Tutor's Comments

A sound understanding of the system. A particularly good point is the comparison with Crown Court cases and the comments on judges' sentencing, appeal rights and the totally untrained jury. The other comments are well substantiated and overall this would be a grade A answer.

A review sheet for this chapter can be found on p. 210.

GENERAL PRINCIPLES OF CRIMINAL LAW

ACTUS REUS and MENS REA

STRICT LIABILITY

PARTICIPATION

INCHOATE OFFENCES

GETTING STARTED

This chapter concentrates on some basic rules which are applied generally throughout the criminal law. In order to prove criminal liability the general rule is that the prosecution must prove two things: the *actus reus* and the *mens rea,* that is guilty conduct and a guilty mind. This is, of course, a very generalised statement, for example there are many 'minor' crimes in which only the *actus reus* need be proved. However, these two concepts are very important in criminal law and it is necessary to explore both of them in detail.

Exceptions to the need to prove *mens rea* are crimes of **strict liability**. Examination questions often focus on whether this concept of strict liability can be justified. There is also the concept of **participation**. This deals with the level of involvement in a crime that is needed for a person to be guilty of that crime. Is the person who supplied tools for a burglary liable for that burglary, even though he/she was not present at the scene?

Finally the chapter explains inchoate offences; these are offences in their own right, although the main crime involved is incomplete. The offender has planned a crime (conspiracy) or tried to do it (attempt) or tried to persuade someone else to commit the crime (incitement).

Examination questions on these topics fall into two categories:

1 essay questions on the concepts involved, usually asking for an explanation and an evaluation of the law;

2 problem or situation questions which set out a series of facts ask what offences are involved; some of these questions may require knowledge of several areas of criminal law (see Chapters 11–13).

ACTUS REUS and MENS REA

ESSENTIAL PRINCIPLES

ACTUS REUS

This is often thought of as the 'guilty act' involved in the offence. However, this is not a full enough or accurate definition. In some cases there is no act but instead a failure to act which makes the defendant liable; in others there must be a consequence which occurs as a result of the act before the defendant is liable and in a few crimes a state of affairs is enough.

OMISSIONS AS *ACTUS REUS*

As a general rule a failure to act is not sufficient for the *actus reus* of a crime. The law generally only makes an accused liable for positive conduct. However there are **exceptions:**

1 **Parliament** can impose liability for an omission in an Act of Parliament, e.g. various traffic laws such as failing to stop after an accident, failing to accord precedence to a pedestrian on a zebra crossing and offences such as wilful neglect of a child. In these cases the legislation has defined the offence in such a way that an omission to do a certain act makes a person criminally liable.

2 **Under the common law** a crime can be committed by an omission where a **duty** to act is recognised. Such a duty can exist in the following circumstances:

   a) **Under a contract** – usually a contract of employment and especially if the failure to fulfil a contractual obligation is likely to endanger the lives of others (*R v Pittwood (1902)*).

   b) **By virtue of relationship** – especially the parent/child relationship. Parents or persons *in loco parentis* are under a duty to care for their child. In *R v Gibbins and Proctor (1918)* a child was denied food and starved to death. The child's father and the woman he was living with were found guilty of murder.

   c) **Voluntary undertaking of the care of another** where that other is incapable of caring for themselves and is totally reliant on the accused. In *R v Stone and Dobinson (1977)* the undertaking was by implication as S's sister had come to live with them in 1972 when she could care for herself. By July 1975 she was incapable of looking after herself and D undertook the task of washing her and providing her with food. In the last few days of her life no care was provided and she died in August 1975. It was held that the defendants were under a legal duty to summon help or to care for her themselves and they were found guilty of manslaughter.

   d) **A duty which exists by virtue of holding some public offices** – a person may be under an obligation to act as a result of his office (*R v Dytham (1979)*). Though the court stated that if the duty to act would be attended with 'greater danger than a man of ordinary firmness and activity may be expected to encounter' an individual may not be held criminally responsible for his failure to act.

   e) **A duty arising from the accused's conduct** – in *R v Miller (1983)* the accused, a squatter, accidentally started a fire in a room. When he realised this he did nothing but leave the room to go to sleep in another room. The House of Lords held that where an accused was unaware he has set in motion a chain of events which could cause or which was causing damage to property but at a time when further (or any) damage could be avoided he became aware of his responsibility for that state of affairs, his failure to correct that situation would constitute an omission punishable by the criminal law.

The duty of doctors

"Doctors' duty"

The position of doctors is a difficult one. A doctor is under a duty to care for a patient unless the patient refuses medical treatment. In this case if the doctor omits to act then that omission cannot form the *actus reus* of any crime if the patient dies. However, where a patient is not in a position to give instructions about treatment then it becomes a question of what is in the patient's best interests. This emerged from the case of *Airedale National Health Service Trust v Bland (1993)* where Bland was in a persistent vegetative state (PVS) having suffered irreversible brain damage in the Hillsborough Stadium disaster. This meant that although he was able to breathe unaided so that he was not on a life support machine, he was not conscious, could not swallow and was fed through a nasal tube. His relations wanted him to be allowed to die by stopping all treatment including the feeding. The trust asked the court for a declaration that this was permissible and the House of Lords decided that stopping treatment was an omission. This meant that it would not be a criminal act unless the doctors were under a duty to continue treatment. In Bland's case there was no hope of recovery so it was held that it was not in his best interest that his life should be prolonged by medical treatment and care and the doctors were not under a duty to continue to prolong his life.

CAUSATION

The *actus reus* may require a consequence as well as the act or omission. In these cases the court has to be satisfied that the accused's conduct caused that consequence. The obvious example is in the offence of an assault causing actual bodily harm (Offences against the Person Act 1861 s. 47) where it must be shown that the accused not only assaulted the victim but that that assault also caused 'actual bodily harm'. In a murder charge the prosecution must prove that the accused's act caused the death. This may be a factual matter as in *R v White (1910)* where the victim was given poison but died of a heart attack. There was no evidence to show that this had been caused by the poison and so the defendant could not be convicted of murder.

Intervening acts

66 Chains of causation 99

A main problem with causation is where the defendant sets in motion a chain of events which finally ends with the forbidden consequence, but there has been an intervening act contributing to the causation of that consequence. This can occur where:

- **the victim takes avoiding action** – e.g. jumps into a river to escape an attacker and then drowns (*R v Pitts (1842)*) or jumps from a building and is seriously injured (*R v Lewis (1970)*). In both these cases it was held that the attacker was liable since the victim's response was predictable. However in *R v Williams and Davies (1991)* the defendants were held not liable for the death of a hitchhiker who jumped from their car. The Court of Appeal said that where the deceased's conduct was not proportionate to the threat it could be said that his action was voluntary and so broke the chain of causation.

- **a third person reacts reasonably to the defendant's threats** – in *R v Pagett (1983)* police officers shot a girl who was being used as a shield by the defendant while he fired at the police. Pagett was held liable for her manslaughter.

- **poor medical treatment fails to save the victim** – in *R v Smith (1959)* a soldier was stabbed in the lung by Smith; the treatment was so poor that it was thought it had affected the victim's chance of recovery by as much as 75%. The Court of Appeal held that Smith was still guilty of murder; his conduct had caused the death and the intervening medical treatment did not break the chain of causation. The court said: 'if at the time of death the original wound is still an operating cause and a substantial cause, then the death can properly be said to be the result of the wound all be it that some other cause of death is also operating'. In *R v Cheshire (1991)* the victim was shot, and died because medical staff failed to recognise a rare complication arising from the treatment given to him. At the time of his death the wounds from the shots were healing well, but it was held that the defendant was still liable for the death. The Court of Appeal said: 'even though negligence in the treatment of a victim was the immediate cause of death the jury should not regard it as excluding the responsibility of the accused unless the negligent treatment was so independent of his acts and in itself so potent in causing death that they regard the contribution made by his acts as insignificant.'

The following have been held *not* to break the chain of causation:

- switching off a life support machine where the patient is pronounced brain dead (*R v Melcherek (1981)*);

- not giving a blood transfusion which could have saved the victim because the victim refused treatment (*R v Blaue (1975)*).

MENS REA

The Latin maxim *actus non facit reum nisi mens sit rea* means that the basis of the common law is that there must be a 'guilty' mind for an accused to be convicted. This maxim applies to almost all common law crimes (for the exceptions see the section below on strict liability). There is also a presumption that statutory crimes need *mens rea* although this can be rebutted (again, see the section on strict liability for further detail). So what does *mens rea* mean? Well it is easier to state what it does *not* mean:

- *mens rea* is not the same as motive;
- it does not mean in 'evil' mind;
- it does not require knowledge that the act was forbidden by the law.

Definition of *mens rea*

A definition has to be very general; *mens rea* is the state of mind expressly or impliedly required by the definition of the offence charged. It is the required blameworthy state of mind of the defendant at the time that the *actus reus* was caused. However, the level of blameworthiness required varies from crime to crime. The main different levels are:

- **specific intention** – otherwise known as intention; and
- **basic intention** – otherwise known as recklessness and which can be sub-divided into:
    - subjective recklessness; and
    - objective recklessness.

Specific intention

This has proved difficult for the courts to define but a good starting point is the Court of Appeal definition given in *R v Mohan (1976)*: 'a decision to bring about, in so far as it lies within the accused's power, [a particular conseqence] no matter whether the accused desired that consequence of his act or not.'

This can also be considered as **direct intent**; in other words the accused has the direct intention of making the consequence happen. A straightforward example is where the defendant wishes to kill the victim and with that aim in mind, stabs the victim in the heart, killing him. Here the defendant clearly has the direct intention required for the crime of murder. The main problem lies where the consequence is a natural and probable consequence of the act but the defendant did not desire that consequence; his aim was something else. This raises whether the consequence was foreseen by the defendant and, if so would that be enough to establish intention.

Foresight of consequences

Prior to 1985 it was thought that intention covered two states of mind:

1 desiring to produce a particular result; and
2 not desiring the result but foreseeing that it was a highly probable result.

This was changed by *R v Moloney (1985)* where the House of Lords ruled that foresight of consequences was not the same as intention; it was only evidence from which intention could be inferred. The House of Lords also tried to give guidelines which judges could use in directing juries on how to approach this problem but within months in *R v Hancock and Shankland (1986)* the House of Lords itself said that the *Moloney* guidelines were unsafe and misleading. In *Hancock and Shankland* it was held that the correct way to explain the matter to a jury was to stress that the probability of the consequence occurring was important in deciding if there was evidence from which to infer intention. It was left to the Court of Appeal in yet another case, *R v Nedrick (1986)* to draw the two decisions of the House of Lords together and attempt to 'crystalise' their effect 'in a way which might be helpful to judges who have to handle this type of case'. The court said that:

- it might be advisable first to explain that a person might intend to achieve a certain result while at the same time not desiring it to come about;
- then to bear in mind that 'the greater the probability of a consequence the more likely it is that the consequence was foreseen and that if that consequence was foreseen the greater the probability is that it was also intended';
- and for the jury to ask themselves two questions:

    1 How probable was the consequence which resulted from the defendant's voluntary act?

    2 Did he foresee that consequence?

- if the consequence was a 'virtual certainty' and the jury were sure that the defendant foresaw the consequence as being a 'virtual certainty' then there would be evidence from which they could infer intention.

A further complication arose in *R v Walker and Hayles (1990)* when the Court of Appeal accepted that a direction, that there had to be a very high degree of probability that the consequence would occur, was adequate. A 'very high degree of probability' does not appear to be the same as a 'virtual certainty'.

Recklessness

In *R v Cunningham (1957)* the defendant was charged with 'maliciously administering a noxious thing so as to endanger life' when he tore a gas meter from the wall in an empty house in order to steal money from it, and as a result gas leaked in to the next-door house making the woman who lived there ill. The court decided that the word 'maliciously' meant either:

- an actual intention to do the particular type of harm that was in fact done; or
- recklessness in the sense that the defendant when acting realised there was some risk of such harm occurring.

"Subjective recklessness"

This second meaning is known as **subjective recklessness** because the defendant realises there is a risk. This meant that Cunningham could not be guilty unless he at least realised that there was a risk that escaping gas could injure someone. Since the word 'maliciously' in everyday language has a rather different meaning the Law Commission, when proposing changes to the law of criminal damage, suggested that the phrase 'intentionally or recklessly' more clearly expressed the legal situation. This phrase was therefore used in the Criminal Damage Act 1971. Initially there were no problems but in *R v Caldwell (1981)* the House of Lords extended the meaning of reckless. Lord Diplock said:

> 'A person is reckless as to whether or not any property would be damaged if he does an act which creates an obvious risk that property would be destroyed or damaged and, when he does that act, he *either* has not given any thought to the possibility of there being any such risk *or* has recognised that there was some risk involved and has none the less gone on to do it.'

The first part extends the meaning of recklessness since it includes situations where the defendant has not realised there is a risk although an 'ordinary prudent individual' would have realised the risk. This is referred to as **objective recklessness** – the courts are no longer considering what the defendant realised; they are imposing an external test of what others would have realised. This can make a defendant criminally liable even though he or she was incapable of realising the risk (*Elliott v C (1983)*). In the 1980s the House of Lords even applied this version of negligence to manslaughter (*R v Seymour (1983)*) but in *R v Adomako (1994)* they reverted to the subjective recklessness test for manslaughter. Objective recklessness appears now to apply only to crimes of criminal damage.

CHILDREN

Children under the age of 10 are considered to be *doli incapax*, that is they are not capable of forming the necessary *mens rea* for any crime. As a result no child under 10 can ever be found guilty of a crime.

For children aged 10 to 13 inclusive there is a rebuttable presumption that they are *doli incapax*. This means that there is an assumption that they cannot form the necessary *mens rea* but the prosecution can prove that the child does in fact know that his or her actions are seriously wrong in which case the child can be found guilty. This view was challenged by the Queen's Bench Divisional Court in *C (a minor) v DPP (1994)* but upheld when the case went to the House of Lords.

COINCIDENCE OF *ACTUS REUS* AND *MENS REA*

Whatever type of *mens rea* is required, there is the rule that both the *mens rea* and the *actus reus* must be present at the same time. In *R v Fagan (1969)* the defendant accidentally drove his car on to a policeman's foot but when this was pointed out to him he then refused to remove his car immediately. It was held that the *mens rea* and the *actus reus* for the crime of assault were present together as, although Fagan did not have the *mens rea* at the time he drove on to the foot, he did when he refused to move and at that time the *actus reus* of the assault was still continuing.

A more difficult situation occurred in *Thabo Meli v The Queen (1954)* where the defendants intended to murder the victim and thought they had done so. In order to cover up their crime they then rolled 'the body' over a cliff. In fact the victim survived both the assault and the fall over the cliff but then died of exposure. The court took the practical view that if a defendant intended to kill and the victim died as a result of the plan then the defendant would be guilty, as both the *actus reus* and the *mens rea* were present at some time during that plan. It would not be sensible to divide up the parts of the plan and then say that the *actus reus* and *mens rea* were not present at exactly the same time.

TRANSFERRED MALICE

If the defendant intends to attack a particular person but by mistake attacks another person, the law transfers the intention from the intended victim to the actual victim. This prevents a defendant from trying to argue that there was no *mens rea* so far as the actual victim was concerned. (*R v Latimer (1886)*). But if the original intention was to carry out a quite different crime then it is not possible to transfer that intention (*R v Pembliton (1874)*).

STRICT LIABILITY

The normal rules of *mens rea* do not apply to crimes of strict liability; the offence is committed by the defendant doing the *actus reus*. Where no intention at all is required, this is known as **absolute liability** and involves the state of affairs situations as in *R v Larsonneur (1933)* and *Winzar v Chief Constable for Kent (1983)*. These situations are rare.

Normally there is a requirement at least to intend to do the act, as shown by *R v Prince (1875)* where the defendant was charged with taking a girl under the age of sixteen out of the possession of her father (Offences against the Person Act 1861 s. 55). Prince knew that the girl was in the custody of her father but mistakenly believed that she was eighteen years old. He was guilty because he intended to remove her from her father's custody; his belief about her age was irrelevant as the offence was held to be one of strict liability.

PRESUMPTION THAT *MENS REA* IS REQUIRED

The courts start by presuming that *mens rea* is required for any offence. As a result there are very few **common law crimes** which do not require *mens rea*; these are:

- public nuisance;
- blasphemous libel;
- criminal contempt of court.

Statutory offences

Again the courts start with the presumption that *mens rea* is required (*Gammon (Hong Kong) Ltd v A-G of Hong Kong (1985)*). However, that presumption can be rebutted. *Gammon* put forward four propositions:

- the presumption that *mens rea* is required is particularly strong where the offence is 'truly criminal' in character;
- the presumption can only be displaced if this is clearly stated or implied by the statute creating the offence;
- the presumption can only be displaced where the statute is concerned with an issue of social concern;
- even where there is an issue of social concern involved, *mens rea* will still be required unless it can be shown that making the offence one of strict liability will help to prevent the offence occurring.

So the courts start by looking at the words of the statute and will only decide that the offence is a strict liability offence if there is no suggestion in the wording that *mens rea* is required. For example, if the words 'with intent' are included then that offence must need *mens rea*.

Social concern

Where an offence is likely to affect the public interest as a whole, then the courts are more likely to decide that the offence is one of strict liability. This covers such matters as:

- pollution;
- public safety;
- laws regulating the sale of food;
- revenue offences.

JUSTIFICATION FOR STRICT LIABILITY

1 **The welfare of the community** – it is seen as a way of encouraging high standards of care in areas where there are potential hazards to the community in general.

2 **Evidential problems** – in many cases it would be impossible to prove *mens rea*: every defendant could say 'I didn't mean to' or 'I didn't know'.

However, it is argued that it is contrary to the fundamental principles of justice to create offences under which people can be found guilty and may be at risk of losing their liberty, even though they had no blameworthy intent.

PARTICIPATION

PRINCIPALS

The **principal offender** is the person who is directly responsible for bringing about the *actus reus* of an offence. It is possible for two or more people to be joint principals as in a bank robbery where one defendant points the gun at the cashier while the other grabs the money. A person is also the principal if he uses an innocent agent to carry out the *actus reus*.

SECONDARY PARTIES

The person who directly causes the *actus reus* is not the only one who can be charged with the offence. Under s. 8 of the Accessories and Abettors Act 1861 anyone who 'shall aid, abet, counsel or procure' is also liable. The *Attorney-General's Reference (No 1) of 1975* stresses that each of the words 'aid, abet, counsel or procure' has a distinct meaning.

Aid

This is any conduct which literally aids the principal to commit the offence and includes:

- being the getaway driver;
- acting as a look-out;
- supplying the principal with tools to carry out the offence.

Abet

This is any conduct which instigates, incites or encourages the principal in the commission of the offence. It includes:

- persuading someone to commit a crime (note that this is also the crime of incitement);
- shouting encouragement.

Counsel

This is where advice is given to the principal before he commits the crime, e.g.:

- suggesting what type of explosive would be most likely to blow open a safe;
- demonstrating how to use skeleton keys to break in to property.

Procure

In the *Attorney-General's Reference (No 1) of 1975* where the defendants had added alcohol to a driver's drink so he drove while over the limit, it was said that to procure means 'to produce by endeavour'. One procures something by setting out to see that it happens and taking the appropriate steps to produce that happening.

THE *MENS REA* OF SECONDARY PARTIES

A secondary party must have knowledge that the principal is going to commit a crime and must have intended to help the commission of that crime.

Knowledge

This does not mean detailed knowledge. The secondary party needs only to know the type of offence involved (*R v Bainbridge (1959), DPP for Northern Ireland v Maxwell (1979)*). In the latter case the House of Lords said that if the crime committed by the principal was one of a number of offences which the secondary party knew might be committed then the secondary party had sufficient knowledge to be guilty.

Unforeseen consequences

If the principal commits a completely different crime from the one originally envisaged by the secondary party then the secondary party will not be guilty. However, there are problems in cases where the secondary party foresaw that the principal might commit a crime, although it was not the crime agreed on. In *Chan Wing-Sui v The Queen (1985),* where the principal had killed during the course of a robbery, it was held that a secondary party was liable for murder if he:

- had agreed that P would kill (or cause grievous bodily harm); or
- knew that it was virtually certain that P would kill (or cause grievous bodily harm); or
- contemplated that P might kill (or cause grievous bodily harm).

In *R v Hyde (1990)* Lord Lane in the Court of Appeal said:

'There are two main types of joint venture where death results to the victim. The first is where the primary object is to do some kind of physical injury to the victim. The second is where the primary object is not to cause physical injury to any victim but, for example, to commit burglary. The victim is killed as a (possibly unwelcome) incident of the burglary. The latter type of case may pose more complications than the former, but the principle is, in each case the same ... If B realises (without agreeing to such conduct being used) that A may kill or intentionally inflict serious injury, but nevertheless continues to participate with A in the venture, that will amount to sufficient mental element for B to be guilty of murder if A (with the requisite intent) kills in the course of the venture.'

Repentance

The secondary party may avoid liability if he withdraws clearly and effectively from the venture before the completion of the offence by the principal. However simply saying 'let's go' and running from the scene is not always enough to avoid guilt (*R v Becerra (1975)*).

INCHOATE OFFENCES

This phrase refers to crimes which have not been completed; there are three of these:

- incitement;
- conspiracy;
- attempts.

In each of these the defendant can be guilty by doing a preliminary act and not the actual offence.

INCITEMENT

This is the encouragement of another to commit an offence. The encouragement can be by any means, e.g. persuading or offering money; it can even be to the world at large as by putting an advert in a paper. The incitement does not actually have to cause the other person to commit the crime, but the incitor must intend that the other person should commit the crime.

CONSPIRACY

Until the passing of the Criminal Law Act 1977 conspiracy was a common law offence. That act abolished common law conspiracy except for three:

- conspiracy to defraud;
- conspiracy to corrupt public morals;
- conspiracy to outrage public decency.

Under the Criminal Law Act 1977 a conspiracy is an agreement between two or more people to carry out a course of conduct that will necessarily involve at least one of them committing a crime (or would have done so but for the existence of facts which made the crime impossible to commit).

Actus reus of conspiracy

The agreement itself is the *actus reus*; nothing more needs to be done. This is true even if the exact plan has not been settled. However, there must be at least two people agreeing excluding the intended victim, the conspirator's spouse or a child under ten years old.

Mens rea of conspiracy

There must be knowledge that the plan necessarily involves the commission of a crime together with an intention to carry out the agreement. It is not necessary, however, to know the full details; knowledge of the essential elements is enough.

ATTEMPTS

An attempt is defined in the Criminal Attempts Act 1981 as doing an act which is more than merely preparatory to the commission of an offence with intent to commit that offence. In other words, trying to commit a crime but for some reason not succeeding. It does not matter that it is impossible to complete the crime (*R v Shivpuri (1986)*).

Actus reus of an attempt

This is 'doing an act which is more than merely preparatory', so to some extent it is a question of fact in each case. It has been suggested that a jury should ask themselves whether the defendant is actually attempting to commit the offence or is only getting ready for the offence. Running on to a race track to interrupt a race (and thus get back a bet) was 'merely preparatory' and not sufficient to convict of attempted theft (*R v Gullefer (1987)*). Similarly, being outside a post office with an imitation gun in a pocket was merely preparatory and not an attempt to rob the post office (*R v Campbell (1991)*).

However, standing on a milk crate looking through a broken window was held to be an attempt to burgle. There was nothing else left to be done before the full crime of burglary, as that would be committed once the defendant entered the building (*O'Brien v Anderton (1984)*).

Mens rea of an attempt

This has to be the *mens rea* for the completed crime or, in some cases, a higher level of intention. For example, for a charge of attempted murder, the prosecution must prove an intention to kill; an intention to cause grievous bodily harm, while sufficient for the completed crime of murder, is not sufficient for an attempt.

EXAMINATION QUESTIONS

1   Analyse the circumstances in which a person may be criminally liable for an omission to act.   (UODLE)

2   'I do not consider that foresight of a high degree of probability is at all the same thing as intention. It is not foresight but intention which constitutes the mental element of the offence.' (Lord Hailsham in *Hyam v DPP (1974)*) Critically discuss the way in which the appellate courts have dealt with the relationship between foresight of consequences and intention.   (UODLE)

3   'The term "reckless" plays a crucial role in determining criminal liability yet its meaning still appears uncertain.' Critically assess the meaning of the term 'reckless' in criminal law.   (UODLE)

4   How satisfactory is the requirement that the offence of attempt includes an act which is 'more than merely preparatory' (Criminal Attempts Act 1981)   (NEAB)

5   Alf tells Del that his neighbours, Ernie and Freda, will be away on holiday over Easter and that they have valuable diamonds in the house. Del suggests that Alf joins him in burgling the house. Alf agrees. Del asks Brian to supply a large screwdriver for 'a job'. Brian agrees understanding Del to mean burglary by 'a job'. A week before the planned burglary, Alf tells Del he does not wish to take part and pleads with him not to do the burglary. Instead Del asks Colin to help him. Colin has a history of violent crime and always carries a knife. Although Del knows this, he considers that there will be little chance of violence being necessary because the house will be empty. Colin and Del use the screwdriver to break into the house. Ernie is asleep in bed having decided not to go away for Easter. He is wakened by the noise and when investigating, Colin stabs him with the knife and kills him.

Assuming that Colin and Del committed burglary, and Colin murdered Ernie, consider the liability of Alf, Brian and Del as secondary parties.   (UODLE)

ANSWERS TO QUESTIONS

OUTLINE ANSWERS TO SELECTED QUESTIONS

Question 1

■ start with the principle that the law generally does not impose liability for omissions;

- point out that some offences can never be committed by omission, e.g. burglary, robbery;
- consider when liability is imposed;
  - by statute (give an example);
  - by the common law; duty arising from contract of employment, relationship, assuming care of another, creating a dangerous situation;
- analyse these by commenting on decisions in cases such as *Gibbins* (why did the duty arise?), *Stone and Dobinson* (why did the duty arise, when can the carer be released from the duty?) and *Miller* (is this decision justifiable? isn't this really a case of separation of *actus reus* and *mens rea*?).

Question 4

This question is focused on the *actus reus* of an attempt as defined by the Criminal Attempts Act 1981 so there is no need to consider the *mens rea* of attempt. However, there must be a detailed discussion of the *actus reus* and an evaluation of the wording in the Act. The following points could be used:

- Explain the difficulties of drawing a line between what acts are 'merely preparatory' and what are enough to be considered an attempt. At what point does an act become 'more than merely preparatory?'
- Use cases to illustrate the problems the courts have had and the dividing line drawn in the cases (*R v Gullefer, O'Brien v Anderton, R v Campbell*).
- Why were *Gullefer* and *Campbell* not considered to have gone beyond preparation? Are these decisions satisfactory?
- What is the law trying to achieve? Is the offence of attempt aimed at prevention of the substantive offence? If so, does the decision in *R v Campbell* create difficulties?
- Should a defendant be criminally liable for 'mere preparation' as well as other later acts?

What other test could be used?

Question 5

This question directs you to consider liability as secondary parties, so there is no need to comment on the actual crimes of burglary and murder. You will not get any extra marks if you do! As there are three participators to consider, it is probably easier to deal with each separately:

1 **Alf** – he agrees to the burglary; does this bring him within 'aid, abet, counsel and procure'? *(A-G's reference No 1 of 1975)*; has he done enough to withdraw from the joint enterprise? (*Becerra*);

2 **Brian** – does supplying the screwdriver make him liable for (a) the burglary, (b) the murder? knowing Del is going to do 'a job' is enough for the burglary (*Bainbridge*), but unlikely to be liable for the murder as it is not in his contemplation;

3 **Del** – he has embarked on a joint enterprise of burglary with Colin; does this make him liable for the murder? Del knows Colin carries a knife but believes the house is empty – the principles in *Chan Wing-Sui* and *Hyde* apply.

STUDENT'S ANSWER WITH TUTOR'S COMMENTS

Question 2

> The courts have experienced innumerable difficulties in trying to limit the *mens rea* requirement for murder to intention only, and murder serves as an ideal example therefore to study intention. Where there has been confusion between motive and intention the appellate courts have inevitably introduced the consideration of foreseeability of consequences in an attempt to infer intention in serious cases. Nevertheless this has created significant complications and uncertainties in what is the most heinous crime.
>
> The eventual ruling in *Hyam v DPP* established that the qualifying *mens rea* for a charge of murder consisted of either intention to cause death or serious bodily injury, or foreseeability that one's actions are likely to do so. It was generally felt, however, that the most heinous of crimes should accordingly have the strictest requirement of criminality and thus *Moloney*

A good introduction focusing on key issues

❝Avoids too much factual detail and concentrates on the law❞

held that only intention to cause death or serious bodily injury would suffice. Nevertheless, in view of jury understanding, Lord Bridge recommended that if death or serious bodily injury were a 'natural consequence' of the accused's actions, and if the accused was aware of this, then intention could be inferred. Unfortunately what Lord Bridge had done was to immediately re-introduce foreseeability as a factor of the *mens rea*. This became apparent when the above direction was used in *Hancock and Shankland* where the accused had 'intended' to stop a taxi by dropping concrete slabs from a bridge. Here Lord Scarman criticised Lord Bridge in *Moloney* for not considering probabilities, and went on to say that an awareness of one's action had a 'high likelihood' of causing death or serious bodily injury, could infer intention. Actually, Lord Scarman had misread *Moloney*: Lord Bridge had actually claimed that the requisite probability was 'little short of overwhelming' on 'a moral certainty'. There is certainly some disparity between the two judges' opinions, and the problem seems to derive from unclarity of distinction between motive and intention requiring further judicial directions to juries. Even judges may confuse motive and intention, as in *Steane*, where the judges erroneously held that in helping the enemy (in war) while under duress one does not intend to help the enemy. Here, a good motive (to protect friends and family) is disparate from criminal intent. Similarly criminal motives do not necessarily infer an intention to kill.

Further confusion has arisen in the subsequent murder cases of *Nedrick* and *Walker and Hayles* where the requisite probability was held to be 'virtual certainty' and 'very high degree of probability' respectively. In the latter case it was held that the difference between the two directions would not amount to misdirection. It is therefore difficult to ascertain why such a direction – further complicating and unnecessarily expanding the law – was made.

❝Good use of knowledge❞

The Accessories and Abettors Act 1861 has led to conviction as a murderer on foresight alone. To be convicted as an accessory (and thus charged as a principal offender) one must intend to assist the principal bring about a prohibited result and do so. This led to the ruling in *Chan Wing-Siu* that when undertaking criminal activities, an accessory who foresaw the principal's (murderer's) actions might possibly involve violence causing at least grievous bodily harm is liable for murder, having intended to assist it.

Thus, in dealing with intention the courts have persisted in incorporating some degree of foresight, even in crimes where intention alone is required for conviction. It appears that in the case of murder the law is in serious need of clarification. It must be established just how foreseeable a consequence must be to be regarded as 'intended'.

Tutor's Comments

A very clear account of the problems. The student has kept focused on the essential points of the question throughout the essay. There is good use of case references, showing wide knowledge and understanding. An A grade answer.

A review sheet for this chapter can be found on p. 211.

DEFENCES IN CRIMINAL LAW

GETTING STARTED

There are various general defences which can mean that a defendant will be found not guilty of the crime. Some defences, such as insanity, are complete defences in that they apply to all crimes; others only apply in certain circumstances or to a limited range of crimes. It is important to be able to understand the key elements of these defences. Examination questions are set on:

■ individual defences in the form of essay questions; or

■ a comparison of two defences; or

■ as a situation problem style question; these will require a knowledge of the crimes involved as well as the defences.

The main point in a situation question is to start by deciding what crimes may have been committed; are the crimes specific intent crimes or basic intent crimes? this may make a difference to the availability of the defences of self-induced automatism, intoxication and mistake.

One of the aspects students often find difficult in these situation style questions is being able to 'spot' which defences are involved. Once you know the key factors of, and cases on, each defence this should not be a problem. The examiner does try to make it obvious, e.g. 'Daphne received a blow on the head which caused concussion. While still semi-conscious …' is pointing you firmly at the defence of automatism. However, it is probably worth building up a 'checklist' on the following lines:

■ epilepsy, mention of any mental illness = defence of insanity;

■ diabetes, sleep-walking = automatism, but may be insane automatism;

■ alcohol, drugs = intoxication, is it self-induced?

■ threatened by armed robber etc = duress.

INSANITY

AUTOMATISM

INTOXICATION

DURESS AND NECESSITY

MISTAKE

SELF-DEFENCE

ESSENTIAL PRINCIPLES

INSANITY

This is a complete defence to all crimes; if a defendant is successful in proving insanity the verdict is 'not guilty by reason of insanity'. The definition of insanity in the criminal law comes from the **M'Naghten Rules (1843)**. These state:

1   that everyone is presumed sane until the contrary is proved; and
2   that to prove legal insanity it is necessary to show that the accused was, at the time of committing the crime, **labouring under such a defect of reason due to disease of the mind, as not to know the nature and quality of his act or, if he did know this, not to know he was doing what was wrong.**

This definition of insanity has been expanded by the courts in cases and it is necessary to understand the effect of its various components. It is also worth comparing the defence of insanity with diminished responsibility (see Chapter 12)

DISEASE OF THE MIND

The courts have defined this phrase very broadly so that it not only includes what are regarded as mental illnesses, but also physical illnesses which affect the mind. In *R v Sullivan (1984)* the House of Lords said that 'mind' meant the faculties of reason, memory and understanding, so that if the effect of a disease was to impair these faculties then that was within the M'Naghten definition. As a result defendants who have committed crimes while suffering from epilepsy, arteriosclerosis and even diabetes have been brought within the definition. Conversely, the definition does not cover some mental conditions.

DID NOT KNOW THE NATURE AND QUALITY OF HIS ACT

This reference is to the physical quality of the act; an insane defendant who believes he is killing a gorilla cannot be convicted of murder even though he is actually killing a man. It also covers the situation where the defendant is acting while suffering from an epileptic fit so that he is unaware of what he is doing.

DID NOT KNOW HE WAS DOING WHAT WAS WRONG

This is an alternative to the above test. If a defendant did know the nature and quality of his act, e.g. he knew he was killing a human being, then he can still show that he comes within the definition of insanity if he can prove that he did not know he was doing wrong. This allows a defence to a mentally ill person who as part of their mental illness believes that they are being attacked and must kill in self defence. However, it does not provide a defence if the accused knows that what they are doing is against the law (*R v Windle (1952)*).

POWERS OF THE JUDGE

Although the verdict is 'not guilty by reason of insanity', the judge will make an order in respect of the defendant. Under the Criminal Procedure (Insanity and Unfitness to Plead) Act 1991 the judge now has much wider powers. He can:

■   order admission to a hospital (with or without a restriction order);
■   make a guardianship order;
■   impose a supervision order with a condition that the defendant attend for treatment;
■   give an absolute discharge.

Note that where the charge is murder the judge must order admission to hospital with a restriction order.

AUTOMATISM

This is an involuntary act of the body without any control by the mind. The accepted definition comes from *Bratty v Attorney General for Northern Ireland (1961)* where it was said that automatism was: '… an act done by the muscles without any control by the mind such as a spasm, a reflex action or a convulsion, or an act done by a person who is not conscious of what he is doing, such as an act done whilst suffering from concussion or whilst sleep walking.'

Unfortunately this is a global definition of automatism and does not explain that the defence has different effects depending on what caused the automatism. It can be:

- **insane automatism** – in which case the rules of insanity apply;
- **non-insane automatism** – this can be considered 'pure' automatism which allows the defendant a complete defence to any crime so that the verdict will be 'not guilty';
- **self-induced automatism** – which has been brought on by the defendant's conduct and so will not always provide a complete defence.

INSANE AND NON-INSANE AUTOMATISM

"Internal factor"

The difference between the two depends on what caused the automatism. If it is caused by a disease or an internal factor then it will be classed as **insane automatism**. This is shown by *R v Sullivan (1984)* where the defendant was acting during an epileptic fit; *R v Kemp (1957)* – arteriosclerosis; *R v Hennessey (1989)* – high blood-sugar levels because of diabetes; and *R v Burgess (1991)* – sleep walking. Before this last case it was always thought that sleep walking would be categorised as non-insane automatism but the Court of Appeal pointed out that if the sleep walking was due to a disorder or abnormality which might recur then it was caused by an internal cause and correctly described as insane automatism.

"External factor"

Where the automatism is caused by an external factor then it is categorised as **non-insane automatism.** In *R v Quick (1973)* it was explained that: 'a malfunctioning of the mind of transitory effect caused by the application to the body of some external factor such as violence, drugs, including anaesthetics, alcohol and hypnotic influences cannot fairly be said to be due to disease.' This covers reflex actions caused by being stung by a swarm of bees (*Hill v Baxter (1958)*); low blood sugar levels which can happen to diabetics if they fail to eat after taking their insulin (*R v Quick*); a traumatic event which caused the defendant to act in a dream-like state as in *R v T (1990)*, where the defendant had been recently raped and this had caused post traumatic stress disorder.

Comment

It is clear that the courts are trying to distinguish between those whose condition is likely to recur and who therefore may need treatment, and those whose automatism was caused by an external factor and is unlikely to recur. However, this has the odd effect that diabetics are classed as legally insane if the cause of their automatism is the disease itself, but as suffering from non-insane automatism if the cause is the effect of the insulin taken to control the disease.

SELF-INDUCED AUTOMATISM

It is clear that in some cases the automatic state has been brought about by the defendant's own actions, e.g. taking alcohol or drugs. In such cases the defendant will not always be able to use automatism as a defence. It is necessary to consider:

- **what crime the defendant has been charged with** – if the crime requires specific intention then the fact that the defendant acted in an automatic state is sufficient to allow a defence; if the crime is one of basic intent (that is the prosecution need only prove that the defendant acted recklessly) then a second question must be asked;
- **whether the defendant knew that his actions were likely to cause an automatic state** – if he did not then he would have a defence except where the automatism had been caused by voluntary intoxication (*R v Bailey (1983)*); however if the defendant knew the probable effect (e.g. being warned clearly by a doctor or chemist about the effects of prescribed medication) there would be no defence to a crime of basic intent.

INTOXICATION

Intoxication covers the effects of drugs and solvents as well as alcohol. It is not a defence as such, but in some cases it will provide a defence because it will mean that the accused did not have the necessary *mens rea* for the crime. The law distinguishes between voluntary intoxication and involuntary intoxication.

VOLUNTARY INTOXICATION

This is where the defendant chooses to take a substance that he knows will cause intoxication. In this case it is necessary to consider what *mens rea* is required for the crime the defendant has been charged with.

Voluntary intoxication and crimes of specific intent

If the offence is one of specific intent then whether the defendant has a defence or not becomes a question of fact:

- **did they have the necessary *mens rea* at the time of the offence?** – a drunken intent is still an intent (*Attorney-General for Northern Ireland v Gallagher (1963)* where the defendant drank to give himself 'Dutch courage' to kill his wife); or

- **were they so drunk that they were incapable of forming the *mens rea* required?** – in *R v Beard (1920)* it was said that if the defendant was 'so drunk that he was incapable of forming the intent required he could not be convicted of a crime which was only committed if the intent was proved.'

Voluntary intoxication and crimes of basic intent

For these crimes recklessness is sufficient to prove the *mens rea*; as a result a defendant who is voluntarily intoxicated cannot use this as a defence. This was stated clearly in *R v Majewski (1977)* where the defendant was charged with assault causing actual bodily harm and assault on a police officer in the execution of his duty. The House of Lords said: 'If a man of his own volition takes a substance which causes him to cast of the restraints of reason and conscience, no wrong is done to him by holding him answerable for any injury he may do while in that condition … It is a reckless course of conduct and recklessness is enough to constitute the necessary mens rea in assault cases.'

INVOLUNTARY INTOXICATION

This covers situations where the defendant did not know he was taking an intoxicating substance; for example where a soft drink has been 'laced' with alcohol. The test in these cases is: did the defendant have the necessary *mens rea* when committing the offence? If so they will be guilty, the involuntary intoxication will not provide a defence (*R v Kingston (1994)*). Where, however, the defendant did not have the necesssary intent they will be not guilty, even if the crime is one of basic intent. This is so because in such circumstances the defendant has not been reckless.

| DURESS AND NECESSITY |

These defences rely on the fact that the defendant has been effectively forced to commit the crime, either through a direct threat by another (duress) or through external circumstances (necessity).

DURESS

The important factors in this defence are:

1 **Nature of the threat** – it must be of death or serious injury; lesser threats do not provide a defence.

2 **The person threatened** – the threat must be to the defendant themselves, or to a close member of their family; there is no authority to say that a threat to kill an unrelated third person will provide a defence. (Note that the Law Commission's draft criminal code does allow for this.)

3 **The crimes for which the defence is available** – duress can be used as defence to all crimes except murder (*R v Howe (1987)*), attempted murder (*R v Gotts (1991)*) and possibly treason (*R v Steane (1947)*).

4 **Unavoidable dilemma** – duress can only be used as a defence if the defendant is placed in a situation where they have no safe avenue of escape (*R v Gill (1963)*).

5 **Subjective and objective tests** – the correct approach to deciding whether the defence of duress should succeed was laid down by *R v Graham (1982)* and approved by the House of Lords in *R v Howe (1987)*; this involves a two-stage test: was the defendant compelled to act as they did because they feared serious injury or death? (the subjective test) and if so, would a sober person of reasonable firmness, sharing the characteristics of the accused, have responded in the same way? (the objective test).

Self-induced duress

In some cases the defendant has voluntarily joined a criminal gang and then been forced to commit further crimes under duress. If the original crimes did not involve any violence then the defendant may use the defence of duress for the later crimes (*R v Shepherd (1987)*). If, however, the defendant knew when they joined the gang that the other members were likely to use violence, duress will not be available as a defence (*R v Sharp (1987)*).

Duress of circumstances

In recent years the courts have recognised that a defendant may be forced to act by the surrounding circumstances. This was shown by *R v Willer (1986)* when the defendant, fearing for his safety, drove on to the pavement to get away from a gang of youths. He was charged with reckless driving but the Court of Appeal said that the jury should have been allowed to consider whether the defendant drove 'under that form of compulsion, that is, under duress'. In *R v Martin (1989)* it was decided that duress of circumstances could be available as a defence if, from an objective viewpoint, the accused acted reasonably and proportionately to avoid a threat of death or serious injury and that the same two-stage test put forward in *R v Graham* applied. In *R v Pommell (1995)* the Court of Appeal said that the defence of duress of circumstances was available for all crimes except murder, attempted murder and some forms of treason.

Comment

1 It can be argued that the objective element should be abolished. Surely the whole purpose of duress is to allow a defence to people who have only committed a crime because they have been threatened with serious injury or death. The reactions of a hypothetical sober person of 'reasonable firmness' are irrelevant; the question to be decided should be: was the defendant so frightened by the threats that they felt they had no other option but to commit the crime.

2 Excluding the defence for the crime of murder is also open to criticism, given that there is a mandatory sentence of life imprisonment if the defendant is found guilty. Why is the defence not available to someone whose family are taken hostage by terrorists and threatened with death unless the defendant helps the terrorists to plant a bomb? The House of Lords in *R v Howe*, when stating that the defence could not apply to a charge of murder, rather 'shrugged off' this problem saying it was 'inconceivable that such persons would be prosecuted'. However, the fact remains that such a person might be prosecuted and would have no defence.

NECESSITY

The courts do not recognise a defence under this heading, although it effectively forms the basis for other defences.

1 **Statutory provisions** – some Acts of Parliament set out defences based on necessity for certain crimes – these include allowing emergency vehicles a defence to breaking the speed limit 'if the observation of the limit would be likely to hinder the purpose for which the vehicle is being used'.

2 **Self-defence** – the essence of this defence is that the defendant is claiming that they acted as they did because it was necessary for their protection.

3 **Duress of circumstances** – as set out above this defence, which might be considered necessity under a different title, is apparently available for almost all crimes.

MISTAKE

To be a defence a mistake must be a mistake about a fact, so that if the facts had been as the defendant believed them to be, it would mean:

■ either there was no *mens rea* for the offence; or

■ the defendant would have been able to rely on another defence.

Simple situations will illustrate these concepts:

■ If A picks up an umbrella from a stand as he is leaving a restaurant in the mistaken belief that it is his own umbrella, he does not have the *mens rea* required for theft as he is not dishonest.

■ If B, in the mistaken belief that V is pointing a gun at him, throws a stone at V and knocks him out, B can plead he should be judged on the basis that his action was in self defence.

Reasonableness of the mistake

Provided the defendant genuinely makes a mistake, there will be a defence even if the mistake is unreasonable. In *DPP v Morgan (1976)* the House of Lords said that:

'If the words defining an offence provide ... that a man is not to be found guilty of it if he believes something to be true, then he cannot be found guilty if the jury thinks that he may have believed it to be true, however inadequate were his reasons for doing so.'

This was also applied in *R v Williams (1987)* where the defendant made a mistake over the need for the use of force in the prevention of crime. So the defendant is judged according to their mistaken view of the facts, regardless of whether their mistake was reasonable or unreasonable.

Drunken mistakes

Here the rule is more complicated. If the mistake negatives the *mens rea* required for the offence then the defendant will have a defence. If the mistake is about another aspect, for example the amount of force needed in self defence, the defendant will not have a defence (*R v Lipman (1970), R v O'Grady (1987)*). The law is trying to balance the needs of the defendant and the protection of victims.

Mistake and crimes of strict liability

For these crimes a mistake, even if reasonable, will not be a defence (*R v Prince (1875), Pharmaceutical Society of Great Britain v Storkwain (1986)*).

SELF DEFENCE

This covers not only actions needed to defend oneself from an attack, but also actions taken to defend another or prevent crime (Criminal Law Act 1967 s. 3). The defence can be a defence to any crime, including murder as the defendant is justifying the use of force. The main rules are:

1 The force used to defend oneself or another must be reasonable in the circumstances. If excessive force is used the defence will fail (*R v Clegg (1994)*).

2 However, in looking at the circumstances, the defendant must be judged on the facts as he believed them to be (*R v Williams (1987)*). This also applies to the use of excessive force (*R v Scarlett (1993)*).

3 In deciding whether the force used was reasonable, the fact that the defendant had only done what he honestly and instinctively thought was necessary in a moment of unexpected anguish is very strong evidence that the defensive action taken was reasonable (*Palmer v R (1971)*).

4 If the force is used after all danger from the assailant is over (i.e. as retaliation or revenge), the defence of self defence is not available.

EXAMINATION QUESTIONS

1 Critically evaluate the principles which govern the law relating to the defence of intoxication. (UODLE)

2 Give a critical evaluation of the law relating to duress and necessity. (NEAB)

3 'Even though the law relating to insanity has recently been reformed, there is still much that could be done to improve it.'

   With reference to the above statement, critically assess the state of the law relating to the defence of insanity. (UODLE)

4 Daphne, while playing hockey, received a blow on the head which caused concussion. While still semi-conscious, Daphne removed a purse from a fellow player's handbag in the changing room. After recovering from the immediate effects of the concussion, Daphne still occasionally suffered from bouts of semi-consciousness due to the blow she had received. Her doctor warned her that drinking any alcohol would greatly increase the likelihood of a blackout. Two days later at a party, Daphne drank one small whisky which caused her to become semi-conscious. She then smashed several crystal glasses on a nearby table. Marjorie tried to restrain Daphne, but Daphne punched her in the face fracturing her jaw.

   Discuss

   Would your answer differ if Daphne was drinking orange juice at the party and Julie spiked her orange juice with whisky? (UODLE)

5 Consider *all* of the following situations:

   ● Nurul, who is driving an open-topped sports car, is stunned by stings from a swarm of bees. The car veers to the wrong side of the road and collides with a parked car.

   ● Diana, who has had an exhausting day, falls asleep as she is driving. Her car collides with a stationary lorry.

- Pippa, who is mentally ill, is driving on the motorway when she begins to think that the car ahead of her is being driven by the devil. She decides to try to force it off the road, and deliberately drives into the side of it.

In each case a charge of driving without due care and attention is brought. Section 3 of the Road Traffic Act 1988 states that:

> If a person drives a motor vehicle on the road without using due care and attention, or without reasonable consideration for other persons using the road, he is guilty of an offence.

No further knowledge of the Road Traffic Act is expected or required for an answer to this question.

Compare, contrast and comment on the issue of criminal liability in these three situations.

(NEAB)

ANSWERS TO QUESTIONS

OUTLINE ANSWERS TO SELECTED QUESTIONS

Question 2

This style of question requires the student to show not only that they know the relevant law but also that they understand it and can weigh up the problems involved. Too many students treat this type of question as an invitation to 'write all they know' and ignore the words 'critical evaluation'.

- give the key principles of the defence of duress;
  - the nature of the threat, the crimes for which it is available, unavoidable dilemma, the subjective and objective tests; do not forget to cite cases in support;
- deal with necessity and remember to link this to duress of circumstances and stress that the essential difference between it and duress proper stems from the source of threat;
- evaluate duress as a defence; points may include:
  - the fact that the threat has to be a serious one and so prevents defendants from relying on lesser threats; this may be a strength rather than a weakness;
  - why the objective test? does this limit the effectiveness of the defence?
  - why is it not a defence to murder and yet is to s. 18 assaults which potentially involve the same *mens rea* as murder; is this not illogical? use an example to illustrate this;
  - is duress of circumstances just necessity under another name?
- evaluate necessity as a defence; the main points will be:

  the lack of a separate defence of necessity; is there a need for it; has the creation of duress of circumstances helped?

Question 4

In this situation style question it is necessary to be able to identify offences as well as defences, so this question actually draws on knowledge of theft and criminal damage (Chapter 13) and assaults (Chapter 12).

- identify the potential offences first; these are:
  - theft (of the purse);
  - criminal damage (of the glasses);
  - malicious wounding (s. 20) / inflicting grievous bodily harm (s. 18) depending on the *mens rea* of Daphne;
- identify the potential defences and apply them to the situation as follows:
  - automatism caused by an external factor (blow to the head) and not self-induced – defence to theft;
  - self-induced automatism (drinking despite doctor's warning); can this be a defence to criminal damage? – no, since criminal damage can be committed recklessly (*Bailey*); can it be a defence to assault? – yes for s. 18, as this is a specific intent crime; no for s. 20 as this is a basic intent crime;

- now consider the effect of Julie's action – this makes Daphne's actions involuntary as the automatism is no longer self-induced – Daphne will be able to use automatism as a defence.

STUDENT'S ANSWER WITH TUTOR'S COMMENTS
Question 3

> **❝ Good opening in view of the statement in the question, because it focuses on both reform and the remaining problems ❞**

The Butler Report 1957 highlighted the need for a less limited view of insanity, and although the Criminal Procedure (Insanity and Fitness to Plead) Act 1991 introduced many changes such as a new range of sentencing options, a different procedure for dealing with those unfit to plead and a greater protection for the vulnerable, it appears unlikely to prevent apparently non-insane people from being found not guilty by insanity and being given unsuitable sentences such as detention in psychiatric hospitals.

In *Kemp (1957)*, a man suffering from arteriosclerosis who caused grievous bodily harm to another after falling unconscious, it was held that no distinction was to be made between a disease of the mind and a disease of the body affecting the operation of the mind.

An epileptic who caused grievous bodily harm to a friend whilst in the latter stages of an epileptic fit was found not guilty by reason of insanity in the case of *Sullivan (1984)*. According to Lord Diplock any mental disability causing a defect of reason that manifests itself in violence and is prone to recur is a disease of the mind.

> **❝ Nice integration of the M'Naghten Rules into the argument ❞**

Following the M'Naghten Rules 1843, a defendant can be said to be suffering from a disease of the mind if when committing the offence a) they do not know the nature or quality of the act or b) do not know the act is wrong. Under such definitions it would appear that the court was correct in finding the defendant not guilty by reason of insanity, but common sense and indeed medical experts would disagree that an epileptic is insane.

Perhaps even more absurd and unjust is the case of *Burgess (1991)* where a sleep walker attacked his girl friend with a video recorder while sleep walking. In the trial the defendant pleaded non-insane automatism, but upon being declared insane he changed his plea to guilty and then appealed raising the issue of non-insane automatism. The appeal was dismissed.

> **❝ Clear account of the difficult legal position of diabetics ❞**

Similarly in the case of *Hennesey (1989)*, the defendant, a diabetic, was stressed, meaning that his medication was insufficient and he suffered an excessive high blood sugar level (hyperglycaemia) and assaulted someone. He, too, had his plea of non-insane automatism rejected and changed to a guilty plea. His appeal was also rejected. This case was particularly astonishing following the decision made in *Quick (1973)* where a diabetic suffering from hypoglycaemia (a low blood sugar level) due to too much insulin was allowed the defence of non-insane automatism on appeal.

There appears to be a complete lack of consistency in the cases especially those involving diabetics. In *Carter (1972)*, a diabetic who was depressed shoplifted and was found not guilty due to her confused and absent-minded state.

As well as the lack of consistency that must be rectified, there must be a provision made by statute that provides protection for those unfortunate people who suffer from disabilities such as diabetes, epilepsy and sleep walking, none of which would be medically defined as 'diseases of the mind'. Until this is done, the law relating to insanity can be said to be in a poor and muddled state despite the recent reforms.

Tutor's Comments

A well focused essay. It shows clear understanding of the case law on insanity and makes sound observations on the difficult areas. Perhaps the essay could expand more on the actual reforms in the Criminal Procedure (Insanity and Fitness to Plead) Act 1991, but even without this the essay would get into the A grade band.

A review sheet for this chapter can be found on p. 212.

OFFENCES AGAINST THE PERSON

GETTING STARTED

This chapter deals with some of the substantive offences involving attacks on the person. The most serious of these is, of course, murder. Murder has never been defined in any Act of Parliament and so we still use the common law definition which was set down in the seventeenth century by Lord Justice Coke. Naturally there have been developments in the law of murder over the last three centuries, but most of these have been as a result of judicial decisions in cases. The major area where Parliament has intervened is regarding the sentence for murder, when they finally abolished the death penalty in 1965. The unlawful killing of a person may be classed as manslaughter rather than murder. The law on both murder and manslaughter is complicated and involves knowing and understanding the effect of decisions in several cases.

The chapter also covers the law of assault, which is mostly found in an old statute, the Offences against the Person Act 1861. This law is unsatisfactory in several respects and the Law Commission has produced proposals for reform but Parliament has shown little interest in enacting these.

Examination questions are asked in two formats:

- on the satisfactoriness of the law; and
- as problems on a given factual situation.

As already pointed out in the previous chapters, some of the problem questions may require knowledge of the topics covered in Chapters 10, 11 and 13.

MURDER

SPECIAL DEFENCES TO MURDER

INVOLUNTARY MANSLAUGHTER

ASSAULTS

ESSENTIAL PRINCIPLES

MURDER

The definition of murder is an unlawful killing of a human being, under the Queen's peace, with malice aforethought, either express or implied, the death following within a year and a day.

ACTUS REUS

The important elements are:

1 that the defendant must have caused the death of another person (a foetus is not included in this definition, although if the child is born alive and then dies of the injuries inflicted when it was in the womb this can be murder *A-G's Reference No 3 of 1994*); and

2 that the death must happen within a year and a day of the defendant's act.

These elements are also required for manslaughter. The rules on causation apply; this means that there must not be an intervening act which breaks the chain of causation. However, medical treatment will rarely break the chain of causation even if it is negligent (*R v Smith (1959), R v Malcherek (1981), (R v Cheshire (1991)*). (See Chapter 11 for a full discussion of causation.)

MALICE AFORETHOUGHT

The key difference between murder and manslaughter lies in the phrase **malice aforethought**. This is the *mens rea* of murder; an unlawful killing without this *mens rea* cannot be murder. So murder is a crime of specific intent and means that the defendant must have the intent either:

■ to kill (express malice); or

■ to cause grievous bodily harm (implied malice).

It is the second part of this that has been questioned. Should a defendant who only intended to do his victim serious harm, but did not want to kill him, be found guilty of murder if his victim dies? The cases of *R v Vickers (1957)* and *R v Cunningham (1981)* have clearly decided that this is sufficient to make the defendant guilty of murder.

Foresight of consequences

Since murder requires specific intention, foresight that death or serious injury is virtually certain to result is not intention but can form evidence from which intention can be inferred. The cases of *R v Moloney, R v Hancock and Shankland, R v Nedrick* and *R v Walker and Hayles* are therefore relevant (see Chapter 10 on general principles of criminal law).

SPECIAL DEFENCES TO MURDER

There are three special defences to murder which reduce the offence to manslaughter. These are:

■ diminished responsibility;

■ provocation;

■ killing in pursuance of a suicide pact.

DIMINISHED RESPONSIBILITY

❝Abnormality of mind❞

This is a defence under s. 2 of the Homicide Act 1957 and covers situations where the person killed while suffering from 'an **abnormality of mind**' which substantially impaired their mental responsibility for acts and omissions in doing or being a party to the killing. The phrase 'abnormality of mind' was explained in the case of *R v Byrne (1960)* as covering the mind in all its aspects, including:

■ the perception of physical acts and matters;

■ the ability to form a rational judgment as to whether an act is right or wrong;

■ the ability to exercise will power to control physical acts.

The Court of Appeal in *Byrne* said that abnormality of mind meant 'a state of mind so different from that of ordinary human beings that the reasonable man would term it abnormal'. The Court of Appeal also said that **substantially impaired** indicated a mental state on the borderline of insanity. However, in *R v Seers (1985)* it was said that 'on the borderline of insanity' was not always the correct way to describe conditions of mind which were covered by diminished responsibility.

Cause of the abnormality of mind

Section 2 of the Homicide Act 1957 states that it should arise from 'a condition of arrested or retarded development of mind or any inherent cause'. External factors such as alcohol cannot be considered, unless they have led to an injury to the brain (*R v Tandy (1988)*). Problems occur where the defendant suffers from an abnormality of the mind, but at the time of committing the offence was also intoxicated. *R v Gittens (1984)* points out that in such circumstances the defence should only be allowed if the jury is satisfied that:

- if the defendant had not taken drink he would have killed as he did; and
- that he would have been under diminished responsibility.

PROVOCATION

This is a defence under s. 3 of the Homicide Act 1957 which allows a jury to consider evidence that the defendant was provoked 'whether by things done or by things said or by both together to lose his self control'. The Act does not however provide a full definition of provocation and it is necesary to look at case law for this. *R v Duffy (1949)* said that 'provocation is some act, or series of acts which would cause in any reasonable person, and actually causes in the accused, a sudden and temporary loss of self-control, rendering the accused so subject to passion as to make him for the moment not master of his mind'.

> **"Sudden and temporary loss of self-control"**

Other cases show that the provocation need not come from the victim, nor need it be deliberately directed at the accused. It may be a one-off incident or it may be a series of things, in which case the final incident may be less serious as it is 'the last straw'.

Timing

It is very important that there is no substantial time lapse between the provocation and the defendant's act, since the definition from *Duffy* makes it clear there must be a 'sudden' loss of self control. In *R v Thornton (1992)*, a wife had suffered abuse from her husband over a period of time. Following the final incident of abuse, she went into the kitchen, sharpened a knife and then returned to the room where her husband was asleep and stabbed him. Because of the time lapse, albeit a short one, the Court of Appeal held that she could not use the defence of provocation. However, in a subsequent case in the same year, *R v Ahluwalia*, where, following years of abuse, the defendant set fire to her husband as he slept, the Court of Appeal although affirming the need for a 'sudden' loss of self-control, did accept that in some cases there could be a 'slow burn' where thinking over the incident made the defendant suffer a 'sudden' loss of self-control.

> **"Slow burn cases"**

Characteristics of the defendant

Section 3 states that a jury, when considering whether the provocation was enough to make the defendant do as they did, shall take into account the effect it would have on a reasonable man. This brings an objective element into the defence. The court is not only concerned with whether the defendant was provoked, but also with how a reasonable person would have reacted. Fortunately this test has been tempered by the decision in *DPP v Camplin (1978)* where the defendant was a fifteen year old boy. The House of Lords held that a jury should think of the reasonable man as:

> '... a person having the power of self control of an ordinary person of the sex and age of the accused, but in other respects sharing such of the acccused's characteristics as they think would affect the gravity of the provocation to him.'

SUICIDE PACT

Where the defendant had made a suicide pact with the victim and both intended to die, then the defendant will have a defence to murder if he was a party to the other's killing. (Homicide Act 1957 s. 4 as amended by the Suicide Act 1961)

INVOLUNTARY MANSLAUGHTER

This is committed where a death is unlawfully caused by the defendant, but the defendant did not have the necessary *mens rea* for murder. It is called involuntary manslaughter to distinguish it from cases where the charge of murder was reduced to manslaughter for one of the reasons above. It now appears that involuntary manslaughter can be committed in two ways:

- by an unlawful and dangerous act (constructive manslaughter);
- by gross negligence.

CONSTRUCTIVE MANSLAUGHTER

There are three elements which must be proved:

- the commission by the defendant of an unlawful act;
- that the act was dangerous in the sense that it was likely to cause harm to another;
- that the act was the cause of death.

Unlawful act

If the act done is lawful then the charge cannot be manslaughter under this heading. An omission is not sufficient to make the defendant guilty (*R v Lowe (1973)*). The act need not be directed at the victim; the principle of transferred malice applies as in *R v Mitchell (1983)* where the defendant punched a man in a queue, that man fell against an elderly lady who died from the injuries she received. Mitchell was guilty of her manslaughter. It also appears that the unlawful act need not even be directed at a person, provided it is dangerous in the sense that it is likely to cause harm to another (*R v Goodfellow (1986)*).

Dangerous act

" Objective test "

The test is an objective one. It was said in *R v Church (1966)* that: 'the unlawful act must be such as all sober and reasonable people would inevitably recognise must subject the other person to at least the risk of some harm resulting therefrom, all be it not serious harm.' The defendant does not have to realise that that the act was either unlawful or dangerous. The only *mens rea* needed by the defendant is an intention to do the act (*DPP v Newbury and Jones (1976)*).

Difficulties have arisen in cases where the victim died from a heart attack brought on by the defendant's act. If a reasonable person would not have realised that any physical harm was likely to happen then the defendant will not be guilty of manslaughter (*R v Dawson (1985)*). However, if a reasonable person would have known that some physical harm was likely to occur, e.g. where a frail and elderly victim was tied up, then the defendant can be convicted of manslaughter (*R v Watson (1991)*).

The act caused the death

The normal rules of causation apply. If there is an intervening act breaking the chain of causation the defendant is not guilty as in *R v Dalby (1982)* where the defendant supplied the victim with heroin, but the victim, himself, injected it.

GROSS NEGLIGENCE MANSLAUGHTER

This is where there is a breach of duty and the defendant's negligence shows 'such disregard for life and safety of others as to amount to a crime against the State and conduct deserving of punishment' (*R v Bateman (1925)*). The leading case on this topic is *R v Adomako (1994)*, in which an anaesthetist failed to realise that a patient's oxygen supply had been disconnected, as a result of which the patient died. The House of Lords held that to decide if a defendant was guilty of manslaughter by gross negligence there had to be:

- a duty of care;
- a breach of that duty causing the victim's death;
- the breach had to be serious; and in considering whether it was serious enough to qualify as gross negligence, a jury had to look at all the circumstances in which the defendant was placed and 'consider whether the extent to which the defendant's conduct departed from the proper standard of care incumbent upon him, involving as it must have done a risk of death to the patient, was such as it should be judged criminal'.

The House of Lords also said that the word 'reckless' could be used in its ordinary meaning and not that given to it in the case of *R v Lawrence(1981)*. Prior to *Adomako*, it had been held that the *Lawrence* direction on recklessness was the correct one and this had unnecessarily complicated the law.

ASSAULTS

There are several different offences involving assault and this section will concentrate on:

- common assault and battery;

- assault causing actual bodily harm;
- malicious wounding;
- wounding with intent.

COMMON ASSAULT AND BATTERY

Although the word 'assault' in general usage is used to cover all attacks, legally there are two separate offences. **Assault** is the putting of another in fear that unlawful force is about to be used on him; **battery** is the application of unlawful force. So if A raises his fist threatening to punch B in the face, that is an assault; the moment the punch lands on B's face it is a battery. Many attacks include both an assault and a battery as in this example, but it is possible for only one to be present. In addition a battery can occur by the application of indirect violence, for example setting a booby-trap which hits the victim.

Mens rea

Both assault and battery are crimes of basic intent. So for assault the prosecution can show either that the defendant intended to put the victim in fear of having unlawful force used on them or that the defendant knew there was a risk that their actions might cause the victim that fear and took that risk. For battery it must be shown that either the defendant intended to use unlawful force or that they knew there was a risk that what they were doing might result in the use of unlawful force.

Both common assault and battery are summary offences triable only at the Magistrates' Court and carrying a maximum penalty of six months' imprisonment.

ASSAULT CAUSING ACTUAL BODILY HARM

This is an offence under s. 47 of the Offences against the Person Act 1861. The offence requires an assault or battery which causes actual bodily harm. So if in the example above when A punched B's face, a black eye was caused, A would have committed this offence. Actual bodily harm covers any injury, except those which are very trivial. It also covers psychiatric illness, but not emotional distress. It is not necessary for the defendant to intend to cause any injury or even to realise there was the risk of injury. If the defendant has the *mens rea* required for assault or battery and uses unlawful force which causes injury, then they are guilty of this offence (*R v Savage (1991)*).

Comment

The fact that there is no need to have any intention in relation to injury means that it can often be just chance which is the deciding factor in whether the defendant is charged with a battery or under s. 47. If by an unlucky chance the defendant causes a graze or a black eye to the victim, then s. 47 is the correct charge, and the offence becomes potentially much more serious as it is an offence triable either way with a maximum penalty of five years' imprisonment.

MALICIOUS WOUNDING

This is the technical name given to an offence under s. 20 of the Offences against the Person Act 1861. It is considered a more serious offence than s. 47, even though it carries the same maximum penalty.

Injury

There must be a 'wound' or 'grievous bodily harm'. Wound means a cutting of the whole skin. The breaking of a bone is not a wound unless the skin is also broken. An internal injury is not a wound even though there is internal bleeding (*JJC v Eisenhower (1983)*). Grievous bodily harm has the straightforward meaning of really serious injury.

Mens rea

This is a basic intent offence so that intention or subjective recklessness that the unlawful act might cause some physical harm is sufficient for the *mens rea*. It is important to note that the defendant does not have to realise that his act might cause serious harm (*R v Mowatt (1968)*).

WOUNDING WITH INTENT

This is the most serious of assault charges. It is defined in s. 18 of the Offences against the Person Act 1861 which states that:

'whosoever shall unlawfully and maliciously by any means whatsoever wound or cause grievous bodily harm to any person with intent to do some grievous bodily harm to any person, or with intent to resist or prevent the lawful apprehension or detaining of any person, shall be guilty of an offence, and being convicted thereof shall be liable to imprisonment for life.'

The same level of injury is needed as for s. 20 offences, that is, a wound or grievous bodily harm. The difference between the two offences lies in the intention. Section 18 is a specific intent crime; it can only be committed if the defendant has the intent to:

■ do some grievous bodily harm; or

■ resist arrest; or

■ prevent the arrest or detaining of another person.

CONSENT AS A DEFENCE TO ASSAULTS

The law recognises that in some situations the consent of the victim will provide a defence to an assault charge. However, this defence is limited. It is available if the assault was in course of 'properly conducted games and sports, lawful chastisement, reasonable surgical interference or dangerous exhibitions etc' (*A–G's reference No 6 of 1980*).

It is *not* available for the following situations:

■ fights to settle differences;

■ sado-masochistic acts which cause injury (*R v Brown (1992)*).

EXAMINATION QUESTIONS

1 a) To what extent are provocation and diminished responsibility defences?

  b) To what extent should they be defences? (UODLE)

2 How satisfactory is the criminal law regarding euthanasia? (NEAB)

3 'Involuntary manslaughter is an offence of ill-defined boundaries covering the middle ground between murder and accidental death.'

  Assess the validity of the above statement by analysing the constituent elements of **constructive** manslaughter and **gross negligence** manslaughter only. (UODLE)

4 Ann's husband and children were killed in a fire two years ago. Since that time, Ann has experienced severe bouts of anxiety and depression for which she has received medical treatment. Recently, Barbara and her family moved into the house next door. From the outset, relations between Ann and Barbara were very poor, principally because Barbara's children were very noisy and abusive. Additionally, Barbara's car, which was always parked in the street below Ann's bedroom window, was fitted with a car alarm which was frequently and unaccountably activated during the night. The morning after one particulary disturbed night, Ann was driving her car down the street when she heard Barbara joking with another neighbour about the car alarm. Ann immediately drove the car on to the pavement and knocked down and killed Barbara. Subsequently, she drove the car for about a mile and stopped it by some waste land on which a number of children, including Howard, were playing. In a complete daze she walked away, leaving the engine running. Howard got into the car and crashed it into a wall whilst attempting to drive it . He later died of his injuries.

  a) Discuss the liability of Ann for the murder of Barbara.

  b) Discuss the liability of Ann for the manslaughter of Howard.

  c) Explain and evaluate the legal provisions designed to secure advice and assistance for those charged with serious criminal offences.

  d) Consider the approach of the judges to the sentencing of offenders and discuss how this might be applied in Ann's case were she to be convicted of manslaughter of either Barbara or Howard. (AEB)

5 Pauline, a woman of 28, has been married to Rodney for seven years. Rodney is an alcoholic and often returns home drunk. While in this state, he often punches and slaps Pauline. This behaviour has been taking place regularly for the past three years. Pauline is

presently suffering from severe depression which she blames on Rodney's behaviour. One evening, Rodney returns home drunk and slaps Pauline on the face. He also tells her that he does not love her any more and intends to leave home for good. Rodney then falls asleep on the sofa. Pauline spends a couple of hours contemplating what has happened and, in a sudden burst of fury, beats Rodney on the head with an ashtray intending to kill him.

Pauline immediately regrets her action and calls an ambulance. Rodney is taken to hospital where he is treated for severe head injuries. Dr Doom injects Rodney with penicillin. Unfortunately, Rodney is allergic to penicillin and he dies.

Pauline is charged with the murder of Rodney. She does not dispute that at the time of the incident she intended to kill him. Consider how Pauline might defend herself against a charge of murder.

(UODLE)

ANSWERS TO QUESTIONS

OUTLINE ANSWER TO QUESTION 4

This style of structured question divides up the areas to be discussed, so make sure that you deal with them separately and label each part clearly.

Part a) The actus reus of murder is present, so the discussion should concentrate on intention and the possible defences of diminished responsibility and provocation.

Part b) Is there an unlawful act which is dangerous so as to bring Ann's act within constructive manslaughter? or is this a gross negligence situation? Also to be considered is Howard's intervening act in attempting to drive the car; almost certainly this would break the chain of causation.

Part c) This requires knowledge of legal aid and advice which are set out in Chapter 8. Consider the Duty Solicitor schemes, the Green Form scheme and the provisions for criminal legal aid.

Part d) This involves knowledge of sentencing, which will be found in Chapter 14. Discuss the aims of sentencing: protection of society, prevention of crime as against reform and rehabilitation.

TUTOR'S ANSWER

Question 5

If Pauline faced a charge of murder then her defences would be provocation and diminished responsibility. As she admits she had the necessary intent to kill him, these are the only two applicable defences and their effect would be to reduce the charge of murder to manslaughter. The two most comparable cases to hers are *Thornton* and *Aluwaliah*. In *Thornton* the defendant was abused by her husband for years and one night, after she was last abused, she stabbed him while he was asleep, killing him. She pleaded provocation. Provocation is defined in s. 3 of the Homicide Act 1957 and requires that the person was provoked to lose their self-control. The common law definition was given in *Duffy* and stated that the provocation was to make the defendant for the moment not master of his mind. Although undoubtedly it was Thornton's bad treatment by her husband that made her act as she did, following the definition she did not do the act immediately after she was provoked, i.e. there was a cooling-off period. Probably the most relevant case for Pauline is the more recent case of *Aluwaliah*. The defendant was again abused and battered by her husband. One night he came home and threatened to burn her with an iron. In the night she poured petrol over his feet and set it alight; he died later in hospital. Her defence in the case argued that she was on a slow fuse and although she did not react straight away, after thinking about it over and over, she lost control of herself. She was still convicted. On appeal, the Court of Appeal accepted that this was possible and agreed it could be a successful use of provocation, but the judge had summed up correctly to the jury, who came to their own conclusion. Although provocation failed for her she was allowed to plead diminished responsibility and this was successful. It is therefore more likely that diminished responsibility will be Pauline's biggest chance of success. This is defined in s. 2 of the Homicide Act 1957 and can be used by someone suffering from an abnormality of mind. The standard definition of abnormality of mind is given in *Byrne* and this should be read out to the jury when diminished responsibility is being pleaded. The definition is basically a condition of mind that any reasonable human being would term abnormal and it covers the inability to think straight and come to rational judgments. Pauline would use the fact that she had been constantly attacked by Rodney which has caused her depression. This should be enough to plead diminished responsibility. It does not cover emotions or fits of rage, but her depression could be said to be an abnormality of mind.

Since it is necessary in all murder cases to prove that the defendant's act caused the death, it is possible that Pauline could defend herself by saying that Dr Doom broke the chain of causation by injecting Rodney with pencillin to which he was allergic. The most comparable case here is *Jordan*. In this case the defendant stabbed someone who was taken to hospital, where the staff were severely negligent. They gave him antibiotics to which he was allergic and too much intravenous drip causing him to catch pneumonia and die. As Dr Doom also injected Rodney with an antibiotic to which he was allergic, it would appear possible to argue that the chain of causation was broken. However, other cases involving medical negligence do not make it likely that this argument would succeed. In *Smith* the victim was stabbed and received what the Court of Appeal described as thoroughly bad treatment which possibly affected his chances of survival by as much as 75%. The Court of Appeal held that Smith was still liable for the victim's death. The original wound was an operating and substantial cause. In *Cheshire* the victim was stabbed and he developed breathing problems partly due to negligence. When he died the stab wounds had healed, but, as in *Smith*, Cheshire was still responsible. The judges said that the chain of causation is rarely broken by negligent medical treatment, and for it to be broken the negligence of the doctors had to be so potent as to make the wounds merely part of history. The wounds have to be more than trivial as in Pauline's case, but they do not have to be the sole cause of death, they can just contribute. If the penicillin was the sole cause of death then she has a good chance of avoiding a murder charge. If it can be shown that his injuries were so severe that it is likely he would have died anyway then her plea of the broken chain will probably fail. As for provocation, it is worth raising the defence but following *Aluwaliah*, it is fairly unlikely to succeed mainly due to the cooling-off period. Although following what the Court of Appeal said, that the slow fuse was possible, she has a better chance of being successful with it. Diminished responsibility is the most likely defence to succeed, also following *Aluwaliah*.

STUDENT'S ANSWER WITH TUTOR'S COMMENTS

Question 1

A clear opening statement

Good use of cases

Part a)
Both provocation and diminished responsibility are defences only to the crime of murder. They do not provide a complete defence, they only reduce the charge from murder to manslaughter.

Apart from being limited in this way, there are other limitations on the two defences and it is necessary to consider them separately.

Provocation is a defence under s.3 of the Homicide Act 1957, which allows a jury to consider whether the provocation was enough to make a reasonable man to act as the defendant did. Provocation is not defined in the section and the definition given in *R v Duffy* is the accepted one. This stated that there had to be something which caused 'a sudden and temporary loss of self-control'. This definition means that there cannot be any significant time lapse between the provocation and the defendant's response. In *R v Thornton* the defendant was not sucessful with the defence as she admitted that she went into the kitchen after her husband's assault and sharpened a knife before going back and stabbing her husband. This short time lapse prevented her using the defence.

Provocation can be words or actions and needed not be intended as provocation as shown by *R v Doughty* when the crying of a 17-day-old baby was held to amount to provocation. Nor need provocation come from the ultimate victim. It can even be self-induced as was seen in the case of *R v Johnson*, where the defendant used the accent and mannerisms of a West Indian and was taunted as being 'a white nigger'.

The main problem in provocation is that there is a two stage test. First the defendant must show that he was actually provoked; this is the subjective test. Secondly the defendant must show that a reasonable man would have also been provoked to act as the defendant did; this is the objective test. Prior to the case of *Camplin*, the courts used to hold that the reasonable man could not be considered as having any of the defendant's special characteristics. But in the case of *Camplin*, where the defendant was a 15-year-old boy, the House of Lords held that the reasonable man was a person having the self-control of an ordinary person of the age and sex of the accused and sharing any other characteristics as would affect the gravity of the provocation. This means the characteristic must be reasonably permanent and so drunkeness is not taken into consideration.

> **Good concise explanation of the Camplin decision**

The characteristic must be relevant to the provocation; for example if the defendant has a scar on his face, that is relevant if he reacts to being teased about his ugly face, but it is not relevant if he reacts to being teased about the fact that he cannot play football.

Diminished responsibility is a completely different defence. It is defined in s. 2 of the Homicide Act as being where the defendant kills while suffering from an abnormality of mind which substantially impairs his mental responsibility for his acts and omissions in doing the killing. The defendant must prove that the abnormality of the mind is from internal causes such as retarded development or injury or disease. Self-induced problems through drinking or taking drugs are not diminished responsibility, unless this has caused brain damage or disease. In *R v Tandy* a mother killed her own daughter while suffering from alcoholism. It was held that the defence of diminished responsibility was available to her if her drinking had become involuntary and had caused injury to her brain.

Diminished responsibility is wider than insanity; it includes what is known as irresistible impulse (*R v Byrne*) where the defendant cannot control his actions although he knows he is doing wrong. However there must 'substantial' mental impairment; this is not clearly defined, for example in *R v Lloyd* the court said it was more than some trivial degree of impairment.

Part b)

> **A valid discussion point**

Since both defences are only available for murder, the first point to consider is whether they should be extended to other crimes, particularly attempted murder and section 18 assaults. It is true that murder is the only crime which has a mandatory life sentence and that by reducing murder to manslaughter, the judge is given discretion in sentencing. However, it would be equally of value to know whether a jury thought there was either provocation or diminished responsibility involved in other serious assault cases, since it could persuade a judge to impose a lower sentence.

> **The reasonable man test is a very important discussion point and could be extended**

For provocation the most important way in which it should be extended is by removing the objective test. Why should it matter whether a reasonable man would have been provoked? Surely the only point a jury should have to consider is whether the defendant, him or herself was provoked to act in that way. This would avoid the complications and uncertainty introduced into the law by the *Camplin* 'characteristics' test.

There is also debate over the time lapse between the provocation and the killing as it is now recognised that some defendants may have a 'slow fuse'. The strict limits imposed in this area have led to comments that the defence is primarily for men as they will react instantly, whereas women, particularly battered women are more likely to gradually build up resentment.

On the other hand, diminished responsibility has been successfully used as a defence where the defendant suffers from PMT and battered-wife syndrome, showing that the courts are fairly progressive in their interpretation of abnormality of mind. In view of the courts' interpretation there is less need to extend the defence of diminished responsibility, but it could be argued that defendants who are suffering from grief do not come within either defence and that diminished responsibility could be widened to include them.

Tutor's Comments

A clear understanding of both defences, although possibly the essay concentrates a little too much on provocation. There is good and accurate use of both statute and case law. The discussion points in part b) are quite wide ranging, again showing a clear understanding of the law. A grade A essay.

A review sheet for this chapter can be found on p. 213.

CHAPTER

13

OFFENCES AGAINST PROPERTY

THEFT

BURGLARY AND ROBBERY

DECEPTION OFFENCES

OTHER OFFENCES IN THE THEFT ACTS

CRIMINAL DAMAGE

GETTING STARTED

All the offences dealt with in this chapter are set out in Acts of Parliament so, when revising, a good starting point is to learn the statutory definitions of the most important crimes. The next stage is to make sure that you understand those definitions, particularly areas which have given difficulty and where there have been major cases decided by the courts. Finally, as is always the position for law examinations, make sure that you can apply your knowledge to factual situations given in problem questions.

Types of question asked in the examination fall into three categories:

- Essay questions on the development of the law and special areas of difficulty; often this type of question will focus on one or more parts of the definition of theft.

- Problem style questions based on a factual situation where the candidate is expected to identify the various offences which have occurred. In this style of question there may be an overlap and there may be offences against the person that need to be identified as well.

- Problem style questions where it is necessary to identify the offences involved, but the main thrust of the question is directed at possible defences (see Chapter 11).

ESSENTIAL PRINCIPLES

THEFT Theft is defined by s. 1 of the Theft Act 1968 which states that:

> 'A person is guilty of theft if he dishonestly appropriates property belonging to another with the intention of permanently depriving the other of it.'

MENS REA OF THEFT

The *mens rea* of theft is dishonesty *and* an intention to permanently deprive. Both these concepts need to be explained.

Dishonesty

The Theft Act itself does not define dishonesty, though it does set out three situations which are *not* to be regarded as dishonest. These are where a person appropriates property:

■ in the belief that he has in law the right to deprive the other of it (s. 2(1)a);

■ in the belief that he would have the other's consent if the other knew about it (s. 2(1)b);

■ in the belief that the person to whom the property belongs cannot be discovered by taking reasonable steps (s. 2(1)c).

In each of these situations the key issue is the defendant's belief; if the defendant acted under one of these beliefs, then the verdict must be not guilty of theft as the element of dishonesty is missing.

The only statement the Theft Act makes about what is dishonest is in s. 2(2) where it says that a person's appropriation of property belonging to another may be dishonest even though he is willing to pay for the property.

Two-stage test As the Theft Act gives so little help on the meaning of dishonest, the Court of Appeal in *R v Ghosh (1982)* explained that there was a two-stage test. First, was what the defendant did dishonest according to the ordinary standards of reasonable and honest people? If so, the second test to apply was, did the defendant realise that what he was doing was dishonest by those standards?

Intention to permanently deprive

If a defendant gives an item back he will not normally be guilty of theft. This is clear from the case of *R v Lloyd (1985)* where a film was taken for a few hours, copied and then returned. However, under s. 6 of the Theft Act 1968, the defendant, even though only borrowing an item, may be held to have the intention of permanently depriving where his intention is to treat the property as his own to dispose of regardless of the other's rights. The Court of Appeal explained that this could occur where a defendant kept an item 'till all the goodness had gone out of it', for example, returning something that is so badly damaged that it is useless.

Note that where the item 'borrowed' is money, the defendant will usually be held to have intended to permanently deprive as the bank notes/cash returned will not be the same ones as those taken (*R v Velumyl (1989)*).

ACTUS REUS OF THEFT

This is the appropriation of property belonging to another. So on a charge of theft it is necessary for the prosecution to prove:

■ that there was an appropriation;

■ that property within the definition in the Theft Act 1968 was taken; and

■ that the property belonged to another.

Appropriation

This is defined in the Theft Act 1968 s. 3 as 'any assumption by a person of the rights of an owner'. This is a very wide definition. In *R v Gomez (1992)* the House of Lords said that it included situations where the other person had consented to the appropriation, if that consent had been obtained by deception. In *Gomez* the property had been handed over in the belief that cheques given for it were genuine, when in fact the cheques were stolen and worthless.

A person can appropriate property even though in the first instance he has come by it innocently, if he later assumes a right to it by keeping it or dealing with it as an owner. This would cover a situation such as where a mother on her return from shopping found that her young child had brought an item out of the shop which had not been paid for. If the mother then decides to keep the item, she is guilty of theft.

Property

This is defined in s. 4 of the Theft Act 1968 as including 'money and all other property, real or personal'. The only restrictions on what is classified as property for the purposes of theft are:

- **land** – this can only be stolen if:
  - the defendant is a trustee or personal representative; or
  - a defendant who is not in possession of the land severs anything from the land; or
  - a tenant appropriates a fixture;
- **mushrooms, flowers, fruit and foliage growing wild** cannot be stolen unless the defendant picks them for reward, sale or other commercial purpose;
- **wild creatures** cannot be stolen unless they are tamed, in captivity or in the possession of another;
- **knowledge** cannot be stolen (*Oxford v Moss (1979)*).

Belonging to another

This does not only mean that the other person has to be the owner. Section 5 of the Theft Act 1968 extends the meaning of 'belonging' so that property is regarded as belonging to any person having possession or control of it. This means that for the purposes of the definition of theft, property belongs to another even if he is unaware that he is in possession of it (*R v Woodman (1974)*). It also means that it is technically possible to steal one's own property if another person has a right over it (*R v Turner (No 2) (1971)*). Section 5 also makes it clear that if someone gets property as a result of another's mistake and is under an obligation to restore the property to the correct owner, then he can steal it from the true owner. This covers situations where as a result of a mistake by a bank too much money is transferred into a person's account (*Attorney-General's Reference No 1 of 1983*).

BURGLARY AND ROBBERY

ROBBERY

This is defined by s. 8 of the Theft Act 1968:

'A person is guilty of robbery if he steals, and immediately before or at the time of doing so, and in order to do so he uses force on any person or puts or seeks to put any person in fear of being then and there subjected to force.'

From this it can be seen that the essential elements of robbery are:

- **theft** – if there is no theft there is no robbery, although there may be an attempt to rob or an assault with intent to steal;
- **force** – but this must be:
  - immediately before or at the time of the theft; and
  - in order to steal.

If the defendant commits a theft, is then caught and uses force to escape, this is not robbery as the force was not used immediately before or at the time of the theft. The theft was already completed by the time he used force.

The amount of force can be quite small; a push may be enough. It is for the jury to decide in each case whether what the defendant did can be described as force (*R v Clouden (1987)*).

BURGLARY

This is defined in s. 9 of the Theft Act 1968:

A person is guilty of burglary if:

a)   he enters any building or part of a building as a trespasser and with intent to commit theft, inflict grievous bodily harm, rape or do unlawful damage therein; or

b)   having entered any building or part of a building as a trespasser he steals or attempts to steal anything in the building or that part of it, or inflicts or attempts to inflict on any person therein any grievous bodily harm.

This means that there are several different ways of committing burglary but the common factors are:

- the defendant must enter a building or part of a building; and
- he must be a trespasser.

Section 9(1)a depends on the defendant's intention at the moment of entering as a trespasser. If it can be proved that he intends to steal, inflict grievous bodily harm, rape or do unlawful damage in the building, then he is guilty of burglary at the moment he enters.

Section 9(1)b is used where there is no evidence of the defendant's intentions on entry and it depends on the defendant's actions once in the building. Under this section the defendant becomes guilty of burglary the moment he steals or attempts to steal in the building or inflicts or attempts to inflict grievous bodily harm to someone in the building.

Building or part of a building

A building literally means any building and includes houses, offices, shops, barns and even garden sheds but it does not include non-permanent things like tents. However, the Theft Act 1968 specifically states that inhabited vehicles and vessels are included in the definition of building, so that it is possible to be guilty of burgling a mobile home or a houseboat.

The phrase part of a building is used to cover situations where the defendant may have the right to be in one part of a building but is a trespasser if he goes into another part. A common example of this is in shops where the general public are allowed into the main body of the shop, but are not entitled to go into areas which are marked 'private' or 'staff only'. In *R v Walkington (1979)* the defendant was found guilty of burglary when he went behind a three-sided counter in a store intending to steal from the till. The court held that this area was clearly for staff only and that the defendant realised this.

As a trespasser

The defendant must know that he has not got permission to be on the premises or be reckless as to whether he is trespassing in the sense that he is aware of facts which mean he might be trespassing. Where the defendant is invited on to the premises, then he is not trespassing (*R v Collins (1973)*), although he may still be treated as a trespasser if he goes beyond the permission given (*R v Jones and Smith (1976)*).

AGGRAVATED BURGLARY

Under s. 10 of the Theft Act 1968, the offence of burglary becomes the more serious offence of aggravated burglary if the defendant has with him at the time of the burglary 'any firearm or imitation firearm, any weapon of offence, or any explosive'. A useful mnemonic for this offence is to remember that the burglar takes his 'WIFE' with him! (Weapon of offence, Imitation firearm, Firearm, Explosive).

DECEPTION OFFENCES

There are several offences involving deception; the difference between them lies in what has been obtained as a result of the deception. Since the common factor is deception, the first point is to be clear what is meant by this.

Deception is defined in s. 15(4) of the Theft Act 1968 as:

'… any deception (whether deliberate or reckless) by words or conduct as to fact, including a deception as to the present intentions of the person using the deception or any other person.'

This covers many situations including using someone else's credit card to pay for goods or paying with one's own cheque when the defendant knows the account is overdrawn and the bank will not honour the cheque. The deception must succeed, that is it must be the reason why the victim handed over property, supplied the services etc. One final point to remember is that a machine cannot be deceived, so that using a fake coin to get cigarettes or chocolate from a machine cannot be any offence involving deception, but will be theft.

OBTAINING PROPERTY BY DECEPTION

This comes from s. 15 of the Theft Act 1968:

'A person who by deception dishonestly obtains property belonging to another, with the intention of permanently depriving the other of it, shall on conviction on indictment be liable to imprisonment for a term not exceeding ten years.'

To be guilty of this offence, the defendant must have obtained property: property has the same meaning as for the offence of theft. Following the case of *R v Gomez (1992)* there is a large overlap with theft and almost all situations which could be charged as obtaining property as deception will also be thefts. But beware, because the reverse is not true; it is quite possible to have a theft where there is no deception and so no s. 15 offence.

OBTAINING A PECUNIARY ADVANTAGE BY DECEPTION

This is an offence under s. 16 of the Theft Act 1968 but it now covers only a very limited area as part of this section (which caused many problems) has been repealed. As a result, obtaining a pecuniary advantage by deception is restricted to where the defendant is:

- allowed to borrow by way of overdraft or to take out any policy of insurance or annuity contract, or obtains an improvement of the terms on which he is allowed to do so (s. 16(2)b);
- given the opportunity to earn remuneration or greater remuneration in an office or employment, or to win money by betting (s. 16(2)c).

OBTAINING SERVICES BY DECEPTION

Under s. 1(1) of the Theft Act 1978 (note that this a *different Act* from the Theft Act 1968), it is set out that:

'A person who by any deception dishonestly obtains services from another shall be guilty of an offence.'

Section 1(2) explains what is meant by obtaining services and says:

'It is an obtaining of services where the other is induced to confer some benefit by doing some act, or causing or permitting some act to be done, on the understanding that the benefit has been or will be paid for.'

Services covers many things such as a haircut or taxi ride or staying in a hotel room. But note that any food dishonestly obtained by deception while staying in a hotel would be the subject of a s. 15 offence of obtaining property.

EVADING A LIABILITY BY DECEPTION

Section 2 of the Theft Act 1978 states that there is an offence where any person by deception:

- dishonestly secures the remission of the whole or part of any existing liability to make payments, whether his own liability or another's (s. 2(1)a); or
- with intent to make permanent default in whole or in part on any existing liability to make a payment ... dishonestly induces the creditor to wait for payment or ... to forgo payment (s. 2(1)b); or
- dishonestly obtains any exemption from or an abatement of liability to make payment (s. 2(1)c).

Section 2(1)a was seen by the Criminal Law Revision Committee as covering situations where someone who owed money told a false story to the creditor, so that the creditor said the debt need not be repaid in full, or even need not be repaid at all.

Section 2(1)b is intended to cover situations where such a creditor is persuaded to put off the date for repayment.

Section 2(1)c covers situations such as showing an out-of-date season ticket or someone else's season ticket and so evading paying the train fare.

<table>
<tr><td>OTHER OFFENCES IN
THE THEFT ACTS</td></tr>
</table>

TAKING A CONVEYANCE WITHOUT CONSENT

Section 12 of the Theft Act 1968 makes it an offence to take a conveyance without the consent of the owner or other lawful authority. It is also an offence to drive or allow oneself to be carried in a conveyance, knowing that it has been taken without consent.

A **conveyance** is anything which is constructed or adapted for carrying people on land, water or in the air. So, although the most common way of committing this offence is by taking a car or other vehicle, it is also an offence to take a motor boat or an aircraft.

No need to prove intention to permanently deprive

This section exists because it is not always possible to prove theft when a car is taken, since the defendant may not have the intention of permanently depriving the owner of the car. A defendant who drives around and then abandons the car undamaged will be charged under this section.

HANDLING STOLEN GOODS

Section 22 of the Theft Act 1968 states that it is an offence for a person to dishonestly handle stolen goods knowing or believing them to have been stolen. Handling is defined as:

- receiving goods; or
- undertaking or assisting in their retention, removal, disposal or realisation.

MAKING OFF WITHOUT PAYMENT

Section 3 of the Theft Act 1978 provides that:

> '… a person who, knowing that payment on the spot for any goods supplied or services done is required or expected of him, dishonestly makes off without having paid as required or expected and with intent to avoid payment of the due amount shall be guilty of an offence.'

This section was passed to deal with situations where a defendant ran off after a taxi ride without paying or left a restaurant without paying for the meal. In such cases it is difficult to prove that there is an offence of obtaining by deception, as the prosecution would need to prove that the defendant had already decided not to pay before the taxi ride or meal was finished.

Intent to avoid payment

The main problem caused by s. 3 is that the prosecution must prove that the defendant never intends paying. This was decided in *R v Allen (1985)*. A person who realises that they have left their money and credit cards at home and leaves without paying but intends to pay in the future is not guilty of an offence.

BLACKMAIL

Under s. 21 of the Theft Act 1968 the offence of blackmail is committed where the defendant:

> '… with a view to gain for himself or another or with intent to cause loss to another … makes any unwarranted demand with menaces …'

A **view to gain or cause a loss** must be of money or other property. In *R v Bevans (1988)* the defendant threatened a doctor with a gun and demanded to be injected with a pain-killing drug. It was held that the drug was property. However, the property does not need to be handed over as the offence is committed when a demand with menaces is made with a view to gain or loss.

An **unwarranted demand** means that the defendant does not believe he has reasonable grounds for making the demand.

Menaces involves making some sort of threat. Clearly, threatening violence is menaces but it does not have to be a threat of violence; other threats such as threatening to damage property or to tell about sexual perversions are included. However, the threats must either be sufficiently serious so that they would affect a normal person, even if the victim was not affected, or they must be threats that the defendant knows are likely to affect the particular victim (*R v Garwood (1987)*).

CRIMINAL DAMAGE

Under the Criminal Damage Act 1971 it is an offence intentionally or recklessly to destroy or damage property belonging to another. Destroying does not mean that the property has to be completely destroyed, but it does have to be made useless for its purpose. Damage includes scratching paintwork on cars and spraying paint on to walls. Recklessly is used in the wider meaning where a defendant is reckless if, either, he realises that there is a risk of damage, or, if an ordinary careful person would realise there was a risk of damage.

Arson

Where the property is damaged or destroyed by fire then the defendant wil be charged with arson.

EXAMINATION QUESTIONS

1   'In the law of theft the concepts of appropriation and dishonesty continue to cause problems for the courts.' Discuss
                                                                                    (UODLE)

2   R, a student, was worried about an examination which he had to pass in order to stay on his course. His conduct has been that of a model student and he has a good record of work for the community. One day he called into the college office to pick up some mail when he saw an envelope containing some examination papers. He immediately hid these papers underneath his coat and took them away to copy them at home before returning them to the office. As he was walking along the road to his house he saw some coins on the pavement which he picked up and put in his pocket. Not long after he saw a wallet with some money in it on a seat in a bus. He discovered that the name and address of the owner was in the wallet and that the owner was employed by the bus company. He did not inform anyone of his discoveries.

Could R be made subject to any criminal proceedings? How might the courts deal with him should he be found guilty of any offence?   (ULEAC)

3   What offences, if any, have been committed as the result of the following occurrences in the Heaton Department Store?

a)   D, who works in the electrical department, borrows an electric drill, without telling his supervisor, for the weekend. When he returns the drill its motor has burnt out.

b)   E, a cleaner of low intelligence, finds a diamond ring in the ladies' cloakroom. She keeps the ring. When this is discovered she says she did not realise it would be possible to find the owner.

c)   F, the flower department manager, picks daffodils growing wild in nearby woods. He sells them in the store and keeps the proceeds.

d)   G, a customer in the self-service food department, takes a number of items from the shelf and places them into a wire basket provided by the store. G then takes a tin of salmon from the shelf and places it into his coat pocket. G is detained by a store detective before he leaves the food department. G admits it was his intention to take the salmon and the other items in the basket from the store without payment.   (UODLE)

4   Bill and Tim go to their local hypermarket. On an earlier visit, the hypermarket manager told Tim he was not to return again as he suspected him of being concerned in a spate of thefts which his store had recently suffered.

As they are about to enter the hypermarket, Bill and Tim agree that they will unplug all the freezers in the store, thus spoiling the frozen foods which they contain. They each enter the store, Bill heading for the freezers in the meat department and Tim heading for the freezers in the dairy produce department.

Bill unplugs several freezers and spoils £1,000 worth of meat. On his way out, he enters a room marked 'STAFF ONLY' and takes £25 from an unattended handbag. As he is leaving the room a store detective challenges him, whereupon Bill strikes him on the nose and makes good his escape.

As Tim is about to unplug the freezer full of cheeses, he is challenged by Mary, a shop assistant. Knowing that Mary is having a secret affair with the manager, Tim threatens to reveal this fact to Mary's husband if she stops him. He then unplugs the freezer spoiling its contents, Mary being too frightened to intervene.

Consider the criminal liability of a) Bill and b) Tim, ignoring any possible offences of conspiracy and secondary participation.   (UODLE)

5   S was asked by T to lend her some sharp knives. S thought that these were to be used to slit pockets of passengers in trains to help T steal their property. In fact T was planning to attack a mail van. She carried out the attack and used one of the knives to slit open a mail bag to check its contents. At that moment she was attacked by one of the security guards and in the ensuing struggle wounded him very badly, so that he is now on a life support system in hospital. What charges might be brought against S and T?   (ULEAC)

ANSWERS TO QUESTIONS

OUTLINE ANSWERS TO SELECTED QUESTIONS

Question 2

All the situations possibly involve theft so start by giving the definition of theft and then deal with each situation separately.

1   The taking of the examination papers: R intends to return them so this cannot be theft – no intention to permanently deprive (*R v Lloyd*); nor is he stealing property by copying the information (*Oxford v Moss*).

2   The picking up of the coins: Is this dishonest? Does R believe that the owner cannot be found by taking reasonable steps? Theft Act 1968 s. 2(1)c.

3   The finding of the wallet: again s. 2(1)c is important in deciding if R is acting dishonestly. Does the fact that the owner's name and address are in the wallet make a difference?

Question 3

Each of these parts involves a different aspect of the definition of the offence of theft so deal with each part separately.

a)   This raises this issue of the meaning of intention to permanently deprive; discuss the effect of s. 6 of the Theft Act 1968 which allows a borrowing to amount to the necessary intention in certain circumstances. Are the facts of what D has done enough to come within s. 6? (Note that the offence of criminal damage could also be involved.)

b)   This involves the issue of dishonesty. Has E acted dishonestly by keeping the ring? The case of *Ghosh* should be considered and also s. 2 of the Theft Act 1968. S. 2(1)c involves a subjective test; does E believe that the owner cannot be traced by taking reasonable steps?

c)   Here the definition of property under s. 4 is important. The general rule being that wild flowers cannot normally be stolen unless they are taken for reward or other commercial purpose. Apply this to F.

d)   This raises the issue of appropriation. Explain s. 3 and consider the cases of *Lawrence, Morris,* and *Gomez*. Deal with the two situations. First the placing of items into a wire basket – is this an appropriation? Then deal with the putting of the tin of salmon into G's pocket – this is a more clear cut situation of theft. Note that G admits he intended taking the items, so there is no need to discuss any other aspect of the offence of theft.

Question 4

First note that you are *not* required to deal with any issues of conspiracy or participation. It is just a waste of time doing so when the examiner has made it clear this is not required.

As there are two people to be considered, it is sensible to divide the answer into two separate parts.

Part a) Bill's liability

1   Criminal damage of the meat in the freezers; this also amounts to theft as all parts of the definition of theft are satisfied.

2   Burglary under s. 9(1)b when he takes the £25; (he has entered a part of a building as a trespasser and stolen).

3   Assault – either a common assault if there is no injury or an assault causing actual bodily harm if the store detective is slightly injured.

4   This is not a case of robbery as the theft was already complete when Bill used force.

Part b) Tim's liability

1   Burglary (s. 9(1)a) at the moment he enters the store, since he is a trespasser and has the intent to commit criminal damage.

2   Blackmail – is there blackmail? Tim uses menaces to Mary with a view to causing a loss to another (the store).

3   Criminal damage when he finally unplugs the freezer and spoils the contents.

STUDENT'S ANSWER WITH TUTOR'S COMMENTS

Question 1

"Accurate but rather brief explanation of s. 2"

The definition of theft in the Theft Act 1968 places great stress on the phrase 'dishonestly appropriates'. The concept of dishonesty is not properly explained in the Act as s. 2 gives three examples of what is not considered dishonest. The only comment on what may be

❝Very limited evaluation❞

❝A good point but needs development❞

dishonest is when it says that a person may still be dishonest even though they pay for the property.

This means that it has been left to the courts to explain the meaning, but the courts have tended to the view that the concept of dishonesty is straightforward and in most cases will not need to be explained. However in *R v Ghosh* the courts held that there were two things to be considered. First, did the jury think that what the defendant had done was dishonest by the standards of ordinary people? If so did the defendant realise he was being dishonest by those standards? These seem quite simple tests to apply.

So far as appropriation is concerned, the starting point is s. 3 of the Theft Act 1968. This says that appropriation is the assumption of the rights of an owner. This could cover almost any conduct and this is the way that the courts are now viewing it. In *R v Gomez* the House of Lords was asked if a person could be guilty of theft when the owner had consented to the appropriation. The Law Lords ruled that this situation was theft.

This makes it difficult to see what the difference is between obtaining property by deception (s. 15) and theft. Surely what Gomez did was obtain goods by deception and the decision seems to have unnecessarily complicated the law and made s. 15 redundant.

However the wide definition given to appropriate has made it easier to convict in shoplifting cases. It is not necessary to wait for a shoplifter to go through a checkout; they are guilty the moment they remove articles from the shelf, if they are being dishonest about it.

Tutor's Comments

Although the relevant sections of the Theft Act are known, the essay lacks details of these. None of the situations in s. 2 is explored. The basic definition of appropriation is given (though not 100% accurately), but again there is no real consideration of s. 3. The two key cases of *Ghosh* and *Gomez* are known but the evaluation of the problems is very simple. Generally the essay is on the right lines but needs more development. A grade D.

A review sheet for this chapter can be found on p. 214.

SENTENCING

GETTING STARTED

In sentencing the main debate is what is the 'correct' sentence for a crime. This has no simple answer and in fact there are two main themes that judges use when deciding a sentence. These are:

1 **Retribution** – looking back to the crime and punishing for it;
2 **Utilitarian** – looking forward and aiming to achieve a useful purpose with the sentence.

During the 1990s sentencing has been drawn into the political arena. For example the Criminal Justice Act 1991 attempted to lay down a framework under which sentencing would become more consistent. At the end of 1995, the Home Secretary announced that he intended bringing in minimum sentences for some crimes and this was seen by the judiciary as an attack on their independence.

In approaching this topic it is useful to be aware of recent trends and any high profile cases that have appeared in the media, but do not base your answers just on these. A balanced view, showing an understanding of the aims of sentencing, is important.

The other aspect of sentencing is the actual types of sentences that are available to the courts, both for adult offenders and young offenders. Again, it is important to be able to make informed comments on the available sentences.

AIMS OF SENTENCING

ESSENTIAL PRINCIPLES

RETRIBUTIVE THEORIES

These are based on the idea that the offender deserves punishment for his or her acts. This was a very popular idea in the nineteenth century, e.g. Kant in *The Metaphysical Elements of Justice* wrote:

> 'Judicial punishment can never be used merely as a means to promote some other good for the criminal himself or for civil society, but instead it must in all cases be imposed on him only on the ground that he has committed a crime.'

The idea regained some popularity in the Criminal Justice Act 1991. That Act was based on the Government White Paper on Crime and Punishment (1990) which stated that the first objective should be denunciation of and retribution for the crime.

Retribution is based on three points:

1 **Revenge** – the idea that society is being avenged for the wrong done; this can be seen in the increased maximum penalties that have been made available for driving offences which cause death.

2 **Denunciation** – this is making it clear to society that certain behaviour will not be tolerated.

3 **Just deserts** – this is the idea that the criminal should receive a punishment suitable to the crime. This has led to **tariff sentences** in some countries where each crime has a set penalty and the court has very little discretion. In our system the Court of Appeal has laid down **guidelines** for certain offences, in particular for rape and for drug offences.

UTILITARIAN THEORIES

The concept behind these principles of sentencing is that punishment must serve a useful purpose. 'Useful' in this context can mean either for the offender or for society as a whole. There are four main principles:

1 **Deterrence –** this can be aimed at the individual who has committed the offence or at other potential offenders. With **individual deterrence** the purpose of the punishment is to make sure that the offender does not re-offend through fear of future punishment. There are several penalties that can be imposed with this in mind, e.g. a prison sentence or a suspended sentence or a heavy fine. The problem with prison is that it does not appear to deter those who have already served a sentence, as about 65% of adult prisoners re-offend within two years of release.

❝Re-offending rates❞

The value of **general deterrence** is even more doubtful as potential offenders are rarely deterred by severe sentences passed on others.

2 **Protection of society** – this involves removing dangerous offenders from society. In Britain today this is achieved through the use of long prison sentences. The Criminal Justice Act 1991 s. 1 states that a prison sentence should only be imposed where the offence is so serious that imprisonment is justified or where the offence is a violent or sexual offence and only such a sentence would be adequate to protect society. There is also a move to using community based sentences that will protect the public, such as curfew orders.

3 **Reformation** – this is where the main aim of the penalty is to reform the offender and rehabilitate him or her into society. This principle of sentence has come to the fore in the second half of the twentieth century with the development of sentences such as probation and community service orders. The Criminal Justice Act 1991 reinforced the use of community based penalties.

4 **Reparation** – this is aimed at compensating the victim of the crime usually by ordering the offender to pay a sum of money to the victim or to make restitution (i.e. return stolen property to its rightful owner). However, there have been some projects where offenders have been encouraged to meet the victim and to do work for them.

BACKGROUND FACTORS CONSIDERED BY THE COURTS

Whichever principle of sentencing is used the court will usually consider both the offence and the background of the offender. In looking at the offence some important points are:

- **how serious was it of its type?** – e.g. how much was stolen? or what injuries were inflicted?
- **was the crime premeditated?** – if so then it is usually considered to be more serious;
- **was the offender in a position of trust?** – again, if this was the case the offence will be considered as being more serious.

So far as the offender is concerned the court will want to know such points as:

- **are there previous convictions?** – although there was an attempt to move away from considering previous convictions in the Criminal Justice Act 1991, this was altered by the Criminal Justice Act 1993 so that now the court may take them into account and also the failure of an offender to respond to previous sentences in deciding the seriousness of the current offence;
- **was the offender on bail when they committed the offence?** – the 1993 Act states that if this is the case the court shall treat that fact as an aggravating factor;
- **what is the family background?** – this may be important in showing both why the offender committed a crime and also indicate whether they are likely to respond to a community based penalty. The court may have a pre-sentence report from a probation officer to help in considering this;
- **are there any medical or psychiatric problems?** – if so this may be an important factor in deciding the appropriate way of dealing with the offender;
- **the age of the offender** – there are restrictions on the types of sentences that can be used for young offenders; also it may not be necessary to inflict a heavy penalty on an elderly person;
- **the financial situation of the offender** – where the court considers that a fine is a suitable penalty then it must enquire into the financial circumstances of the offender and take them into account when setting the level of the fine.

ADULT OFFENDERS

There are many sentencing options available to the courts when dealing with offenders over 21 years old. These include:

- an immediate term of imprisonment;
- suspended prison sentence;
- fines;
- community service orders;
- probation orders;
- combination orders combining community service and probation;
- curfew orders;
- discharges which may be either conditional or absolute.

In addition, for appropriate offences, the courts have the power to make an order excluding an offender from a certain place or banning him from driving. There are also special powers for dealing with mentally ill offenders.

PRISON SENTENCES

For the crime of murder the only sentence a court can impose is life imprisonment. For other crimes Parliament has laid down a maximum prison sentence, but it is for the court in each individual case to decide if imprisonment is necessary and if so what length of time the offender should serve in jail. It is very rare for a court to give the maximum sentence although this has occurred in some cases of rape where the maximum is life imprisonment. The maximum sentence that can be imposed by a Magistrates' Court is six months for one offence and six plus six, making twelve months, for two or more offences.

The United Kingdom sends a higher percentage of its population to prison than any other European Union country. The number of offenders in prison has risen steadily. The government attempted to reduce the number of defendants sent to prison for relatively minor offences by setting out statutory guidelines on the use of prison sentences in the Criminal Justice Act 1991. This states that a prison sentence should not be imposed unless the offence is so serious that only imprisonment is justified or the offence is a violent or sexual offence and only such a sentence would be adequate to protect society.

Release on licence

Prisoners do not serve the whole of their sentence as those who receive less than four years will be automatically released after serving half of their sentence. Those receiving four years or more will be automatically released after serving two-thirds of the sentence and may be released on licence at any time after serving at least half the term of imprisonment. Except for those serving less than a one year sentence all prisoners are supervised after release.

Prisons are seen as a way of containing violent offenders but there are problems:

❝ Problems of imposing prison sentences ❞

■ too many petty offenders are sent to prison;

■ there are variations in sentencing practice at both Magistrates' Courts and Crown Courts so that both the chances of being sent to prison and the length of sentences vary in different areas;

■ there have been serious disturbances within prisons, one of the worst incidents occurred in 1990 at Strangeways Prison;

■ too many prisoners are able to abscond;

■ there are insufficient constructive activities to give prisoners skills and so help them on their return to the community;

■ the re-offending rate for released prisoners is too high.

The Chief Inspector of Prisons, Judge Tumim has said:

'Most prisoners … are male and under 30. Their offences are connected with stealing cars, burglary and occasionally drugs, but they are not given to violence. They were failures at school and they know too little to lead useful lives outside … They need to be taught working skills and they need social training to cope with the problems of drink, drugs, Aids, and above all their own offending behaviour.'

Suspended prison sentences

These can be for a maximum term of two years' imprisonment and the maximum period during which it can be suspended is also two years. The effect of a suspended sentence is that the offender does not actually go to prison unless another crime is committed during the period of suspension. The use of suspended sentences is limited by the Criminal Justice Act 1991 to cases where the offence is so serious that an immediate custodial sentence would have been appropriate but there are exceptional circumstances in the case that justify suspension of that sentence.

FINES

This is the most common way of disposing of a case in the Magistrates' Court, where the maximum fine is £5,000. About 20% of offenders appearing in the Crown Court are also fined; this court has no limits on the amounts it can fine offenders.

Unit fines

An attempt was made in the Criminal Justice Act 1991 to match fines not only to the seriousness of the offence but also to the ability of the offender to pay, by the introduction of unit fines. Magistrates had to decide on the number of units the offence merited and then multiply those units by the weekly disposable income that the defendant had available. In theory this appeared a sound idea but in practice there were major problems, partly occurring because defendants failed to fill out forms correctly when giving details of their financial situation. The scheme was abandoned after only ten months. Courts, however, are still obliged to consider both the seriousness of the offence and the offender's financial circumstances when setting the amount of a fine.

COMMUNITY PENALTIES

Probation Order

This places the offender under the supervision of a probation officer for a period of between six months and three years. During this time the offender must keep in regular contact with the probation officer and must lead an 'industrious and honest' life. Other conditions may be included by the court such as a residence order, requiring the offender to live at a certain address or a treatment order requiring the offender to attend for medical or psychiatric treatment.

Community service order

This requires the offender to work for between 40 and 240 hours on a suitable project organised by the probation service. The exact number of hours will be fixed by the court and those hours are then usually worked in eight-hour sessions, often at weekends.

Combination order

This is a combination of up to 100 hours of community service and a probation order.

Curfew orders

Under these an offender can be ordered to remain at a fixed address for between two and twelve hours in any 24-hour period. This order can last for up to six months and may be enforced by electronic tagging where suitable.

DISCHARGES

The courts also have powers to discharge an offender on the condition that no further offence is committed during a set period of up to three years. This method of dealing with offenders is set out in the Powers of the Criminal Courts Act 1973 and is intended to be used where it is thought that punishment is not necessary. If a offender re-offends within the time limit the court can then imposed another sentence in place of the conditional discharge as well as imposing a penalty for the new offence. Conditional discharges are widely used by Magistrates' Court for first-time minor offenders. There is also the possibility of an absolute discharge but these are rarely used. The effect of such a discharge is that no penalty is imposed. They are likely to be used where an offender is technically guilty but morally blameless.

YOUNG OFFENDERS

This term includes all offenders under the age of 21. However, there are various different sentences available for those under 18, under 16, under 14 and under 12. The main aim in sentencing young offenders is reformation and rehabilitation. Offenders under 18 years old are normally dealt with in the Youth Court.

CUSTODIAL SENTENCES

Young offenders' institutions

An offender aged 18 but under 21 can be sent to such an institution for a minimum of twenty-one days and a maximum determined by the maximum prison sentence available for an adult. If an offender reaches 21 while still serving a sentence he or she will be transferred to an adult prison.

For those under 18 there are limits on custodial sentences, except for offences for which an adult can be imprisoned for at least fourteen years, when s. 53 of the Children and Young Persons Act 1933 allows long periods of detention to be ordered. Apart from this, offenders aged 15 to 17 can be sent to a Young Offenders' Institution for a minimum of two months and maximum of two years. Persistent offenders aged 12 to 14 can be sent to special secure units.

 **Re-offending rates**

Custodial penalties do not appear to have any reformative effect. Home Office research in 1994 revealed that, for male prisoners, 82% of 17 to 20 year olds re-offended within two years of being released, while the figure for those aged 15 to 16 was even higher at 92%. However, there also statistics to show that persistent offenders are likely to re-offend regardless of whether they are given a custodial sentence or a community based sentence.

Community penalties

Offenders aged 16 to 21 can be given the same community penalties as adults. That is:

- probation order;
- community service order;
- combination order;
- curfew order.

In addition an **attendance centre order** may be made. This involves attendance at a special centre for two or three hours a week up to a maximum of 36 hours.

Those under 18 can be given a **supervision order** where the offender is placed under the supervision of the local social services. Extra 'strings' may be attached to such an order including a night restriction order or residence in secure accommodation.

Fines

Any offender may be fined although the maximum amount varies with age as follows:

- 10–13 year olds £250;
- 14–17 year olds £1,000.

Where an offender is under 16 years old the court may order the offender's parents to pay the fine.

Discharges

These may be used for any offender and in fact are commonly used for first-time young offenders who have committed minor crimes.

EXAMINATION QUESTIONS

1 How successful have been recent attempts by Parliament to impose greater controls over judges in sentencing? (ULEAC)

2 Discuss the aims pursued in the sentencing of criminal offenders. (AEB)

3 a) Discuss the options open to a sentencer, explaining what these different sentencing options are intended to achieve.

    b) Comment on how a sentencing court will decide on the most suitable disposal for an individual offender. (NEAB)

4 Bernard, aged 16, is convicted by the Midshire Youth Court of causing criminal damage.

    a) What sentencing powers does the court have in respect of him?

    b) Why are there differences in the sentences available for young offenders and adult offenders? (UODLE)

5 Explain and evaluate the sentencing options available to the courts in dealing with young offenders. (WJEC)

ANSWERS TO QUESTIONS

OUTLINE ANSWER

Question 3

Part a) This requires a list of the main sanctions available to the court and a discussion of what each is aimed at. Probably the easiest way to tackle this question is to list the options in the first paragraph and then discuss each one separately.

1 **List of options** – custodial sentences; community penalties of probation, community service, combination order and curfew orders; fines; discharges.

2 **Custodial sentences** – main aim protection of the public and prevention of crime; also thought to deter potential offenders.

3 **Community penalties** – main aims reform and rehabilitation in the community.

4 **Fines** – aims of retribution and deterrence.

5 **Discharges** – punishment thought not to be needed; appearance in court felt to be sufficient deterrence.

Part b) Comments on this should include:

1 Consideration of the seriousness of the crime.

2 Consideration of the defendant's past record.

3   The background of the defendant – family and work.

4   Any mitigating or aggravating features.

TUTOR'S ANSWER

Question 4

Part a) Bernard's age means that he is categorised as a young person and the court has specific powers for this age group. The options open to the court include both custodial and non-custodial sentences. Bernard could be sent to a Young Offenders' Institution for a minimum of two months up to the Youth Court's maximum power of six months. This is unlikely unless Bernard has previous convictions and the criminal damage is very serious.

The other options for the court are to impose a community penalty or a fine or to give Bernard a discharge. There are several community penalties the court can consider; first it is possible to place Bernard on probation but he must agree to this and agree to be bound by its terms and conditions. A probation order can last for three years during which time the offender must keep in touch with his probation officer and abide by any other conditions such as a residence order that the court thinks fit to add to the probation order. As Bernard is only 16 the court may use a supervision order rather than a probation order. This would place him under the supervision of the local social services and his consent for this is not needed. As with probation the court may add in extra requirements.

Another possible sentence is a community service order under which Bernard will have to do supervised work unpaid on a community project for the number of hours specified by the magistrates in the Youth Court, the minimum being 40 hours and the maximum being 240 hours. It is also possible for the court to order a combination order that is up to 100 hours of commmunity service and a probation order. Another option is a curfew order where the court can specify a period of between two and twelve hours in any 24-hour period when the offender must remain in a particular place (usually the home). This can last for up to six months and might be used if the crime is part of a pattern of offending at a particular time of day. The curfew can be monitored by electronic tagging.

As Bernard is a young offender there is also the option of making an attendance centre order of a maximum of 24 hours. Attendance is usually for three hours on a day at the weekend. He can be ordered to pay a fine up to a maximum of £1,000 and he can be ordered to pay a sum of money to the owner of the property damaged by way of compensation.

Finally he may be given a conditional discharge, which lasts for a specified time up to three years or an absolute discharge. This latter is not very likely but it is quite possible that Bernard may be given a conditional discharge especially if he is a first time offender.

Part b) There are many reasons why there are differences in sentences for young offenders and adults. These reasons fall into two groups; the ideological aims of sentencing and the practicalities of what is possible.

So far as sentencing aims are concerned, the courts put the emphasis on reformation when dealing with young offenders. In fact s. 44 of the Children and Young Persons Act 1933 requires courts to have regard for the welfare of the child. For this reason there are limits on custodial sentences, especially for offenders under the age of 15 and a greater variety of community based solutions are available. The premise is that the younger the offender, the greater the chance of reform and so educative means should be used. Adult offenders are more likely to be set in their ways and persistent offenders not so amenable to reform. The courts will consider a wider set of sentencing aims when dealing with an adult and may decide to give a custodial sentence as a deterrent or to protect society.

When the court does decide that a custodial sentence is necessary for a young offender, that sentence will be served in a separate institution from adult offenders. The regime will involve more education and training. There is also the reason that adult offenders would corrupt youngsters as prisons are often seen as 'universities of crime'.

On the practical side fines are set at maximum levels that young offenders can pay. As young offenders of Bernard's age are usually students a fine of £5,000 would be impractical. For those under 16 the court can make the parents take responsibilty for the payment of the fine and indeed for their child's behaviour. With older offenders this is not feasible.

Another practical aspect is that education is important for young offenders and, although there are facilities within the custodial institutions, the courts prefer to keep offenders within their local community and maintain continuity in their education; this is not a factor in sentencing adults.

STUDENT'S ANSWER WITH TUTOR'S COMMENTS
Question 2

Courts do take into consideration many factors when sentencing including the seriousness of the offence and the defendant's personal circumstances. However, there are underlying principles on sentencing and what effect the judge wishes to have. Principles on sentencing are divided into two main groups. These are those based on retribution which look back to the crime and how it should be punished and those which are utilitarian and look forward to the future and what effect the sentence may have on the offender's future behaviour.

66 Good opening 99

Retribution is based on the idea that, as a person has done wrong, he must be punished. It can also be called giving the offender his just deserts. People in society like to see a person punished in proportion to his crime, that is, the more serious the crime the greater the punishment should be. This was the idea behind unit fines introduced in the 1991 Criminal Justice Act. These aimed to take into account the seriousness of the crime together with the offender's financial means. They were scrapped in 1993 after criticism in the press and by magistrates about inconsistent and absurd results. Unit fines have been replaced by entry points giving guidance to magistrates on what the appropriate penalty should be for an offence which is an average one of its type.

66 Good use of unit fines but a weak explanation of entry points 99

There has been much debate about whether a defendant's past criminal record should be taken into account when sentencing. Some people believe that the other crimes have been punished and that should be an end of them; they are not relevant to the present case. Othes think that a first offender should be dealt with more leniently than a persistent one. Now the sentence does tend to increase with each offence but the judge does have discretion in this. Some American states, however, have a method of tariff sentencing which uses a table based on the type of crime and the previous conviction 'score'. The judge reads off the appropriate sentence from this table and can only alter it within a very narrow range.

66 It is always acceptable to compare with other legal systems 99

The view of society towards a particular offence will be taken into account when sentencing. Public denunciation had an effect on drink driving. Over twenty years ago it was considered as normal to drive after drinking and not viewed as criminal by most people. Today it is seen as serious and the courts are using harsher penalties to reflect this especially where the driving has caused death.

Another aim of the courts when sentencing is deterrence. Can the offender be effectively put off from committing further crimes by the punishment given for this offence? To this end the courts may decide to use a custodial sentence in the belief that the experience of going to prison or, for young offenders, a Young Offenders' Institution will be so unpleasant that the offender will not want to repeat it. In practice this does not work as around 65% of adults released from prison re-offend within two years, while for young offenders the figure is even higher. Deterrence probably does not work as most crimes are committed on the spur of the moment.

66 Well balanced discussion of deterrence 99

When sentencing the judge will also think about protecting society as this is an important aim where the offence is a violent one or the offender is dangerous. The ultimate way of protecting the public is the death penalty which is no longer used in this country although it is used in other countries including some of the American states. In Britain in some cases the judge has no option but to impose a life sentence. This can only be reviewed by the Home Secretary, who has the power to let the offender out on licence.

With young people in particular the court may want to aim at reformation. This may lead to a probation order which may be combined with a treatment order to help rehabilitate those with drink or drug problems. Another option is a community service order under which the offender has to perform between 40 and 240 hours' work on some community project.

It can be seen that there are many different aims that can be pursued when sentencing offenders and the aim used in a particular case will depend on the nature of the offence, the personality of the offender and the aim that the judge considers most appropriate.

Tutor's Comments

A clear understanding of the main sentencing aims. The essay also tries to link these aims with actual sentences by way of explanation. A sound essay which merits an A grade.

A review sheet for this chapter can be found on p. 215.

FORMATION OF A CONTRACT

GETTING STARTED

The law of contract concerns the enforceability of agreements. The courts do try to uphold contracts wherever possible, but two basic questions arise when considering enforceability:

- Is there evidence of true agreement between the parties?
- Is it reasonable for the court to uphold this agreement?

This chapter will help to answer these questions, by examining exactly what is needed to form a contract, that is to provide the court with evidence of agreement.

The main themes of questions set on this topic are:

- the difficulty of identifying offer and acceptance;
- whether consideration has been provided to enforce the agreement;
- assessing whether the parties to the agreement intended it to be legally binding;
- the capacity of the parties to enter into a contract;

Do remember that some questions, especially the problem kind, may involve more than one area of contract law, e.g. consideration and legal intent.

OFFER AND ACCEPTANCE

CONSIDERATION

LEGAL INTENT

CAPACITY

ESSENTIAL PRINCIPLES

Numerous agreements are formed every day, and many of these will amount to legal contracts. It is not normally necessary to enquire into them, as the people involved are happy with what they have agreed, and most people honour their word. However, when agreements go wrong it is then sometimes necessary for the courts to intervene, and to establish whether a contract exists, the courts try to identify **an offer from one party followed by an acceptance by the other**.

OFFER

❝Offer defined❞

A working definition of an offer is useful when answering examination questions. A suggestion is: **an expression of willingness to contract on certain terms, made with the intention that it will become binding on acceptance**.

❝The 'shopping' principle❞

Such a definition helps to differentiate between a true offer and other, more casual, statements, generally known as **invitations to treat**. A display in a shop window is generally held to be an invitation to treat, the customer making the offer by proposing to buy an item, and the seller being free to accept or reject the offer. This position was confirmed in the case of *Fisher v Bell (1961)* where a shopkeeper avoided prosecution for 'offering for sale' flick-knives in his window by successfully claiming that the display was only an invitation to treat. The case of *Pharmaceutical Society of Great Britain v Boots (1952)* extended the principle to supermarkets. Here the display of goods on shelves is an invitation to treat, the customer making an offer by presenting the selected items to the cashier and the cashier accepting (on behalf of the owners).

This general 'shopping' principle applies to other trading situations, e.g. catalogues, circulars, timetables. In *Partridge v Crittenden (1968)* a small advertisement at the back of a journal for the sale of some birds was held to be an invitation to treat, leaving the seller free to accept or reject any potential customers who replied. This upholds the idea of **freedom to contract**, and also avoids the problem of exhausted stocks.

+ Grainger + sons v Gough (1896) = circulation of price list

Auctions and tenders

Similarly in auction sales the display of goods is an invitation to treat (and could be regarded as the auctioneer's 'shop window'), the bidders making a series of offers, and the auctioneer accepting on behalf of the owners by the fall of the hammer (*Sale of Goods Act 1979*). An example of the shopping principle in auctions can be found in *Payne v Cave (1789)*.

When goods are sold by tender, again the invitation to tender is an invitation to treat, the tenders being the offers, the seller deciding which one to accept – (see *Spencer v Harding (1870)*).

Dealing with machines

When dealing with a machine the position has to be different. Vending machines, car park barriers, etc. are obviously unable to consider an offer and cannot decide to accept. Therefore for practical reasons the offer is considered to be made by the owners of the machine by holding it in readiness for use, the acceptance being made by the customer operating the machine in some way. This was the case in *Thornton v Shoe Lane Parking (1971)* which concerned an automatic barrier in a car park.

General offers

Another situation where the general 'shopping' principle does not apply is when a general offer is made to the world at large. A well-known example is *Carlill v Carbolic Smoke Ball Co (1893)*, where the advertisement of a product to cure various ills was held to be a general offer which was accepted by Mrs Carlill (among others) who bought the product, used it as directed, and still contracted flu. Whilst the company was only able to form contracts with individuals, the initial offer could be made to the 'whole world', and would ripen into a contract with anyone performing the requirements for acceptance.

Termination of an offer

An offer can be terminated in various ways:

■ **Acceptance or refusal** – here the offer is no longer available.
■ **Counter offer** – this introduces new terms, and is like a new offer, cancelling the original offer (see *Hyde v Wrench (1840)*). Not be confused with a request for further information, which leaves the original offer open (see *Stevenson v McLean (1880)*). A series of counter offers on standard forms may amount to a 'battle of forms' (see *Butler v Ex-Cell-O (1979)*).

- **Revocation** – must be communicated before acceptance (see *Byrne v Van Tienhoven (1880)*), this can be through a third party, but reliability may be a problem (see *Dickinson v Dodds (1876)*). If the offer is a general one, then the revocation should be given as much publicity of the same kind as the original offer, although this is not observed much in practice (see *Shuey v United States (1875)*). Revocation of a continuing act of acceptance cannot take place while the act continues (see *Errington v Errington (1952)*).

- **Lapse of time** – if not stipulated by the offeror, this will arise after a reasonable time, bearing in mind such factors as the nature of the goods, type of market, etc. (see *Ramsgate Hotel v Montefiore (1866)*).

- **Death** – but in certain circumstances the estate may act in place of the deceased party, if the contract is not of a personal nature (see *Bradbury v Morgan (1862)*).

- **Failure of a precondition** – for example the goods to be exchanged must be substantially in the same condition as when viewed (see *Financings v Stimpson (1962)*).

ACCEPTANCE

Acceptance is the second half of a contract, and can be defined as: **agreement to all the terms of the offer.**

Where no method of acceptance is stipulated, the general rule is that it is by the same method as the offer, although there may be good reasons why this is not used. If a method is stipulated, then this should normally be used, but another method which is no less advantageous to the offeror may be valid (see *Yates v Pulleyn (1975)*).

The general rule is that acceptance must be communicated, and should not be assumed, although in some circumstances this may be waived, as in *Carlill*, where the general offer was accepted by conduct. The issue arose in *Felthouse v Bindley (1862)*. Here an uncle, wishing to buy his nephew's horse, wrote saying, 'If I hear no more about him, I consider the horse is mine at £30.15s'. Despite the nephew's willingness to sell, this was not enough to form a binding contract.

METHOD OF ACCEPTANCE

Postal rule

Where acceptance is made using the post, the **postal rule** generally applies. The rule, based on the case of *Adams v Lindsell (1818)*, is that **acceptance by post is valid immediately on posting**. This is a rule of convenience, and does not apply where the method of communicating is more or less instantaneous, such as by telephone, fax, etc. (see *Entores v Miles Far East Corporation (1955)*).

Ignorance of the offer

Where a person performs all the required acts of acceptance, but does so in ignorance of the offer, there will be no contract, as the offeree must act at least partly in response to the offer. Compare the Australian case of *R v Clarke (1927)*, where the defendant gave information leading to the arrest of a criminal to avoid prosecution, having completely forgotten about a reward, with that of *Williams v Carwardine (1833)*, where similar information was given partly to ease the plaintiff's conscience, but also to claim the reward.

SOME NON-STANDARD SITUATIONS

Collateral contract

A second, or **collateral contract** may exist within, or alongside, another contract, as in *Esso v Commissioners of Customs and Excise (1970)*. Here a promotional campaign which promised motorists a 'world cup coin' in return for the purchase of a certain quantity of petrol was held to be a collateral contract, standing beside the contract of sale. This use of a collateral contract allows the customer to claim entitlement to rights under a sales promotion, and is therefore a useful aid to protecting the consumer.

Multipartite agreement

A **multipartite agreement** may exist where a number of parties have made identical contracts with one person. They may then be deemed to have obligations toward each other. This arose in *Clarke v Dunraven (1897)*, where the competitors in a yacht club race, who had all made identical agreements with the yacht club secretary, were deemed to have obligations to each other in the case of damage to another boat.

Difficulty of identifying offer and acceptance

Sometimes it is difficult to identify a specific offer and acceptance, even though it is clear that a contract exists. This was the case in *Brogden v Metropolitan Railway Co (1877)*. The plaintiff had for some time supplied coal to the defendant company under an oral contract (which, of course, is just as valid and binding on the parties as a written one). The defendant company decided to form a written agreement, and sent a copy of it to the plaintiff who made an amendment, signed it and sent it back. It was not read, but placed in a drawer. Some time later a dispute occurred, and the problem arose as to whose terms formed the contract. Clearly there was a contract, but the court found it very difficult to isolate an offer and acceptance. At the very latest this would have been when the plaintiff began to supply coal after the forming of the written agreement. The case shows the need for precise terms, and also the difficulties of identifying an offer and an acceptance.

See figure 15.1 for a simple revision of the stages of agreement.

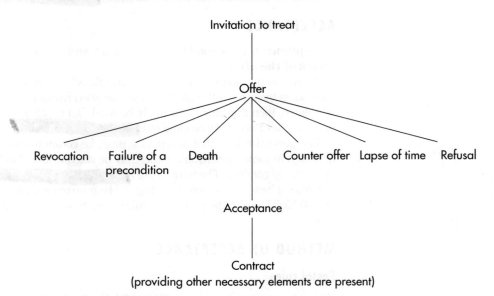

Figure 15.1 The stages of agreement

CONSIDERATION

Consideration is the 'thing' exchanged in a contract, and may take many forms. It is often money for goods or services, but may be less obvious. A classic definition is found in the case of *Currie v Misa (1875)*:

> 'A valuable consideration ... may consist either in some right, interest, profit, or benefit accruing to the one party, or some forbearance, detriment, loss, or responsibility, given, suffered or undertaken by the other.'

However, it may be easier to think of consideration as the price of a bargain, and this was the basis of Pollock's definition, adopted by the House of Lords in *Dunlop v Selfridge (1915)*:

> 'An act or forbearance of one party, or the promise thereof, is the price for which the promise of the other is bought.'

This definition also brings out the point that consideration can be a promise to do or to give something, as well as an act.

GENERAL PRINCIPLES

Various aspects of consideration have been established by case law:

❝Must be sufficient but need not be adequate❞

■ Consideration must be **sufficient** which means that it must be recognisable in some way to the court, and usually of some economic value. However, it does *not* need to be **adequate**, or a fair monetary bargain. So, in *Thomas v Thomas (1842)* a woman was allowed to live in a house for £1 per year. This was obviously not adequate, but was sufficient to form a binding contract.

❝Must not be past❞

■ Consideration must not be **past**, that is it must be given at the time of the promise of the other party, not an action already done in the past. In *Re McArdle (1951)* work already done on a house was held not to be good consideration for a later promise to contribute to the cost. However, if something is done at the request of the other party, and it could be understood by all that payment would be made at the end, then apparently past consideration may be valid. In *Lampleigh v Braithwait (1615)* a man obtained a pardon from the king for his friend, who afterwards promised to pay him £100 for his trouble. It was held that the pardon was obtained at the other party's request, and it could be understood that some kind of payment would be made.

❝Must not be illegal❞

■ Consideration must not be **illegal**. In *Foster v Driscoll (1929)* smuggling goods into the USA was held not to be good consideration.

❝Must not be an existing duty❞

The performance of an existing duty will not generally be good consideration, whether this arises under the law of the land or in an existing contract. In *Collins v Godefroy (1831)* a lawyer's promise to appear in court, when he was already obliged to do this as a witness, was held not to be consideration. In *Stylk v Myrick (1809)* the promise of some sailors to sail a ship home short-handed was not consideration, as they were obliged to do this anyway. However, something 'extra' may be good consideration, such as doing more than the law of the land or the contract stipulates. Examples include:

■ providing a larger police patrol than usual (*Glasbrook v Glamorgan (1925)*);

■ sailing a ship home extremely short-handed (*Hartley v Ponsonby (1857)*);

■ keeping a child well looked after (*Ward v Byham (1956)*);

■ performing the same duty to another party, and thus running the risk of being sued twice (*Scotson v Pegg (1861)*).

In *Williams v Roffey (1990)* the principle was developed further. Here the court held that where performance of an existing duty enabled the other party to obtain some practical advantage or avoid a disadvantage, this would be good consideration. In the case a firm of builders avoided the consequences of being late completing, and did not have to look for new carpenters.

❝Part payment of a debt❞

Where a debt is owed, merely paying part of it, even with the agreement of the creditor, does not discharge the whole debt. However, if with the creditor's agreement something 'extra' is added to the part payment this may then discharge the whole debt – see *Pinnel's Case (1602)*.

The Court of Appeal in *Re Selectmove (1994)* has made it clear that for the present the principles in *Williams v Roffey* will not be extended to part payment of a debt.

❝Promissory estoppel❞

Where one party promises to excuse the other party from their duties, but then goes back on this promise in an unfair way, the court may not allow this, following the equitable doctrine of promissory estoppel, established in the case of *Central London Property Trust v High Trees House (1947)*.

LEGAL INTENT

PRESUMPTION IN COMMERCIAL CONTRACTS

Apart from the basic requirements of offer, acceptance and consideration in forming a contract, the law requires a general intention to be legally bound. In fact, in commercial situations, it is *presumed* that such an intention exists, thus providing some protection for the consumer (see the cases of *Carlill* and *Esso* above). This presumption can be rebutted, but evidence of the intention *not* to be bound must be made clear (see *Rose and Frank v Crompton (1925)* and *Kleinwort Benson v Malaysia Mining Corporation (1989)*).

An everyday example of this rebuttal is found in football pools coupons (see the case of *Jones v Vernons Pools (1938)*).

PRESUMPTION IN SOCIAL AND DOMESTIC ARRANGEMENTS

On the other hand, in social and domestic arrangements, the presumption is that there is no intention to contract, and an example is seen in the agreement between the husband and wife in *Balfour v Balfour (1919)*. This allows people to go about their everyday domestic lives without unintentionally finding themselves bound by a contract. Again, the presumption can be rebutted, as in the cases of *Merritt v Merritt (1970)*, where the couple were separated, and *Simpkin v Pays (1955)*, where the presence of a lodger meant that an agreement between a grandmother and granddaughter was also enforceable.

CAPACITY

A further requirement in forming a binding agreement is that the parties should have legal capacity to contract. Most adults do have this status, but certain people in society have limited capacity, generally for their own protection.

CORPORATIONS

Corporations are generally limited by whatever means they are created, so that a chartered corporation, such as a university, may be limited by the charter, a statutory corporation may be limited by statute, and a registered company may be limited by its registration document (the memorandum of association). There are also practical limitations, in that a university, for example, cannot in reality have a hair cut! If any of these corporations should contract outside its limitations, the court could declare its actions *ultra vires*, that is, outside its powers, and therefore unlawful.

DIPLOMATS

Diplomats have a certain immunity from prosecution and law suits, and by the same argument are generally unable to enforce contracts.

PERSONS OF UNSOUND MIND AND DRUNKARDS

For their own protection, those who are of unsound mind or drunk at the time of making a contract are not generally liable. However, they must pay a reasonable price for contracts made during periods of lucidity, and will also be liable for contracts for necessaries (see below under minors).

MINORS

Those under 18 years of age are generally not liable for contractual obligations, although they can enforce a contract against an adult. This general rule protects minors from their youth and inexperience.

Necessaries

However, minors must pay a reasonable price for **necessaries**. These are more than absolute basics to sustain life, and are defined in s. 3(3) of the Sale of Goods Act 1979 as 'goods suitable to the condition in life of the minor or other person concerned and to his actual requirements at the time of the sale and delivery'. This means that an item may be a necessary to one person but not to another, depending on lifestyle and circumstances. A further point is that items may be of the type which would be necessaries if the minor was not already well supplied with them. A case illustrating this is *Nash v Inman (1908)*, where an undergraduate obtained eleven fancy waistcoats. They may have been considered necessaries, but were held not to be as the father had already supplied the son with clothing.

Services

Necessaries can also include services, as seen in the case of *Chapple v Cooper (1844)*, where a young widow was held liable for her late husband's funeral costs.

❝Reasoning❞   This ensures that traders and retailers are not deterred from supplying minors with the basic essentials of normal living, but also discourages them from selling expensive luxurious items to minors on credit.

Employment and training

Contracts of employment and training are binding on a minor if on the whole they are for the minor's benefit. They can then be seen as a kind of necessary. In *Doyle v White City Stadium (1935)* a trainee boxer agreed to hand over any prize money. However, his training contract was, on the whole, held to be beneficial to him, and therefore enforceable. On the other hand, in *De Francesco v Barnum (1890)* a young dancer was found to have entered into a wholly oppressive training contract, and this was held to be unenforceable.

Continuing obligation

Where a minor has entered into a contract of an ongoing nature, such as a tenancy or partnership agreement, this can be repudiated up to the age of 18, or within a reasonable time afterwards (see *Edwards v Carter (1893)*).

Loans to minors generally are not enforceable at common law, although a reasonable amount may be payable for the amount spent on necessaries (see *Lewis v Alleyne (1888)*).

Minors' Contracts Act 1987

❝Remedies❞   Two important provisions in this Act have helped to remedy the imbalance which was felt to exist between minors and adults. First, under s. 2, guarantees given by an adult to support a loan to a minor are now enforceable. Secondly, s. 3 gave to the court a new power of restitution. This enables the court, where 'it is just and equitable to do so', to require the minor to hand back any property acquired under an unenforceable contract, or any property representing it. This is not a perfect solution to any problems created by minors' contracts, but is much fairer than the previous position.

EXAMINATION QUESTIONS

1 Critically examine what in law will amount to an 'offer'. (UODLE)

2 Does the present law relating to minors' contracts strike the correct balance between the respective interests of minors and the adults who enter into contracts with them? (UODLE)

3 Critically examine the ways in which an offer may be terminated. (UODLE)

4 E is a world famous operatic soprano who was made an offer by F to perform in London for one major concert for a fee of £10,000. E replied to this offer saying that she would only appear for a £12,000 fee. F refuses to consider this demand and he makes a new offer to E of £11,000. E reluctantly accepts this offer verbally but nothing is put in writing regarding the transaction. Two days before the concert E contacts F to inform him that she will not be appearing in London as she has received a far better offer to appear in New York. F is distressed and threatens E with legal action, but E counters this by claiming that there is no contract as nothing appears in writing.

How does the law regard F's position, and what remedies are available to him? (ULEAC)

5 Whilst out shopping for himself and his neighbour, Jim notices the following promotional campaign in the window of a shop called Wizelectrics: 'Any customer purchasing a model Super 99 video recorder will receive a Minilux portable television free of charge.'

Jim is tempted to treat himself to a video recorder under the promotion, but decides to go home to review his finances. On the way he delivers some shopping to his elderly next door neighbour, Mrs Earnest. She is grateful to Jim and promises him £15 for his recent kindness to her. However, she does not pay him.

Later that week Jim, persuaded by the promotion, decides to buy a video recorder from Wizelectrics. He pays, and the shop assistant places the video recorder on the counter for him to take, apologising that the last television has been given away that morning and that there are no more available at present.

Advise Jim regarding both the television and the money from Mrs Earnest. (UODLE)

ANSWERS TO QUESTIONS

OUTLINE ANSWERS TO SELECTED QUESTIONS

Question 1

Briefly introduce, showing the need for identification of an offer and acceptance to show evidence of a binding contract.

Provide a working definition of an offer.

Compare an offer with an invitation to treat, with examples from cases:

- shop windows (*Fisher v Bell*);
- supermarkets (*Pharmaceutical Society v Boots*);
- small advertisements, circulars, timetables, etc. (*Partridge v Crittenden*);
- auctions and tenders (*Payne v Cave, Spencer v Harding*).

Discuss situations where the initial proposal is likely to be an offer:

- advertisements of a nature which is likely to be a general offer (*Carlill v Carbolic Smoke Ball Co*);
- dealing with machines (*Thornton v Shoe Lane Parking*);
- promotional campaigns (*Esso v Commissioners of Customs and Excise*).

Discuss counter offers (*Hyde v Wrench*) and 'battle of forms' situations (*Butler v Ex-Cell-O*).

Discuss non-standard situations, such as collateral contracts (*Esso*) and multipartite agreements (*Clarke v Dunraven*).

Consider the difficulty sometimes of identifying an offer (*Brogden v Metropolitan Railway Co*).

Question 2

Introduce by defining minors, outline the general position of minors not being liable and comment on the reason for this (to protect the minor).

Examine the various forms of necessaries, for which the minor may be liable:

- goods (*Nash v Inman, Sale of Goods Act 1979*);
- services (*Chapple v Cooper*);
- contracts of employment, training and education, if beneficial to the minor (*Doyle v White City Stadium, De Francesco v Barnum*).

Outline contracts of continuing obligation (*Edwards v Carter*) and the general position on loans (*Lewis v Alleyne*).

Show how, in protecting a minor, an adult could be treated very harshly under the common law:

- only reasonable payment for necessaries was recoverable;
- luxurious items could be retained by the minor with no payment to the retailer;
- loans need not be repaid;
- guarantees were not enforceable.

Then show how the Minors' Contracts Act 1987 attempts to remedy this imbalance, and give the adult, too, some protection:

- the common law continues to protect an adult who supplies necessaries to a minor;
- for luxury goods the court now has the power, at its discretion, to order restitution of the goods or any property representing them;
- guarantees are now enforceable.

Compare the previous common law position with the present position since the Minors' Contracts Act and make some conclusion over the point raised in the question of balancing protection of minors and adults who deal with them.

TUTOR'S ANSWER

Question 3

An offer is a fundamental element in the formation of a contract, and is an aid to the court in determining whether a binding agreement exists. It may be defined as a willingness to contract on certain terms, with the intention that it will become binding on acceptance. It is likely that occasions will arise when termination becomes necessary, or when the offeror has a change of mind, but some way of regulating this is needed. This will then uphold the idea of freedom to contract, and at the same time ensure fairness between the parties.

The most obvious way of terminating an offer is by the offeree either accepting or refusing it. Acceptance of all the terms will form a binding contract. Some difficulties may arise with acceptance by post, as the offeror may not be aware of the acceptance, and consequently be unsure as to whether the offer is still open. However, one party must bear some burden of communication, and English law places it on the offeror. Refusal appears straightforward. If the offeree clearly rejects the proposal there is no problem, but difficulties arise when only one or more of the terms are rejected by the offeree. This may give rise to a counter offer situation. A counter offer is a new proposal or alteration to the terms of the offer. The effect of this is to terminate the original offer, leaving it no longer open to acceptance at a later time. A similar situation arose in *Hyde v Wrench*, where a farm was offered for sale at £1,000. When the potential buyer tried to accept at £950, the court held that a counter offer had been made, and the offer of £1,000 had been terminated.

This must be distinguished from a mere enquiry, such as that which arose in *Stevenson v McLean*. Here a question as to whether a seller would be prepared to accept payment by instalments was held not to be a counter offer, but just an enquiry, leaving the original offer still open to acceptance. This raises the problem of differentiating between the two. Probably a change of stated terms will be a counter offer, whilst querying an additional point which has not already been established will be a mere enquiry.

If the offeror wishes to withdraw an offer, this will amount to revocation. This is allowed provided that the revocation is communicated to the offeree before acceptance takes place. In *Byrne v Van Tienhoven* the situation was further complicated by the application of the postal rule. Revocation may be communicated by a third party, and an example of this is *Dickinson v*

Dodds. Here a potential buyer of a house attempted to accept after being told by a third party that the seller no longer wished to sell. The court held that the revocation was valid, because the buyer in fact knew as clearly as if the seller had told him personally. However, the case left unanswered the question of the reliability and motives of the informant, and whether this can be assessed.

The revocation of a general offer raises further problems. It would be impractical for the offeror to be obliged to communicate with everyone who may have seen the original offer, for example in a newspaper, or on a poster. There is no direct English authority on this, but the American case of *Shuey v US* suggests that revocation should be made in the same way and with the same amount of publicity as the original offer. However, this would not necessarily be seen by exactly the same people who saw the original offer, so problems could still arise. In practice, this method of revoking a general offer is not widely used. With many advertisements and promotional campaigns the public generally assume that if a notice is removed then the offer is no longer open.

Lapse of time may bring an offer to an end. If the offeror does not stipulate a time limit, then the offer will end after a reasonable time, and in a dispute the courts will decide what is reasonable, taking into consideration such factors as the nature of the goods, e.g. perishable food, the market, e.g. heavy demand, and fluctuating prices, e.g. shares. Again, case law is limited, but in *Ramsgate v Montefiore* an offer for shares was held to have lapsed after five months.

Failure of a pre-condition will terminate an offer. For example, a buyer would expect goods to be in the same condition at the point of sale as they were in at the time of the offer being made. The issue arose in *Financings v Stimpson,* where a car was stolen and badly damaged between the offer and the acceptance. The offer was held terminated, in fairness to the buyer.

The death of a party will normally bring the offer to an end, but if it did not concern services of a personal nature, and merely the exchange of goods, *Bradbury v Morgan* suggests that the offer may continue through the personal representatives of the deceased, with money being paid into or out of the estate.

In auction sales the rules of offer and acceptance apply, so the bidder may revoke his bid, provided that he does so before the fall of the hammer. Similarly, a tenderer may withdraw his tender, provided that he communicates with the person inviting tenders before acceptance takes place.

With contracts involving machines similar rules apply. The offeror must communicate – so, for example, with a vending machine selling cold drinks, a notice could be placed on the front and the machine switched off. In a *Thornton v Shoe Lane* situation in a car park a 'closed' or 'full' sign could be placed at the entrance, providing there is a way for cars to avoid entry.

Where an offer is accepted by a continuing act revocation poses difficulties. An example was given in *Errington v Errington* of a person almost completing a long walk, only to be told that the reward was no longer available. The case concerned a father who offered that a house would belong to a young couple eventually, if they repaid the remainder of a mortgage regularly. It was held that the offer could not be revoked while they maintained the payments, that is while acceptance was taking place. However, if payments ceased, the offer would end.

So it can be seen that the basic principles of terminating an offer aim to bring about fairness between the parties. Some difficulties still remain, however, particularly with some aspects of revocation.

STUDENT'S ANSWER WITH TUTOR'S COMMENTS

Question 5

> **“Identifies the main issues”**
>
> On advising Jim, the areas of law which are relevant are past consideration and offer.
> On advising him about whether or not he will be able to force Mrs Earnest to pay him £15 the law relating to past consideration is relevant. As a general principle past consideration is not consideration. Mainly because when parties enter a contract they have to agree on what benefit they will both give up – the consideration.
>
> In the case of *Re McArdle* a bungalow was left to the children when the parents died. One daughter in law decided to redecorate the house. After doing so other members of the family said they would pay her some money to split the expenses of redecorating. They later refused to pay. The court held that she could not enforce payment because the promise was made after she had carried out the work and she had therefore given no consideration for it.

"Reasoning in Lampleigh v Braithwait?"

This contrasts with the case of *Lampleigh v Braithwait* where Braithwait had killed a man. He asked Lampleigh if he would intercede with the king and get him a pardon. Lampleigh was successful. Braithwait promised him some money The court found for the plaintiff and Braithwait had to pay.

So on advising Jim whether Mrs Earnest has to pay him, if he is to go by the first case he cannot enforce payment. However if he was to follow the second case (*Lampleigh v Braithwait*) he may receive the £15.

"Rather categorical here"

It can also be said that he was already under a duty to look after his neighbour and so did not really do anything out or the ordinary. This was illustrated in *Ward v Byham* where the father of an illegitimate child paid the mother maintenance in return that she kept the child well looked after and happy. It was held that making sure the child was well looked after was her statutory duty, however keeping it happy constituted an extra consideration. As Jim is under no duty to look after Mrs Earnest he may be able to receive the £15 payment.

When Jim saw the advertisement in the shop window it was not an offer but merely an invitation to treat. When parties enter an agreement one party accepts the other party's offer. Terms of an offer must be certain. Sometimes what seems to be an offer is merely an incentive or an encouragement for the making of an offer – an invitation to treat.

"Good – argument the other way"

The general rule is that advertisements for the sale of goods are invitations to treat. This was illustrated in the case of *Partridge v Crittenden* where the appellant was charged under legislation protecting birds of offering to sell 'bramblefinch cocks and hens for 25 shillings each'. It was held that he was not guilty of a statutory offence and it was only an invitation to treat.

So if Jim was to go by this case he would not be able to do anything about the television. However it does not mean that all advertisements offering things for sale cannot amount to an offer if the facts justify it.

In *Carlill v Carbolic Smoke Company* the company advertized that their smoke balls would prevent anybody who used them from catching influenza. Mrs Carlill used them correctly but still caught the flu. On their advertizing campaign the company stated that they would give £100 to persons who caught the flu. Mrs Carlill sought the £100. The defendants claimed that the reward of £100 was not legally binding and was merely an 'advertising puff'. The Court of Appeal found for the plaintiff, stating that the fact that they had deposited £1,000 in the bank showed a willingness to be bound by the agreement.

Relating this to Jim's problem it can be said that Wizelectrics intended the offer to have legal effect as they obviously had a supply of Minilux portable televisions.

This is also supported by the case of *Esso Petroleum v Commissioners of Customs and Excise* – world cup coin case. On the question of whether the customer had any legal right to the coin it was held that the promise of a world cup coin for every four gallons of petrol bought was legally enforceable.

"Coverage of points quite good. Application to the facts is a little weak"

On advising Jim it can be said that he may be able to receive the £15 from Mrs Earnest and is entitled to the television set. If not now then maybe at a later date because I'm sure Wizelectric can order some more television sets. This is supported by the decision in Carlill v Carbolic Smoke Ball Co.

Tutor Comments

The student has covered the main points, but sometimes has not developed them very far, and has often only applied them to the question in a very brief way. For example, in considering the possibility of the statement about the television being an offer, there is no consideration of the facts. Why would a company give away televisions? To generate sales. Therefore they could be offering a television in exchange for the increase in sales generated by a customer. Similarly, discussion is needed on the relationship with Mrs Earnest, along the lines of '… if she requested the shopping to be done, and implied that she would pay, then consideration may exist …'. This is about a grade C answer.

A review sheet for this chapter can be found on p. 215.

CONTENTS OF A CONTRACT

THE TERMS WHICH FORM A CONTRACT

TYPES OF TERMS

EXEMPTION CLAUSES

PRIVITY OF CONTRACT

GETTING STARTED

If problems arise once a contract has been formed, it is usually necessary to refer to the terms which form the contract in order to settle disputes. Questions which may arise from this in real life are:

- What are the terms of the contract?
- Which terms are the more important ones?
- Are there any exemption clauses which may be valid?
- Who can enforce the contract?

The main themes of examination questions set on this topic concern:

- terms which may have been implied into the contract (if a term is definitely part of the contract, you will normally be told this in the question);
- the way in which courts differentiate between different types of terms;
- the validity of exemption clauses;
- privity of contract.

Again, remember that some questions, especially the problem kind, could involve more than one area. Privity, for example, could be a minor aspect of a problem question, or could form an essay question on its own.

THE TERMS WHICH FORM A CONTRACT

ESSENTIAL PRINCIPLES

We have seen in Chapter 15 that a contract may be formed in a number of ways, and it does not really matter in theory whether the contract is made orally or in writing. However, when a dispute arises, the parties may wish to refer to the terms of a contract. If terms are written down, seen and understood by both parties, and they have signed the contract, there is often little doubt as to what the terms actually are. However, a contract is often composed of terms which are not written, or not seen by a party, and may be partly written and partly oral. Here difficulties arise in determining exactly what the agreement was.

TERMS AND REPRESENTATIONS

Generally, a statement made well before a contract is formed will be a **representation**, and one made during a contract will be a **term**, but other factors may be also taken into consideration. The distinction is important because the remedies for breach of a term are different from those for misrepresentation.

Term or representation?

Points to consider include:

- How soon before the contract was the statement made? In *Routledge v McKay (1954)* a statement made a week before selling a motorcycle was held to be a representation.
- Does the representor have special knowledge? In *Oscar Chess v Williams (1957)* a private seller of a car was not expected to have specialist knowledge, so statements concerning the car were only representations. However, in *Dick Bentley v Harold Smith (1965)* a car dealer's statements were held to be terms.
- Is special importance placed on an issue? In *Bannerman v White (1861)* the answer to a special enquiry about the treatment of hops was held to be a term.
- How persuasive is the statement? In *Ecay v Godfrey (1914)* a seller said that a boat was sound, but suggested a survey be made by the buyer. This statement was not considered to be a term, as it was not very persuasive.

INCORPORATING TERMS INTO CONTRACTS

A term will be incorporated into a contract if:

- the affected party is aware of the clause; or
- reasonable steps have been taken to bring the clause to the party's attention.

Is the term included?

Again, various factors have arisen through cases, and these include:

1. The degree of notice. This has often arisen where a customer has been given a 'ticket' of some kind, and the court enquires whether the 'ticket' is the kind of document that a reasonable person would read and retain. In *Chapelton v Barry (1940)* a clause on a receipt for a deckchair on the beach was held not to be incorporated into a contract, as it was not the kind of document a person would normally read. However, in *Parker v S E Railway (1877)* a clause on a receipt for a bag left with a cloakroom attendant was held to be incorporated, because the person leaving the bag would need to read and retain the ticket in order to reclaim the bag.

   So the questions that the court will ask are: **'Did the plaintiff read, or was he aware of, the term?'** and, if not, **'did the defendant do what was reasonable to give the plaintiff notice of the term?'**

2. Whether there was a 'course of dealings'. In *Hollier v Rambler Motors (1972)* there was not, as a customer had only taken his car to a garage three or four times in five years. However, in *British Crane Hire v Ipswich Plant Hire (1975)* a course of dealings did exist as the parties were in the same trade and therefore both knew the usual trade practice.

3. The time at which notice was given. In *Olley v Marlborough Court (1949)* a notice on the back of a hotel door was held not to form part of the contract which had just been made in the hotel entrance. It came too late.

A useful case to read

The case of *Thornton v Shoe Lane Parking (1971)* already encountered in Chapter 15, involving a clause inside a car park, which was only apparent after forming the contract, sums up many of these points in an interesting context, and is worth reading in some detail.

WRITTEN CONTRACTS

The parol evidence rule

The rule in L'Estrange v Graucob

Where parties have taken the trouble to put their contract into writing, it is generally presumed that they mean the document to be binding, without additions or amendments. This is the basis of the parol evidence rule, which states that **oral or other evidence will not be admitted to contradict or amend a written contract** *(Goss v Lord Nugent (1833))*. This is reinforced by the rule in *L'Estrange v Graucob (1934)* which says that **if a person signs a contract he is bound by it, even though he may not have read the terms**. However, many circumstances arise in practice where even a written contract is incomplete in some way, and terms may have to be implied into it.

IMPLIED TERMS

Terms can be implied into a contract in three main ways:

- by custom;
- by statute;
- by the courts.

TERMS IMPLIED BY CUSTOM

Custom may arise in commercial contracts, and we have seen above how a 'course of dealing' may lead to a term being incorporated. In addition, custom may exist in a particular region.

TERMS IMPLIED BY STATUTE

Where an Act of Parliament declares that a term will form part of a contract, then it will be implied whether the parties intend it or not. A particularly important example is The Sale of Goods Act 1979 (as amended), where terms are implied concerning the state of goods sold (see especially ss 12–15). These are covered in more detail in Chapter 22, as they particularly affect consumer contracts. Note that part of the Act has now been amended by The Sale and Supply of Goods Act 1994, which applies to contracts made after 3 January 1995.

TERMS IMPLIED BY THE COURTS

The courts will themselves intervene in certain circumstances, to imply a term if it is not covered by custom or statute. In *Samuels v Davis (1943)* the courts held that a set of false teeth should be fit for the purpose for which they were bought, even though this was not implied into the contract by statute, as they were not strictly goods. Generally the courts will intervene:

Officious bystander test

1. To give effect to the clear and obvious intention of the parties. This point arose in *Shirlaw v Southern Foundries (1939)*, where it was said that a term to be implied must be one which goes without saying. It must be such that if a bystander were to ask the parties, 'Didn't you mean to include this term?', they would immediately answer, 'of course'. This has become known as the **officious bystander test** and was applied in *Spring v National Amalgamated Stevedores and Dockers Society (1956)*.

Business efficacy test

2. To give business efficacy to the contract, in other words to make it work. This reflects the courts' general aim to uphold contracts where possible, rather than to destroy them. However, they will only imply a term in this way where it is clearly intended to prevent injustice and give effect to the general intention of a contract. This **business efficacy test** is illustrated in *The Moorcock (1889)* where, in a contract to use a jetty on the Thames, a term was implied that the river bed was in a condition not to endanger the vessel. It was suggested by Lord Denning in *Liverpool City Council v Irwin (1976)* that a term concerning the maintenance of services to a block of flats should be implied where it was reasonable. This was generally rejected, and it was said that a term should only be implied where the nature of the contract implicitly required it.

COLLATERAL CONTRACTS

Sometimes a collateral contract makes a term operative on a contract with which it would be otherwise inconsistent. In *City of Westminster Properties v Mudd (1959)* a tenant renewed a lease only after being assured that he would be able to sleep in a room annexed to the property. This was held to override a clause restricting use to business purposes.

CONDITIONS AND WARRANTIES

All terms in a contract are not of the same importance. The more important, fundamental, terms are called **conditions**, whilst the less important ones are called **warranties**. When a condition is breached the innocent party can choose whether to **affirm** (or continue with) the contract and claim damages, or to **repudiate** (or end) the contract.

"The two types compared"

The difference is seen in two cases with similar facts, coming to court in the same year. In *Poussard v Spiers and Pond (1876)* a singer was engaged to perform in an opera but fell ill, missing rehearsals and the first performances, and forcing the producer to employ a substitute. It was held that she had breached a condition, entitling the producer to repudiate, because the breach 'went to the root of the matter'. In *Bettini v Gye (1876)* a singer engaged for a season similarly fell ill and missed some rehearsals, but recovered in good time for the performances. This was held to be a breach of warranty, giving rise to damages.

WHEN A TYPE OF TERM IS SPECIFIED WITHIN THE CONTRACT

Sometimes the parties may refer to a term within the contract as a condition, but this is not necessarily conclusive. A party may not be aware of the legal significance of what is an ordinary English word, and the courts will need to be sure that the parties intended the legal consequence of labelling a particular term a condition. In *Schuler v Wickman Machine Tool Sales (1973)* one term out of twenty was labelled as a condition of the agreement. However, in the circumstances the court held it to be a warranty.

TERMS SPECIFIED BY STATUTE

As seen above, some terms are implied into certain contracts by statute. Where a statute says that a term will be a condition then this is conclusive. Again, see Chapter 22 for more detail.

CONSIDERATION OF THE TERMS BY THE COURTS

If custom and statute do not apply then issues are resolved by case law, and we have seen that some terms which are clearly of fundamental importance are conditions, while others of lesser importance are warranties. Some terms do not fit easily into these two categories, as their importance is not apparent until they are breached, and these are known as **innominate terms**.

"Innominate terms"

THE *HONG KONG FIR* CASE

This kind of term arose in *Hong Kong Fir v Kawasaki Kishen Kaisha (1962)*. A charterparty (agreement to hire a ship) stated that it would be 'in every way fitted for ordinary cargo service'. In fact the engines were old and developed trouble and the staff found to be incompetent, causing considerable delay. However the court looked at the effect of the breach, and found that the goods could still be carried, and the delay compensated by appropriate damages. It was considered that this type of term did not lend itself to traditional analysis, and Diplock LJ said that the breach would be considered serious enough to justify repudiation if the effect was **to deprive the party not in default of substantially the whole benefit of the contract**. This is a different approach from that traditionally taken by the courts, and looks at the consequences of the breach, before deciding whether to treat the term as a warranty or as a condition.

"The principle applied"

The principle was applied in the case of *The Hansa Nord (1975)*, where the slight deterioration of a cargo of citrus pellets was not serious enough to allow the buyer to repudiate. It was also used in *Reardon Smith v Hansen Tangen (1976)*, where the court would not let the buyers use a technical breach to escape from a subsequently unwanted contract.

"Contrasting cases"

These cases contrast with others, such as *The Mihalos Angelos (1970)*, where a ship was not ready to load and thus held to be in breach of a condition. It was said that the charterer and owner meet on equal terms and need definite rules on which to work. A similar outcome resulted from irregularity of payments under a charterparty in *The Chikuma (1981)*. It was felt that in such commercial contracts the parties need to know where they stand and avoid long and expensive litigation.

The approach in *Hong Kong Fir* is a useful one, but to some extent leads to uncertainty. The courts appear to be using it with some caution, bearing in mind the need for certainty in some cases.

EXEMPTION CLAUSES

An exemption clause in a contract is one which seeks to exclude or limit in some way one party's liability toward the other. Over a period of time these clauses had been used in an oppressive way, where a person in a weak bargaining position had little say in the formation of a fair contract. The courts have therefore sought to limit the use of such clauses, and in addition Parliament has made substantial changes to the common law position through the Unfair Contract Terms Act 1977.

The validity of exemption clauses should be examined in three stages:

1 Incorporation.
2 Construction.
3 Legislation.

INCORPORATION

❝Is the clause part of the contract?❞

An exemption clause, just like any other term of a contract, must be incorporated as part of the contract. For this, see again the section above on incorporating terms into a contract. The main points are:

- the term must not come too late (*Olley v Marlborough Court (1949)*);
- it must be brought to the notice of the other party in a reasonable way (*Thornton v Shoe Lane Parking (1971)*);
- the parties may have formed a 'course of dealing' (*Hollier v Rambler Motors (1972)*).

CONSTRUCTION

❝Does the clause cover this damage?❞

Construction means interpretation, so the courts will examine whether the clause can be interpreted to cover the damage which has arisen. Two rules are used:

1 The **main purpose rule**. The courts will not allow an individual term to defeat the main purpose of the contract. In *Glynn v Margetson (1893)* a clause which allowed a ship to call at any port in Europe or North Africa would have defeated the purpose of a contract to ship oranges in good condition from Spain to Liverpool.

2 The ***contra proferentem* rule**. Any doubt or ambiguity in an exemption clause will be interpreted against the person seeking to rely on it (or proffering it). In *Houghton v Trafalgar Insurance (1954)* the word 'load' in a car insurance policy was held not to extend to an excess of passengers.

LEGISLATION

Unfair Contract Terms Act 1977

The Unfair Contract Terms Act 1977 has radically changed the idea of freedom to contract, and given much protection to the consumer. Two important concepts are:

- **business liability** (s. 1(3)) – liability will generally arise from things done by a person in the course of business or from business premises;
- **a consumer** (s. 12) – a person 'deals as a consumer' if he is not acting in the course of business and the other party is doing so.

Main provisions

The two main provisions regarding exemption clauses are:

- a contract term cannot now exclude or restrict liability for death or personal injury resulting from negligence (s. 2(1));
- a contract term can only exclude or restrict other liability resulting from negligence if it is reasonable to do so (s. 2(2)).

REASONABLENESS

❝Fair in the circumstances❞

Reasonableness is interpreted to mean fair given the circumstances known to the parties at the time, and given the resources to meet the liability. The possibility of insurance cover will also be taken into account.

Other factors which the court may take into account include:

- the bargaining power of the parties, and whether an alternative source was available;

- any inducement to agree to the term, e.g. a favourable price;
- trade custom and previous dealings;
- the difficulty of the task.

❝Examples of unreasonableness❞

In the case of *Green v Cade (1978)* a term requiring rejection or complaints concerning a consignment of seed potatoes to be made within three days of delivery was held unreasonable regarding a defect which could not be discovered on inspection at the time of delivery. In *George Mitchell v Finney Lock Seeds (1983)* concerning the supply of cabbage seed, a clause limiting liability to the purchase price of about £200 was held unreasonable, given that the damage sustained by the failure of the crop was over £61,000. In *Smith v Bush (1989)* a surveyor was not allowed to exclude liability for negligence in valuing a property, following the above guidelines.

❝European directive❞

The **European Directive on Unfair Terms in Consumer Contracts (93/13)** came into effect at the beginning of July 1995. This states that if a term in a consumer contract is not individually negotiated, then it is unfair if it causes a 'significant imbalance' in the rights and duties under the contract, to the detriment of the consumer, 'contrary to the requirement of good faith'. Interestingly, there is also a requirement that written terms should be drafted in 'plain, intelligible language'. Exactly how English law will put this into action remains to be seen.

PRIVITY OF CONTRACT

❝Basic rule❞

Privity is the relationship between the parties to a contract, and in English law it is very closely connected with the requirement of providing consideration. The basic rule is found in *Dunlop v Selfridge (1915)* and is that **only a person who is party to a contract can sue on it**. Dunlop, who made tyres and sold them to a wholesaler, Dew, could not sue Selfridge, a customer of Dew, for breaking a price agreement, as they had not contracted with Selfridge (see Figure 16.1).

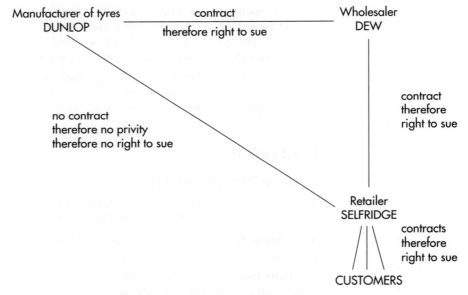

Figure 16.1

❝Reasoning behind the rule❞

The rule seems very reasonable when considering the imposition of a duty on a third party. A person would not generally wish to be subject to a duty to which they had not freely agreed. However, when considering giving a benefit to a third party the rule seems less fair. In *Tweddle v Atkinson (1861)* a man was not able to enforce payment due to him under a contract, even though the contract was formed specifically for this purpose.

The kind of problems caused by the doctrine can be seen in the case of *Jackson v Horizon Holidays (1975)*. Mr Jackson wanted to claim compensation for himself and his wife when their holiday was not as expected. Only Mr Jackson was party to the contract, but on this occasion the Court of Appeal allowed damages for the other family members.

ESTABLISHED EXCEPTIONS

There are a number of established exceptions to the doctrine of privity:

- **statute** – this overrides the common law, e.g. Law of Property Act 1925, regarding assignments;
- **agency** – where a person acts on behalf of another (*The Eurymedon (1975)*);

- **collateral contracts** – a way of getting around the doctrine – (*Shanklin Pier v Detel (1951)*);
- **covenants which 'run with the land'** – both restrictive (*Tulk v Moxhay (1848)*) and positive (*Smith and Snipes Hall Farm v River Douglas Catchment Board (1949)*);
- **price restrictions** – where this is allowed, currently only for medicaments.

ATTEMPTS TO AVOID THE DOCTRINE

Various attempts have been made to avoid the strict doctrine of privity.

Extending *Tulk v Moxhay*

Applying the rule in *Tulk v Moxhay* (see above) to allow covenants to run with chattels (things other than land) was as first allowed in *Lord Strathcona SS Co v Dominion Coal Co (1926)*, but later restricted to charterparties in *Clore v Theatrical Properties (1936)*, and then felt to have been wrongly decided in *Port Line v Ben Line Steamers (1958)*.

Implying a trust

Attempting to show that rights under a contract were held on trust, and therefore enforceable by the third party, who would be a beneficiary of the trust was at first allowed in *Les Affreteurs Reunis v Walford (1919)* but restricted or disapproved in following cases, such as *Re Schebsman (1943)* and *Green v Russell (1959)*.

Using the Law of Property Act 1925

Attempting to apply s. 56 of the Law of Property Act 1925, which apparently allowed a person who was not party to a contract to acquire rights in the property which formed part of the contract, is a liberal interpretation which has not generally found favour in the courts. It was not allowed in the case of *Beswick v Beswick (1968)*. Mrs Beswick tried to enforce payment of a weekly sum of money owed to her by her nephew under an agreement between the nephew and her late husband. She was not allowed to receive the money by implying a trust, nor by use of s. 56, but as administratrix of her late husband's estate.

RECOMMENDATIONS FOR REFORM

It does seem somewhat unfair that somebody like Mrs Beswick is unable in contract law to claim the benefit which was intended for her. As long ago as 1937 the Law Revision Committee recommended that a person in her position should be able to claim a benefit where it was expressly intended. No action was taken, and this was reported upon again by the Law Commission in 1991 (Paper 121, *Privity of Contract – Contracts for the Benefit of Third Parties*, November 1991). They again recommended that a third party should be able to obtain a benefit under a contract where it is clear that the parties intended this to be legally enforceable. This was thought to be preferable to extending the exceptions as issues arose, and would go a fair way to providing justice while leaving the law of privity intact.

EXAMINATION QUESTIONS

1   Is it correct to say that the importance the courts will attach to any particular term of a contract will be determined by the intentions of the contracting parties?   (UODLE)

2   As a hobby, Anneliese designs, and makes, costumes and scenery for amateur theatrical productions. She places an order for a quantity of costume material with a wholesaler, Clothcut, which, bearing in mind the current state of the market, offers her the choice of: (a) supply of the goods by a guaranteed delivery date at a price of £170, or (b) supply of the goods at a price of £120 with the following clause included in the contract, 'We exclude liability for late delivery of goods'. Anneliese chooses to obtain the material under option (b), but when the material is over six weeks late, she blames Clothcut and says that she will sue.

Anneliese has also bought a machine for attaching buckles from a supplier called Banglers. The machine malfunctions, firing a heavy duty staple into Anneliese's hand, resulting in considerable pain and absence from work for three days. When Anneliese looks at the contract for the machine, she finds that it includes a clause which reads: 'The company will not be responsible for any loss or injury, however caused.'

Advise Anneliese as to any rights she may have against both Clothcut and Banglers.

(UODLE)

3 G has decided that he no longer needs his very expensive leather coat so he decides to make a gift of it to his friend, H. H is delighted with the gift and G promises to have the coat properly cleaned by an expert before he hands the coat over to H. G approaches I, who inspects the coat and agrees to clean it at a cost of £30. I writes to G the following day confirming the agreement and informing him that he takes no responsibility for damage caused to any article during the cleaning process. Whilst I is cleaning the coat, chemicals in the cleaning materials are mixed in error and the coat is ruined. Both G and H are angered by this, but I disclaims any responsibility, referring G to his earlier letter.

What are the legal rights of G and H, if any? Comment upon the liability of I.   (ULEAC)

4 Hillview Farm Limited made an oral contract for the purchase of 20 tons of early seed potatoes from Growmore Seeds Limited, a company they had dealt with for many years. The seed potatoes were delivered together with a standard form invoice which had been agreed between the Seed Trade Association and farmers' organisations. On the front of the invoice in bold print was 'For Conditions of Sale see reverse'.

Clause 3 in the contract states: 'Any complaint as to quality, description or suitability of seeds, bulbs, corms, tubers, trees or plants (hereinafter referred to as Seeds or Plants) or non-delivery of the correct quality in accordance with the contract must be made to the seller within three days of delivery and if made verbally confirmed in writing within ten days.'

Clause 6 states '… we will at our option, replace the defective seed or plant, free of charge to the buyer or will refund all payments made to us by the buyer in respect of the defective seed or plant and this shall be the limit of our obligation. We hereby exclude all liabilities for any loss or damage arising from the use of any seed or plant supplied by us and for any consequential loss or damage arising out of such use.'

The reason for the three day provision was that seed potatoes are extremely perishable and deteriorate very quickly if not stored correctly.

Growmore Seeds Limited had on some previous occasions made *ex gratia* payments in excess of the seed cost in circumstances which they thought to be justified.

Hillview Farm Limited planted the potatoes and the crop completely failed. It was discovered after tests that the reason for the failure was partly caused by the seed potatoes being contaminated with a virus which could not be detected by normal inspection and partly caused by seed potatoes not being early seed potatoes as ordered but a less hardy variety which should be sowed much later in better weather.

Advise Hillview Farm Limited as to the legal basis of any action it may wish to pursue and whether it can claim for the loss of the expected value of the crop on the open market.

(NEAB)

5 What is the extent of the rule that only a party to a contract may sue on it?   (WJEC)

6 What arguments can be adduced for and against reforming the law relating to privity of contract.   (UODLE)

ANSWERS TO QUESTIONS

OUTLINE ANSWERS TO SELECTED QUESTIONS

Question 2

Introduce the topic of exemption clauses. There are two situations to consider:

- whether Clothcut's exemption clause was reasonable;
- whether Banglers' exemption clause was valid.

For both situations it is necessary to go through the steps of incorporation, construction and legislation. So it would be sensible to outline the relevant law on exemption clauses generally, and then apply it to each situation.

- Incorporation – was the term introduced at the point of contract or later? Was the clause brought to Anneliese's attention – see cases on this, for authorities. With both of these incidents you are told that the clause is *in* the contract. Anneliese had a choice in the contract with Clothcut, so this indicates that she was well aware of the clause in question. With the contract with Banglers the clause is only discovered afterwards, so you can comment on the fairness of the way in which the clause may have been incorporated.

- Construction – does the term cover damage arising? (again, see the cases on this). There is not really a problem over this.

- Legislation – the first incident with Clothcut raises the issue of reasonableness. As this is a consumer contract (this is Anneliese's hobby) an exemption for liability other than for death or personal injury is only allowed if reasonable (Unfair Contract Terms Act 1977 s. 2(1)). One of the factors to be taken into account is whether there was an incentive to accept the clause, e.g. a low price for goods. This clearly arose here. The problem is whether this delay is still reasonable, as there must come a point when a delay is unreasonable. There is no clear answer to this, but the issue must be raised. Again, look at cases in the section on reasonableness in this chapter.

- The second issue regarding legislation arises in the contract with Banglers. First, Anneliese will be protected under the Sale of Goods Act 1979, as amended by the Sale and Supply of Goods Act 1994, and will be entitled to repudiate the contract and ask for her money back. A term requiring the goods to be of satisfactory quality will be implied into the contract. Secondly, she is also protected by the Unfair Contract Terms Act 1977 which provides in s. 2(1) that exemption of liability for personal injury will not be allowed. Anneliese could therefore sue for full damages for the malfunction of the machine and compensation for her injury.

Question 6

- Introduce the topic of privity and outline the principles (see *Dunlop v Selfridge*).

- Show some of the difficulties, e.g. in the case of *Jackson v Horizon*.

- Work quickly through the established exceptions. Do not dwell on these. It is creditworthy as legal knowledge, but is well established and does not cause any real problems.

- Consider in turn the attempts to avoid the doctrine, in order to provide justice. These should raise matters of critical analysis, such as the 'floodgates' argument (if one plaintiff is successful, many more will follow), and the idea of not using one area of law to avoid another.

- Discuss the recommendations for reform.

STUDENT'S ANSWER WITH TUTOR'S COMMENTS

Question 1

> **Good introduction. Identifies the different terms and the reasons for them, and refers directly to the issue raised in the question of whether the courts place importance on the intentions of the parties.**

> **Uses appropriate cases to illustrate the difference between conditions and warranties and again considers the part played by the intentions of the parties.**

> **Considers the effect of a breach of each type of term.**

In contracts, certain terms are more important than others. Those that are fundamental to the contract are known as conditions and the less important ones as warranties. The need to distinguish between these terms arises from the obvious need for different remedies if they are breached. Generally it will be obvious from contracts which terms parties intend to be the most important, but in certain circumstances this may not be clear.

Two cases which outline the differences clearly are *Poussard v Spiers and Pond* and *Bettini v Gye*. Both contracts were made with singers who subsequently fell ill; one missed several rehearsals but recovered in time for final rehearsals and the performances and the other missed half of the performances. Clearly the parties' original concerns were that the singers should perform, and rehearsals were a less important matter. Therefore it was found that the singer who had missed only rehearsals had breached only a warranty, but the one who had missed performances had breached a condition. The intentions of the contracting parties were clear and the courts took this into account.

If a warranty is breached the innocent party is merely entitled to damages, but if a condition is breached, they may either affirm and claim damages or repudiate and claim damages for obligations already incurred. If parties' intentions are clear, the type of remedy most suitable to the breach will be clear.

The labelling of terms may appear to be a clear way for parties to show their intentions but in *Schuler v Wickman* this was held to be inconclusive. A term labelled 'condition' was the only one of twenty terms, but the court held that if the parties had intended the word

Discusses terms specified within the contract

Further example with argument the other way

Reference to statute

Very clear explanation of innominate terms

Appraisal of the use of the approach by the courts

Further critical analysis relevant to the question

Sound reasoned conclusion, again addressing the specific issues raised in the question

condition to be strictly interpreted they should have stated so. This was perhaps because it may not have been the intention of the parties for the term to have been a condition and they may merely have failed to understand the legal significance of the word.

An example of where parties' intentions were considered by the courts is *Lombard v Butterworth* where rental instalments were consistently paid late despite a term stating that punctual payment was 'of the essence'. The court held that this was a breach of condition since the parties had made their intention clear.

Sometimes statute may provide that certain terms will be either warranties or conditions. Here the intentions of the parties are irrelevant and the courts will refer to the statute. An example is the Sale of Goods Act 1979 in which it states that there will be a condition in every consumer contract that goods are of merchantable quality.

If statute does not make provision, case law will apply. In *The Mihalos Angelos* it was held that a party was entitled to repudiate a contract. It was said that ship owner and hirer met on equal terms and that they sought a firm foundation of rules on which to build.

In the *Hong Kong Fir* case a new approach was established for considering the importance of terms. Here it was said that a particular term could have been breached in a small or large way, and that it did not lend itself to traditional analysis. This type of term is known as an innominate term and in this case the court looked at the effect of the breach before deciding if it was serious enough to be a breach of condition or was only a breach of warranty. The court decided that although a ship had been delayed a long time, the innocent party did not want to repudiate the contract since their cargo would eventually arrive. They merely wanted damages for the delay and therefore the term was treated as a warranty.

This approach was applied in *The Hansa Nord* and the *Hansen Tangen* case, and in both cases the courts found that the breaches were not serious and that parties were not entitled to repudiate. In the latter the court said that a small technical breach should not allow repudiation as this would lead to injustice.

The use of the new approach should be carefully considered since in certain cases it may be more suitable to use traditional analysis. In *The Chikuma* it was held that conditions should be strictly interpreted in order to avoid lengthy litigation. Again in *Bunge v Tradax* it was held that the breach of a term requiring notice of readiness to load should entitle parties to repudiate since they wished to form a new contract and get their job done as quickly as possible. Where parties have equality of bargaining power (e.g. charterparties) the traditional approach is often more suitable.

The problem of referring to the intentions of parties is that it creates uncertainty in the law and this means that out of court settlements are more difficult and predicting the worth of the case may be hard. However the benefit is that cases are decided justly and parties can get a satisfactory outcome.

It is often the case that whichever approach courts use to decide a case, the outcome will be the same. If the *Hong Kong Fir* approach were applied to *Poussard v Spiers and Pond* or *Bettini v Gye*, the outcome would probably still have been the same. By looking at the intentions of the parties, the courts are taking a more modern approach which will possibly lead to fairer individual outcomes. The *Hong Kong Fir* approach was used in the *Bachelors Peas* case, well before the *Hong Kong Fir* case, and the court clearly felt then that it was fairer to look at the intentions of the parties than the interpretation of the clause individually.

The importance of a contractual term will not always be determined by reference to the intentions of the parties. However, this is becoming more and more common in modern cases, and though it is not always in the interests of certainty, it provides justice in individual cases.

Tutor's Comments

This is an excellent answer. It is comprehensive in its coverage of the legal principles involved and makes very good use of case citations to illustrate and develop points. It addresses directly the issues raised in the question, and contains a very pleasing amount of critical analysis which is both accurate and perceptive. A good A grade answer.

A review sheet for this chapter can be found on p. 217.

CHAPTER 17

VITIATING FACTORS

MISREPRESENTATION

MISTAKE

DURESS AND UNDUE INFLUENCE

ILLEGALITY

GETTING STARTED

A contract may be apparently well formed, with the necessary ingredients of offer and acceptance, consideration and legal intent, between parties who have capacity to contract, but with some other element present which means that the contract is not as intended in some way. In some circumstances the party who feels wronged may be able to end the contract. The elements which have this effect on a contract are known as vitiating factors. This chapter will examine the vitiating factors as follows:

- **misrepresentation** – where a party is led into a contract by an untrue statement beforehand;
- **mistake** – where one or both parties have made a false assumption in forming the contract;
- **duress and undue influence** – where one party enters into the contract under unfair pressure;
- **illegality** – where a contract involves something unlawful or is against public policy.

The main themes of questions set on this topic are:

- What kinds of statements will amount to a misrepresentation and what remedies are available?
- What kinds of false assumptions will result in the contract being avoided?
- The extent to which the courts will allow a contract to be set aside as a result of unfair pressure.
- When a contract will be avoided for illegality and when public policy will override the interests of the parties.

MISREPRESENTATION

> "Misleading untrue statements"

ESSENTIAL PRINCIPLES

We have seen in Chapter 16 that many statements made prior to the forming of a contract are not **terms** but merely **representations**. These do not form part of the contract, but may nevertheless be important in helping a party to decide whether to go ahead and form the contract. In many cases such statements will actually persuade, or induce, a party to enter into a contract. It could then be very unfair if these pre-contractual statements turned out to be untrue.

Where someone has been misled into forming a contract in this way by facts which prove to be untrue a remedy may be available for **misrepresentation**. Misrepresentation can be defined as follows: 'A misrepresentation is an **untrue statement of fact**, made by one party to a contract to another, which, while not forming a term of a contract, has **an inducing effect** on it.'

ACTIONABLE MISSTATEMENTS

To be actionable there must be a misstatement of fact, and *not*:

■ a mere commendation (or advertising 'puff');

■ a statement of opinion;

■ a statement of future intentions;

■ a statement of law.

Mere commendation

It is sometimes difficult to distinguish between a permissible advertising gimmick and an actionable false statement. In *Dimmock v Hallett (1866)* an auctioneer's description of land as 'fertile and improvable' was held to be a mere advertising flourish and not actionable.

Opinion

A statement of opinion may be recognised by being hedged around with words such as 'I think' or 'we believe', or common sense could tell the listener that the maker of the statement is only stating a personal view. In *Bissett v Wilkinson (1927)* a seller of land in New Zealand said that it would support 2,000 sheep. This proved to be untrue, but not actionable, as the land had not previously been used for sheep farming and the buyer knew that the seller had no expertise in the field.

However, if the person stating their opinion is an **expert** in the field, or the only one who could have such information, then what is said may be actionable. This was so in *Esso v Mardon (1976)* where a representative from Esso gave professional advice to a person opening a petrol station which turned out to be totally wrong. This was held to be actionable because of the skill and expertise of the maker of the statements.

Future intentions

While stating what may be intended in the future is not generally actionable, if it is proved that a party never intended to carry out promises made, then an actionable misrepresentation may arise. In *Edgington v Fitzmaurice (1885)* a company prospectus stated that new shares were being issued to raise money to expand and improve buildings, whereas it was shown that it was intended all along that the money would be used to pay off debts. Bowen LJ said that, in some circumstances ,'the state of a man's mind is as much a fact as the state of his digestion'.

Statement of law

If a person misstates the law to another this will not generally be actionable (although a solicitor who misstates the law may be liable to his client).

SILENCE AND MISREPRESENTATION

> "Silence generally not misrepresentation"

We have seen that a misrepresentation is an untrue statement of fact. The issue then arises as to whether such a statement could be made by a person remaining silent. The general position is that silence does not amount to a misrepresentation. There is no duty to talk to the world at large, and no liability in general for not disclosing facts (although one may feel morally bound in some circumstances). The principle of *caveat emptor* applies – let the buyer beware. This was so in *Fletcher v Krell (1873)* where a woman who was interviewed for a post as governess did not disclose that she had previously been married (this was important at that time).

However, this is rather a sweeping general proposition, and many modifications have arisen in case law, some of which are listed below.

Misleading conduct

Lord Campbell said in *Walters v Morgan (1861)* that conduct could lead to misrepresentation, and may be in the form of 'a single word, or … a nod or wink, or a shake of the head or a smile'.

Concealing a defect

If a defect is deliberately concealed a misrepresentation may arise, as in *Scheider v Heath (1813)* where a ship was partly submerged to conceal a rotten hold.

Half-true statement

In *Dimmock v Hallett* the seller of land said that all his farms were let, but omitted to say that all of the tenants had given notice to leave, and this was held to be a misrepresentation because it was incomplete and therefore misleading.

Changed circumstances

If circumstances change between statements being made and a contract being formed, the statements may be misleading if no further updating information is given. In *With v O'Flanagan (1936)* a doctor who became ill whilst negotiating the sale of his practice was held liable in misrepresentation, as he did not inform the buyer that his takings had dropped by a huge amount.

Fiduciary relationship

A fiduciary relationship is where one party places trust in the other and relies on it. This imposes a greater duty than usual to disclose relevant information. In *Hedley Byrne v Heller (1964)* it was found that there was a fiduciary relationship between a banker and a firm to whom he was giving undertakings about the creditworthiness of a mutual client. One also arose in the case of *Esso v Mardon* (above), between the Esso representative and the garage manager. In both cases one party had special knowledge that caused them to be in a position of trust. In such cases remaining silent over an issue could be a misrepresentation.

Contracts *uberrimae fidei*

An even closer relationship, that of *uberrima fides*, or utmost good faith, is said to exist in some contracts. This is where one party places total trust in the other, because the one being trusted holds all the relevant knowledge or information. It arises in insurance contracts. If a person wishes to insure property, such as a car or a house, the insurance company is normally informed about it by a statement from the customer. It is imperative that this is a full disclosure of all material facts, as the insurance company is relying on the customer telling the truth. If the customer lies in some way, this could be a misrepresentation. This arose in *Seaman v Fonereau (1743)* when a ship captain did not report being in a position of danger, and in *Bufe v Turner (1815)* when a house owner did not report the circumstances of a fire.

INDUCEMENT

The untrue statement must have induced, or persuaded, the other party to enter into the contract (this forms part of the definition of misrepresentation). If the other party did not place importance on the untrue statement then a claim cannot be based on it. In *Attwood v Small (1838)* the purchasers of a mine relied on their own surveyor's report, rather than the claims of the owner. Although these were later found to be incorrect, they did not form an actionable misrepresentation.

If a party has the opportunity to check facts and does not, they can still claim misrepresentation. In *Redgrave v Hurd (1881)* a buyer did not take up the opportunity to inspect accounts, but successfully claimed misrepresentation of the value of the business.

MISREPRESENTATION PASSED ON VIA A THIRD PARTY

Once an untrue statement has been made from one party to another, it is usually considered 'spent', so it is no longer a misrepresentation if the second party passes it on to a third. However, if the first party *knows* that the wrong information is likely to be passed on, then an actionable misrepresentation may arise. This was so in *Pilmore v Hood (1838)* when the seller of a pub wrongly stated the takings, knowing that the information was likely to be passed on to another person who bought the business.

TYPES OF MISREPRESENTATION

Fraudulent misrepresentation

Before the 1960s the law only recognised one type of misrepresentation, that being **fraudulent misrepresentation**. If a person had deliberately lied, perhaps in order to induce a sale, then the other party could rescind, or end, the contract, and sue in the tort of deceit. Fraudulent misrepresentation was defined in *Derry v Peek (1889)* as a false statement made (i) knowingly, or (ii) without belief in its truth, or (iii) recklessly as to whether it be true or false. This has traditionally been quite difficult to prove, the courts regarding fraud seriously, and therefore looking for more than mere negligence or foolishness.

Misrepresentation Act 1967

Then, following the decision in *Hedley Byrne v Heller*, where there was a special relationship, Parliament recognised the need for a further remedy, and passed the Misrepresentation Act 1967, acknowledging that a misrepresentation may arise out of negligence, or carelessness, or even innocently, but still cause harm or inconvenience to the other party. This is now the normal route to a remedy for most parties suffering from a misrepresentation.

REMEDIES FOR MISREPRESENTATION

For any misrepresentation there is the possibility of **rescinding** the contract, which means ending it *ab initio* (i.e. going back to the starting point). This could be barred in several ways:

- **affirmation** – where the misrepresentee indicates willingness to continue with the contract – *Long v Lloyd (1958)*);
- **lapse of time** – where the misrepresentee waits an unreasonably long time before bringing an action (*Leaf v International Galleries (1950)*);
- **restitution impossible** – where the goods cannot be restored (handed back) to the other party in their original state (*Vigers v Pike (1842)*);
- **supervening third party rights** – where a third party now has the goods (*White v Garden (1851)*);
- **some other circumstance** where the court decide to award damages in lieu under the Misrepresentation Act 1967.

DAMAGES

For fraudulent misrepresentation a claim may be made for damages in the tort of deceit, or if a special relationship exists, following *Hedley Byrne v Heller*. However, it is now much easier to sue under the Misrepresentation Act 1967.

 **Damages under the Misrepresentation Act 1967**

Section 2(1) provides a remedy for a misrepresentee without proving fraud, where a remedy *would* have been available, had fraud been proved. This is known as the **fiction of fraud**. The section provides the remedy of damages for a misrepresentee **unless the misrepresentor can show** that he believed in his statements and that this was reasonable. This is unusual, in that once an untrue statement is shown to exist, the burden lies on the misrepresentor to prove his innocence.

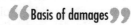 **Basis of damages**

Damages are assessed on a tort basis, following the decision in *Roycott v Rogerson (1991)*.

Section 2(2) of the Act allows the court to award damages, at their discretion, in lieu of rescission.

MISTAKE

Mistakes may be made by either party during the formation of a contract which, inconvenient though they may be, do not affect the validity of the contract. However, some mistakes are much more fundamental and could make the contract void. The cases where this has arisen can be categorised in various ways. Here they will be referred to in four groups:

- **common mistake** – where both parties are labouring under the same false assumption;
- **mutual mistake** – sometimes known as shared mistake, where the parties are at cross purposes;
- **unilateral mistake** – where only one party is mistaken and the other is aware of this;
- **mistake over documents**.

COMMON MISTAKE

Here the parties are in agreement, but their contract is based on an assumption which is false. Two main groups of cases have arisen in this way:

- cases where the mistake is over the **existence** of the subject matter;
- cases where the mistake is over the **quality** of the subject matter.

Non-existent subject matter

Where the mistake is over existence of the subject matter of the contract, the situation is known as *res extincta* (the thing is destroyed). In *Couturier v Hastie (1856)* a sale was agreed over a cargo of corn which was still on its way to the UK, but unknown to the parties it had been sold at Tunis to prevent deterioration. The subject matter (the corn) did not therefore exist to form the basis of a contract. In *Galloway v Galloway (1914)* a separation agreement was made between a husband and wife, but when they found that they had not been legally married, the agreement was held to be void.

The common law is now reinforced by s. 6 of the Sale of Goods Act 1979.

Mistake over title

An extension of the principle of *res extincta* is *res sua* (the thing is his own). It will rarely arise, but in the case of *Cooper v Phibbs (1867)* a lease was drawn up to transfer a fishery and, unknown to both parties at the time, the buyer was already the owner.

Mistake over quality of subject matter

The general position is that where the mistake of the parties merely results in a **bad bargain** for one of them, the contract will not be void. This is consistent with the principle that the law only requires sufficiency of consideration, not the normal market value. This arose in the leading case of *Bell v Lever Bros (1932)* where a company thought that they were obliged to make a large settlement on dispensing with the services of a senior member of staff, whereas the payment need not have been made.

The point is perhaps more easily seen in the case of *Leaf v International Galleries (1950)*. Here a painting was sold, with the buyer and the gallery who sold it both thinking that it was painted by Constable. In fact it was proved, some years later, to be a copy. The court held that the contract could not be avoided, as the painting itself was the subject of the contract, and did exist. The reasoning seems quite logical, if it is considered what would happen if the situation was reversed. If a painting was bought in a jumble sale, which some years later turned out to be a valuable one, the buyer would not wish to avoid the contract!

MUTUAL MISTAKE

In cases of mutual mistake, the parties are not really in agreement, as they make different assumptions in forming the contract. In such cases, if there is total ambiguity the contract is held void. In *Raffles v Wichelhaus (1864)* an agreement was made to buy a cargo of cotton, on a ship named 'Peerless' in Bombay. There were actually two ships of the same name loaded with cotton in Bombay, and the court held the agreement too ambiguous to enforce.

Where there is some 'extra' factor the contract may be allowed to continue. In *Wood v Scarth (1858)* a lease was drawn up for a pub and, after a conversation with the seller's clerk, the buyer accepted, believing the only payment to be the rental of £63. The seller had also intended a premium of £500 to be paid. Here the contract was upheld, because of the 'extra' evidence of the statements of the clerk.

UNILATERAL MISTAKE

This is where only one party has contracted on the basis of a false assumption. The other party will normally know of this mistake, and in some cases will have encouraged it.

The courts again take the view that merely being mistaken over the quality or value of the goods is not fundamental enough to avoid the contract. This was one argument raised in *Smith v Hughes (1871)* where the court said that even if the seller knew that the buyer was mistaken over the quality of the oats which he bought, this would not render the contract void.

On the other hand, some mistakes may be so fundamental and obvious that one party will be *taken* to have known about the mistake of the other. In *Hartog v Colin and Shields (1939)* a mistake over price was so obvious and fundamental to a buyer that he was deemed to have been aware of it, and the contract was held void.

Mistake as to identity

This is an aspect of unilateral mistake, and in many cases has occurred when one person has posed as someone else in order to persuade a seller to part with goods on credit.
The cases fall into two groups:

- *inter absentes* – where the parties are not in each other's presence, but deal 'at arm's length';
- *inter praesentes* – where the parties meet face to face.

Dealing at arm's length

An example of *inter absentes* is *Cundy v Lindsay (1878)* where a firm supplying a quantity of handkerchiefs was held to have been fundamentally mistaken in dealing with a rogue posing as someone else in a letter in order to obtain goods. The contract was held void.

In each other's presence

A series of *inter praesentes* cases have been the subject of some debate. In *Phillips v Brooks (1919)* the principle was applied that identity was not crucial to a contract where a person was face to face with the other party. In the case a rogue posed as someone else to obtain jewellery on credit, paying with a cheque which was dishonoured, and then selling the jewellery to a third party for cash before disappearing. Apart from the mistake issues, there was a fraudulent misrepresentation, but rescission was barred as a third party had bought the goods. The court held that the mistaken identity was not crucial enough to avoid the contract, and that the seller was taken to contract with the person before him.

Ingram v Little (1961) involved similar facts, except that this time three elderly ladies were selling a car. Here the court felt that the mistaken identity was crucial to the contract, and held it void, the car being returned to the ladies.

In the more recent case of *Lewis v Avery (1971)* Lord Denning examined the two previous cases, and felt that the legal principles in *Phillips v Brooks* were to be preferred. Where parties are *inter praesentes* they would intend to deal with the person before them, identified by sight, hearing, etc., and their contracts would be binding.

MISTAKE RELATING TO DOCUMENTS

The general rule is that if parties sign a written document they are bound by it (*L'Estrange v Graucob* (see Chapter 16)). However, if a party has been induced to sign under a misrepresentation or some unfair pressure, then the contract will be voidable. In addition, two measures exist which may help where a written contract is not in accordance with the parties' intentions:

- the plea of *non est factum*;
- rectification.

Non est factum

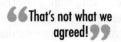
❝I didn't mean to sign it!❞

In very limited circumstances the plea of *non est factum* – which literally means 'not my deed' – may be available. In *Foster v Mackinnon (1869)* an elderly man with poor eyesight was induced to sign a document, being told that it was a guarantee. When it was found to be a bill of exchange in favour of the plaintiff the defendant successfully pleaded *non est factum*. However, the plea will not be allowed too easily, lest it be used as an excuse to escape an unwanted contract. In *Saunders v Anglia Building Society (1971)* Mrs Gallie was unsuccessful in her claim, as the document which she signed was not very different from what she intended to sign, and she was considered to be somewhat careless in not reading it through first.

Rectification

❝That's not what we agreed!❞

Rectification is a measure used by the courts to amend a written contract so that it reflects more accurately the parties' previous oral agreement. This will be an exception to the general principle of the parol evidence rule (see Chapter 16) and the courts will need good evidence of the previous oral agreement. In *Joscelyne v Nissen (1970)* an agreement over who should pay expenses was rectified because of the evidence of regular payments having been made by one party.

DURESS AND UNDUE INFLUENCE

It has long been recognised at common law that a party might have been coerced, or pressed, into a contract. The resulting contract cannot be regarded as a true agreement between parties.

DURESS

66 Sign this or else ... 99

Duress was originally a narrow common law doctrine and limited to situations where a contract was formed under the threat of violence to the person or unlawful constraint. It also extended to threats to those close to the person, such as family. In *Cumming v Ince (1847)* an old lady's 'agreement' to settle property on a relative was held void as it was formed under the threat of confinement to a mental hospital.

66 Threats to property 99

At common law threats to property were not within the definition of duress (*Skeate v Beale (1840)*). However, more recently the approach to this has changed somewhat, and in *The Siboen and the Sibotre (1976)* it was suggested that some very serious threats, such as the threat to burn down a house or slash a valuable painting, may amount to duress.

Economic duress

Threats to property have led to the extension to the doctrine to encompass a threat to a party's financial situation. There is obviously greater difficulty in defining the boundaries of this type of threat, and in differentiating between duress and legitimate commercial pressure, but some principles are emerging through case law:

- In *North Ocean Shipping v Hyundai Construction (1979)* – also known as *The Atlantic Baron* the court recognised the possibility of economic duress, based on unreasonable commercial pressure in a valuable shipping contract.
- In *Pao On v Lau Yiu Long (1980)* it was held that the threat of a breach of contract alone would not necessarily lead to economic duress, as this was a normal problem of commerce.
- In *Universe Tankships of Monravia v ITWF (1982)* – also known as *The Universe Sentinel* – a threat to 'black' a ship by a union unless certain financial and other conditions were met was held to be economic duress. This is obviously a very substantial threat, as it prevented the owners of the ship operating, and involved very valuable contracts.
- In *Williams v Roffey (1991)* the possibility of economic duress was considered concerning a contract between builders and carpenters, but none was found on the facts.
- In *Atlas Express v Kafco (1989)* a threat to breach a contract to transport goods meant that a small firm with a contract to supply Woolworths could not operate. This was held to be economic duress, the value of the contract being of importance given the relative size of the firms involved.

The effect of duress

The effect of common law duress was to render the contract void. However, the courts, when dealing with economic duress, are using their discretionary powers to a large extent, and this, together, perhaps, with a desire to be fair and consistent, has led to the courts making contracts formed under economic duress voidable, and therefore subject to such things as lapse of time and third party rights.

UNDUE INFLUENCE

Because the common law doctrine of duress was so narrow, the courts developed, through equity, the doctrine of **undue influence**. This arises where there is unfair pressure on a party to enter into a contract which does not amount to duress. The cases can be divided into two categories:

- where there is **no special relationship** between the parties;
- where there is a **fiduciary, or special, relationship**, either a) generally, e.g. parent-child, solicitor-client , or b) on this particular occasion.

Proved undue influence

Where there is no special relationship, the burden is on the party claiming undue influence to **prove** it.

Presumed undue influence

Where there is a recognised fiduciary relationship between the parties, undue influence is **presumed**. In *Allcard v Skinner (1887)* it was found to exist between a nun and her mother superior.

However, the presumption is rebuttable if evidence exists that the weaker party was free to exercise independent will in entering the contract. In *Re Brocklehurst (1978)* it was suggested that proving one or more of the following points may rebut the presumption:

- full disclosure of all material facts, i.e. an explanation of the possible consequences of entering the contract;
- independent advice;
- adequate consideration;
- spontaneity of a gift.

The effect of undue influence

As undue influence is an equitable doctrine, the effect of it is to render the contract voidable. Equitable principles will therefore apply, as well as the bars to rescission, and in *Allcard v Skinner* (above) the nun was unsuccessful because of a long time delay.

The 'banking' cases

There has arisen in recent years a series of cases concerning banking issues. These have raised a number of issues surrounding the doctrine of undue influence, and would repay careful reading of a fuller nature than can be undertaken here. The following principles emerge:

- The relationship between a banker and client is not necessarily a fiduciary one, but in *Lloyds Bank v Bundy (1975)* the court held that in going beyond everyday duties into a position of particular trust a bank may 'be crossing the line into the area of confidentiality'. In the case an elderly farmer placed total trust in the bank and allowed his house to be used as security for a business loan to his son. The charge on the house was set aside on a finding of undue influence.
- The relationship between husband and wife is not generally a fiduciary one (*Midland Bank v Shepherd (1988)*) but in *BCCI v Aboody (1989)* undue influence between a dominant husband and much younger wife was proved on the particular facts.
- Where a fiduciary relationship is established, undue influence will only be presumed if there is also a manifest, or obvious, disadvantage to the weaker party (*National Westminster v Morgan (1985)*).
- The case of *Barclays Bank v O'Brien (1993)* raised several important issues. A spouse or cohabitee *could* be affected by undue influence (or misrepresentation) by the other partner. The doctrine of notice will apply in such cases, i.e. the bank should be aware of the rights of the weaker party (here Mrs O'Brien) unless adequate steps have been taken to ensure that she received independent advice. The House of Lords held that the effect of the misrepresentation in this particular case was to set aside the whole transaction. Similarly, in the case of *TSB v Camfield (1994)* the whole loan was set aside.
- The problem of sharing loss where neither party had acted with any devious intention arose in *Cheese v Thomas (1993)*.
- Banks will probably only be obliged to take reasonable steps to ensure that independent advice is received (see *Banco Exterior v Mann (1994)* where the husband and wife used the same solicitor, and *Midland Bank v Serter (1994)* where the wife used the bank's solicitor).

ILLEGALITY

Some contracts, although well formed, may contain an element of unlawfulness, e.g. a contract to rob a bank. The law will obviously not enforce such a contract, but the whole area of illegality in contract law goes far beyond obvious criminal activity, into the area of public policy.

Some contracts are **illegal when formed**, such as *Re Mahmoud and Ispahani (1921)* where linseed oil was sold to a dealer without a licence, contrary to statute.

Other contracts are well formed, but become **illegal in their performance**, such as *Anderson v Daniel (1924)* where a consignment of manure was delivered without the requisite labelling.

Some contracts are **illegal by statute**, as *Re Mahmoud and Ispahani* (above), and others are **illegal at common law**, such as *Everet v Williams (1725)* where an agreement between highwaymen to rob a coach and share the swag was held illegal.

Contracts not actually illegal, but prejudicial to the state, preventing the administration of justice, promoting sexual immorality, defrauding the Revenue or promoting corruption in public life will not be legally binding, e.g. *Parkinson v College of Ambulance (1925)* where an agreement was made to obtain a knighthood in exchange for a generous donation to charity.

Contracts which are not actually illegal may be allowed to stand but remain unenforceable, such as wagering agreements, contracts prejudicial to marriage, and those in restraint of trade.

RESTRAINT OF TRADE

This is an area of illegality which arises more often in examination papers.

Any contract which restrains trade by restricting a person's freedom to work is *prima facie* contrary to public policy and therefore void, *unless* it can be justified in some way. These restraints are normally found as a term either in a contract of employment or in a contract for the sale of a business.

Not every such term will be void then, only those which are not found to be reasonable:

- between the parties; and
- with regard to the public interest.

Reasonableness may involve such areas as:

- Protection of trade secrets, as in *Forster v Suggett (1918)* where a restriction on a manager's freedom to work in the manufacturer of glass, which involved secret processes, for five years after the end of a particular employment, was held valid.
- Protection of clientele, as in *Fitch v Dewes (1921)* where a solicitor's clerk was prevented from working within a seven-mile radius of Tamworth town hall.
- In the sale of a business, the need for the public to be served by businesses, and the state of the market – in *Nordenfelt v Maxim Nordenfelt (1894)* a world-wide restraint for 25 years was upheld, given the nature of the business of manufacturing guns and ammunitions.
- Exclusive dealing arrangements must be shown to be reasonable – in *Schroeder Music v Macaulay (1974)* such a restraint on a song writer was held to be unreasonable, and in the two cases of *Esso v Harper's Garage (1968)* one arrangement was held valid for four years, but another for 21 years was held unreasonable.

When a restraint of trade is found to be unreasonable, then it will be void to the extent that it contravenes public policy. Severance may be possible, if the offending clause can be removed without altering the basic meaning of the contract. The court traditionally will not rewrite the contract, but merely strike out offending words (known as the **blue pencil test**), retaining the general nature of the contract. However, there is an apparent slight relaxation of this strict approach, by interpretation of the offending clause in a way which makes it reasonable (see *Littlewoods v Harris (1978)*).

Injunction is an important remedy in this area, preventing the actions of a party and thus enforcing a restraint clause.

EUROPEAN LAW

It should be noted that European law has had a great impact on this area of law, as it involves the principles of free competition and free movement within the European Union. Article 85 of the Treaty of Rome makes void any practices which adversely affect competition within the European Union.

EXAMINATION QUESTIONS

1 Is it correct to say that every untrue statement which induces a contract will amount to a misrepresentation in law? (UODLE)

2 Critically examine the remedies available to a person who has entered a contract on the strength of a misrepresentation. (UODLE)

3 Last month in H's showroom G saw a saloon car which he was interested in buying. H realised that G was keenly interested in the car and he informed G that the car had only one careful previous owner, that it was five years old with an engine capacity of 2,000cc, and that its total mileage was 40,000. This was exactly what G wanted so he agreed to purchase the car for a sum of £2,500. He paid H the money in cash and took the car away. One week later G showed the car to his friend who was a motor mechanic. This friend inspected the vehicle and informed G that the engine was not the original but that it was ten years old and had been fitted to this newer body. He further told him that the engine capacity was in fact only 1,500cc and the true mileage was in excess of 120,000. G later discovered that the previous owner of the car had constantly driven the car badly and had not

maintained it in a proper manner. These facts were known to H but he had never bothered to investigate further, being anxious to complete the sale.

In what ways does the law give any protection to G in these circumstances? (ULEAC)

4   On Friday, Jane advertises her car for sale in the local newspaper. As she has no technical knowledge of cars, she relies on the vehicle registration document and describes the car as a 1990 white Vauxhall family saloon. Wendy sees the advertisement, contacts Jane and views the car. Wendy's inspection of the car is brief, but she specifically asks Jane the age of the car. Jane shows her the registration document that states the first registration as 1990. Wendy offers Jane a cheque which she is at first reluctant to accept but does so after Wendy produces a driving licence as identification. Unknown to Jane, Wendy is part of a gang dealing in suspect cars and the cheque is worthless. Wendy gives the car and registration document to Martin, a garage owner who is also part of the gang and tells him that it is a 1990 car. On Sunday, Martin contacts Paula, who he knows is looking for a second-hand car of this type. He describes the car to her as a White 1990 Vauxhall saloon. Paula views the car at the garage and buys it for cash.

On Monday, when Jane visits the bank with the cheque, she discovers that the cheque is worthless.

On Wednesday, Paula discovers that the car is in fact a 1988 version which had been imported into Britain and not the 1990 version as described by Jane, Wendy and Martin.

a)   Advise Jane:

   i)   what action she might bring against Wendy if she can be found;

   ii)   whether she can recover the car from Paula if she cannot bring an action against Wendy. (15)

b)   Advise Paula what possible actions she has against Martin. (10)

(NEAB)

5   Sheila consults her bank manager, Ms Suet, over her plans to sell her house. Sheila is a widow and she frequently consults Ms Suet on financial and personal matters. When told that Sheila intends to sell her house, Ms Suet offers to buy it at the current market price. Sheila accepts the offer and the sale is completed. Six months later house prices have risen by 25% and Sheila is seeking to have the sale of the house set aside, on the grounds that Ms Suet had taken advantage of her position as Sheila's bank manager.

Advise Sheila. (UODLE)

6   Mortimer visits Ravinder, the manager of Centrebank, and discusses with her the possibility of borrowing money to fund a business venture. Mortimer takes some application forms home and persuades his wife, Ophelia, to sign them. She does so, under the impression that the loan is £30,000 on a short-term basis. Centrebank later makes the money available using a house owned by Mortimer and Ophelia as security.

After some time it becomes obvious that Mortimer's business venture is failing. To her dismay, Ophelia learns for the first time that the loan is for £80,000. Centrebank wishes to sell the house to recover the amount loaned.

How, if at all, would Ophelia be able to defend her position? (UODLE)

ANSWERS TO QUESTIONS

OUTLINE ANSWERS TO SELECTED QUESTIONS

Question 1

■ Introduce the topic of misrepresentation and define it. Discuss the importance of distinguishing between misrepresentations and contractual terms, because of the different remedies available.

■ Discuss what kinds of untrue statements will (and, to some extent, will not) amount to a misrepresentation, i.e. one of fact, not opinion, law, etc.

■ Examine the issue of whether silence can form an actionable misrepresentation, and look at issues surrounding it, e.g. conduct, half-true statements, change of circumstances, etc.

■ Consider whether the present state is satisfactory regarding silence.

- Consider inducement, as without it a statement will not form a misrepresentation.
- Form a reasoned conclusion. Refer back to the question.

Question 6

- Introduce the topic of undue influence and explain that there is not automatically a fiduciary relationship between banker and client. If Ophelia is to succeed in this area then she will need to prove that she suffered from undue influence on this occasion.
- From *Lloyds v Bundy* the parties could have 'crossed the line' into an area beyond ordinary banking transactions.
- Nothing in the question suggests that the situation is like *BCCI v Aboody*.
- The problem is similar on facts to *Barclays v O'Brien*, so give a reasonably full account of that case.
- See if there are any differences between this problem and *Barclays v O'Brien*, or any particular similarities, and apply the law from the case to the problem. Consider the relationships between banker and client, husband and wife, and the need for the bank to satisfy itself that Ophelia had received independent advice. Remember that in *Barclays v O'Brien* it was held that Mrs O'Brien had suffered from a misrepresentation over the size and period of the loan, and the contract was set aside on this basis.
- Consider briefly the issues in the more recent cases and apply them.
- Form some conclusion. Remember that this does not need to be definitive (e.g. Ophelia will win), but may take the form of: 'If it is found that Ophelia has suffered from either undue influence or misrepresentation, as in *Barclays v O'Brien*, then the court would be able to set aside the contract for the whole of the loan.'

STUDENT'S ANSWER WITH TUTOR'S COMMENTS

Question 2

> 66 Good – misrepresentation defined and types outlined 99

Misrepresentation could be defined as an untrue statement of fact, made by one party to a contract to another, which, while not forming the term of the contract, has an inducing effect on it. There are various types of misrepresentation. It is necessary to distinguish between fraudulent misrepresentation, negligent and wholly innocent misrepresentation. This is mainly because of the remedies available.

> 66 Fraudulent misrepresentation defined and remedies explained 99

Fraudulent misrepresentation was explained in the case of *Derry v Peek*. According to Lord Herschell in this case 'fraudulent' is a false statement that is 'made knowingly, or without belief in its truth, or recklessly as to whether it be true or false'. The essence of fraud is absence of honest belief. The courts regard fraud seriously and will therefore look for more than mere negligence or foolishness.

Two remedies are available for fraudulent misrepresentation. The plaintiff can either claim damages or rescind the contract. Damages for fraud are based on the tort of deceit. Here the object is to restore the plaintiff to the position he would have been in if the contract had never existed. This is unlike the usual basis for damages in contract which compensates for loss of bargain. The plaintiff may also apply for an order to have any property handed over to be restored to him.

There are two types of negligent misrepresentation: negligent at common law and negligent misrepresentation under the Misrepresentation Act. At common law, before 1964, there was no general remedy for negligent misrepresentation. Damages were restricted to cases where fraud was proved (*Derry v Peek*). Any non-fraudulent misrepresentation was regarded as 'innocent' and damages were not available for such innocent misrepresentation.

> 66 Damages under *Hedley Byrne* explained. A very brief account of *Esso v Mardon* would be helpful 99

In 1963 the House of Lords stated, *obiter*, in *Hedley Byrne v Heller* that in certain circumstances damages may be recoverable in tort for negligent misstatement causing financial loss. The liability depended on a duty of care arising from a 'special relationship' between the parties. The term 'special relationship' could mean the duty of care in tort. A relationship will also be considered to exist where the representee possesses relevant knowledge or skill, and would expect the other party to rely on this (*Esso v Mardon*).

Under the Misrepresentation Act 1967, s. 2(1) provides a remedy for negligent misrepresentation, where the burden of proof shifts to the misrepresentor to prove his innocence. Under s. 2(2) the court has discretion to allow damages instead of rescission where appropriate.

Damages may not be claimed for wholly innocent misrepresentation, i.e. one that is neither fraudulent or negligent. The only remedy for wholly innocent misrepresentation is rescission, which may be accompanied by an indemnity. However s. 2(2) of the Misrepresentation Act 1967 gives the court a discretion to award damages in lieu of rescission where the misrepresentee would be entitled to rescind. Therefore damages under s. 2(2) cannot be claimed, but they may be awarded by the court. Section 2(3) of the Act states that when the court award damages under s. 2(1) any damages awarded under s. 2(2) in lieu of rescission are taken into account.

Rescission is clearly a serious and drastic remedy, and the courts will not allow it in certain circumstances, particularly where it would be obviously unreasonable to attempt to return to the original position.

Bars to rescission prevent parties from rescinding in several circumstances. Affirmation will occur when the injured party has indicated, once the misrepresentation has been discovered, that he is willing to carry on with the contract. An act of affirmation can also be made by implication of conduct. In *Long v Lloyd* the plaintiff wanted to rescind the contract after the second journey when the vehicle broke down completely. The defendant had agreed to share the cost of repair for the breakdown of the vehicle during the first journey. It was held that he could not do so since he had affirmed the contract.

If a misrepresentee discovers the fault a long time after the contract has been made, if the misrepresentation is fraudulent the time allowed to discover the fraud does not count provided that he acts within a reasonable time of discovery. On the other hand, if the misrepresentation is not fraudulent, the time allowed to bring the complaint to court and ask for rescission begins at the point of contract, as in *Leaf v International Galleries*. The plaintiff was induced to buy a picture by a non-fraudulent misrepresentation that it was a Constable. It was held that he had lost the right of rescission.

The injured party will lose the right to rescind if the parties cannot be restored to the original state. However 100% restitution is not required but something near to it. In *Vigers v Pike* a lease of a mine which had been entered into as a result of a misrepresentation could not be rescinded as there had been considerable extraction of minerals since the date of the contract.

Rescission cannot be ordered where a third party has acquired rights in the goods, *bona fide* and for value (i.e. in good faith and for consideration). In *White v Garden*, Parker had bought some iron from Garden and paid Garden with a false bill. Parker then sold the iron to White, a *bona fide* third party. Garden discovered that the bill was false and repossessed some of the iron from White. White sued and succeeded. Rescission was barred by the third party rights.

Remedies for misrepresentation vary according to the type of misrepresentation. The 'injured' party can generally claim damages either in the tort of deceit or under the Misrepresentation Act 1967 or can rescind the contract.

Tutor's Comments

This answer covers the basic material on remedies for misrepresentation extremely well. It is well learned and clearly understood, and would attract high marks for legal knowledge. Rescission is fully explained, and the route to damages is clear. However, there is nothing on the basis of assessment of damages (see *Royscott v Rogerson*). The area which needs attention is critical analysis, for example a comment on lapse of time could be made: 'There must be a reasonable time limit where no fraud is involved and the parties act in good faith. Also, if the buyer had bought a painting which had gained in value, would he still wish to rescind?' In order to answer the question '*critically* examine ...' some more comment is needed on whether the measures available provide a satisfactory outcome for a misrepresentee. However, this is a very creditable attempt, and overall a good B standard.

A review sheet for this chapter can be found on p. 218.

CHAPTER 18

THE ENDING OF A CONTRACT

GETTING STARTED

This chapter will examine the ways in which a contract may be brought to an end, and the remedies which the law provides for those who may have suffered from a breach of contract.

- The basic question which arises when considering the ending of a contract is *how* it can be, or has been, discharged.

- Once a contract has ended the injured party will seek a remedy, so the final question is to decide which remedy is appropriate.

The main themes of examination questions on these topics are:

- deciding which method of discharging the contract is appropriate;

- considering exactly what will amount to performance;

- the consequences of breach;

- the extent to which the doctrine of frustration may be applied;

- whether damages will suffice, whether they are too remote, and how they should be assessed;

- the circumstances in which equitable remedies will apply.

Again, especially with some examination boards, issues from this area may arise in combination with other topics.

DISCHARGE

REMEDIES

ESSENTIAL PRINCIPLES

Discharging a contract means bringing it to an end in some way. The way in which this is done is often important because of the burden of any loss which may fall on either, or both, parties. A contract may end in one of the following ways:

- **performance** – when a contract is completed;
- **agreement** – when parties agree to change or end a contract;
- **breach** – non-performance, or untrue statements within a contract;
- **frustration** – when an event outside the control of the parties ends a contract.

These will be considered in turn.

PERFORMANCE

> **❝Performance must be exact and complete❞**

It seems at first sight very obvious to say that a contract is discharged when both parties have performed their obligations. However, what precisely amounts to performance is not always straightforward. The general rule is that performance must match **exactly** and **completely** what the parties agreed. The harshness of this rule when applied strictly is seen *in Re Moore Co and Landauer Co (1921),* where the plaintiff's performance did not match his obligations **exactly**, as although the correct goods were delivered, they were in the wrong size cases. In *Cutter v Powell (1795)* a seaman died mid-voyage, so his performance was not **complete**. Because of the hardship which could result from the rule a number of exceptions have evolved through case law.

Severable contracts

The contract in *Cutter v Powell* is an example of an entire one, that is one which can only be performed by each party carrying out their obligations completely. Where, on the wording and construction of the contract, it is divisible into various obligations which can be carried out and paid for, regardless of whether performance is complete, it is known as a **severable contract**. Compare the following contracts:

- *Vlierboom v Chapman (1884)* – a cargo was to be carried from Batavia to Rotterdam, but was only taken to Mauritius. This was an entire contract, and nothing was payable unless the task was finished.
- *Ritchie v Atkinson (1808)* – a cargo was to be carried at £5 per ton. When only part of it was taken it was held that payment could be paid in proportion to the quantity carried.

Substantial performance

It has long been established that if a party has substantially performed their obligations under the contract (i.e. carried out most of them) then they can enforce it. In *Boone v Eyre (1779)* a plantation was sold, but the slaves were missing, yet the contract was held to be substantially performed. See also *Hoenig v Isaacs (1952).* Full payment is made subject to a deduction to remedy the defect. For substantial performance to be considered the breach must only amount to breach of warranty or a non-serious breach of an innominate term, not a condition.

Acceptance of partial performance

If not enough has been performed for substantial performance, then the parties may agree to accept partial performance. In *Christy v Row (1808)* delivery of coal was accepted (in fact, it was requested) by the defendant at a different destination, and this was held to be acceptance of partial performance with the defendant liable for payment. There must be a genuine choice for the other party (*Sumpter v Hedges (1898)*). Payment is made on a *quantum meruit* basis, that is in proportion to the work done.

Prevention of performance

If one party prevents the other from completing performance, then the injured party can either sue for damages for breach of contract, or claim payment on a *quantum meruit* basis for work done so far (*Planche v Colburn (1831)*).

Tender of performance

This is a proposal to perform, and in certain circumstances can be the equivalent of performance. In *Startup v Macdonald (1843)* an attempt to deliver oil on the last day of the month, on a Saturday evening, amounted to tender of performance, as the recipient refused to take delivery at that time, and damages were payable. Note that time of delivery is now covered by the Sale of Goods Act 1979 and must be at a reasonable time.

Time of performance

The time taken to perform obligations may be vital to one party. If this is made known, or is obvious, then time is said to be 'of the essence'. This could then be a condition of the contract. Otherwise performance must be within a reasonable time, and again this is covered by the Sale of Goods Act 1979.

Vicarious performance

If a party arranges for someone else to carry out duties under the contract, this could be vicarious performance, that is performance **on behalf of another**. If the other party has given consent to this, there is no problem. If no consent has been given, then vicarious performance will only satisfy the contractual obligations if it is reasonable. Obviously, if performance is of a personal nature, e.g. to paint a portrait or perform in a concert, then duties cannot be delegated. However, if a contractual duty was to supply a coach for an outing, then this probably could be sub-contracted, provided a coach of similar specification was supplied. If obligations are not met satisfactorily, the other party is entitled to refuse consent to delegate. In *Edwards v Newland (1950)* consent to delegate the storage of goods was refused, as the owner of the goods had chosen the contractors for their skill and integrity.

AGREEMENT

66 Changing or ending the contract **99**

In the same way that a contract is formed by agreement, it can be discharged by agreement. To vary or end the contract, both parties must provide consideration. This could be as simple as agreement to receive fewer goods in return for agreement to receive less money. An example is *Berry v Berry (1929)* where a deed of separation was modified by a new contract.

BREACH

66 Non-performance or defective performance **99**

A breach of contract arises when there is non-performance, defective performance, or an untrue statement within a contract. Breach can be:

- **actual** – where one party has not performed, or
- **anticipatory** – where one party indicates, before the date on which performance is due, that performance will not take place – the other party can then sue immediately (see *Hochster v De la Tour (1853)* where a courier was told that his services would not be needed for the summer season).

The consequences of breach will depend on the type of term breached:

- **repudiatory breach** – if a condition is breached, the innocent party may choose to end the contract, or agree to continue with it and claim damages;
- **non-repudiatory breach** – if a warranty is breached, the innocent party may only claim damages.

For more detail on this see Chapter 16 on types of terms.

Breach may be implied from actions or statements, if a party makes it obvious that performance will not be taking place – (*Frost v Knight (1870)*).

FRUSTRATION

The doctrine of frustration provides a remedy where, during the life of the contract, and without the fault of either party, some event occurs, which makes further performance impossible or illegal or which makes the contract radically different from what was originally undertaken.

The contract is then discharged and both parties are relieved of further duties. The idea of frustration is to provide a fairer sharing of the burden of loss than may be possible through breach. However, the courts must be aware in allowing the doctrine that parties do not simply use it to escape from an unwanted contract, or to create an unfair position for the other party on discharge.

66 Obligations were once very strict **99**

At one time the law took a very rigid view of a party's obligations under a contract. They were considered 'absolute' in the sense that even if some event occurred completely outside a party's control, making it impossible to fulfil their duties, liability would remain with that party.

This sometimes harsh approach is evident in the seventeenth-century case of *Paradine v Jane (1647),* but an inroad into this rigid stance came with the case of *Taylor v Caldwell (1863),* where a concert hall was hired, but it burned down before the date of hire.

The three aspects of the definition of the doctrine of frustration, which arise from the definition will be considered in turn:

- impossibility;
- illegality;
- radical change in circumstances.

Impossibility

A contract may become impossible in three ways:

1 **The subject matter is destroyed** – the case of *Taylor v Caldwell* (above) is a good example of this. Because the hall was destroyed in the fire during the life of the contract, and by no fault of either party, the contract became impossible to fulfil.

2 **The subject matter is unavailable** – if the person or thing required for the performance of the contract becomes unavailable, the contract will be frustrated. An example is *Morgan v Manser (1948)* where a compere, Charlie Chester, was called away for war service. This case also shows that a factor to consider is the length of time of unavailability in proportion to the whole of the contract.

3 **A party dies** – if the contract is of a personal nature, then the death of the party performing the personal obligation will frustrate the contract.

Note that if a particular method of carrying out the contractual duties is essential to the performance of the contract, and this method then becomes impossible, the contract will be frustrated. However, if the situation is just that the change of method is less convenient or more expensive, then this will not amount to frustration (see *Tsakiroglou Co Ltd v Noblee Thorl GmbH (1962)* (below)).

Illegality

Frustration will discharge a contract if, during its lifetime, the law is changed in such a way that the basis of the contract becomes illegal. This is likely to happen if:

- legislation is passed during the currency of the contract (after it is made but before it is performed);
- if war breaks out during the currency of the contract, and performance would amount to trading with the enemy (which would be illegal).

Radical change in circumstances

This group of cases probably shows one of the boundaries of the doctrine of frustration, and many of them arose out of the postponement of the coronation of King Edward VII (because of illness). A contract will be frustrated where, because of surrounding circumstances and events it becomes futile. Note that it is not impossible, or illegal, just completely pointless. Compare *Krell v Henry (1903)* where a room hired under a contract was no longer needed, with *Herne Bay Steam Boat Co v Hutton (1903)* where a contract to hire a boat for a pleasure trip and to see the king's naval review still had some point to it.

Limits to frustration

To avoid abuse of the doctrine, certain limits or restraints are imposed by the courts.

- An important limitation arises through the case of *Tsakiroglou Co Ltd v Noblee Thorl GmbH (1962)* which involved the use of the Suez Canal. The principle emerged that if a contract merely becomes more onerous, that is more difficult or expensive, or takes longer to perform, then this will not amount to frustration.

- As frustration arises, by definition, when neither party is at fault, it follows that if a party induced the frustrating event, then it cannot be relied on to discharge the contract (*Maritime National Fish Ltd v Ocean Trawlers Ltd (1935)*).

- If an event which is alleged to have frustrated the contract is expressly provided for in a clause in the contract, then this takes effect and the doctrine of frustration does not apply. But note that such clauses are interpreted narrowly (*Metropolitan Water Board v Dick, Kerr and Co (1918)*).

- Where an event is foreseen, or should have been foreseen because a party has special knowledge, the doctrine of frustration may not apply (*Walton Harvey v Walker and Homfrays (1931)*).

The legal effect of frustration

The Law Reform (Frustrated Contracts) Act 1943

The legal effect of the contract being frustrated is that it is discharged regarding any remaining contractual obligations, but not *ab initio* (from the beginning). The area is now covered by **the Law Reform (Frustrated Contracts) Act 1943**. **(**Note that the Act only deals with the effects of frustration. It is still necessary to rely on the common law to decide if a contract is frustrated or not.)

The Act was passed to apportion fairly the losses when a contract is discharged by frustration. Its main provisions are as follows:

- Money paid before the frustrating event is recoverable, and money payable before the frustrating event ceases to be payable (s. 1(2)).

- If the party to whom money has been paid or is payable had incurred expenses in performance, before the frustration, the court may award them such expenses up to the limit of the money paid or payable before the event (s. 1(2)). However, if nothing was paid or payable before the frustrating event, they will not be able to recover expenses.

- Where a party has gained a valuable benefit (other than money) under the contract before the frustrating event, they may be required to pay a just sum for it. This will apply whether or not anything was paid or payable before the frustrating event (s. 1(3)). However, Goff J suggested in *B P Exploration Co (Libya) v Hunt (No 2) (1983)* that where subject matter is totally destroyed, e.g. by fire, the valuable benefit will be nil.

The Act does not apply to charterparties, contracts of insurance or contracts for the sale of specific foods which are frustrated by the goods perishing.

REMEDIES

DAMAGES

The most usual remedy for an innocent party to seek as a result of a breach of contract is damages, and may be claimed as a right at common law.

What can be recovered?

Damages can be:

- **liquidated** – where the amount to be awarded in a particular breach has already been decided by the parties;

- **unliquidated** – where no fixed amount has been decided – these can be **nominal** (a minimum amount), **exemplary** (an unusually large amount), or **substantial** (the normal claim).

BASIS OF DAMAGES

Loss of bargain basis

The normal basis for awarding damages in contract is for loss of bargain. The court aims to put the plaintiff into the position which would have been achieved if the contract had been performed correctly (*Robinson v Harman (1848)*). This supports the view that the idea behind the law of contract is to uphold contracts where possible.

Reliance basis

In some circumstances – these are exceptional – damages are awarded on a tortious basis, and the aim then is to restore the injured party (as far as possible) to the position which would have existed if the contract had not been formed. The plaintiff is compensated for expenses incurred in reliance on the contract, which have been wasted by the defendant's actions. This approach is used in awarding damages for misrepresentation.

CONTRIBUTORY NEGLIGENCE

What if both parties are to blame?

Whilst it is established that in tort damages can be apportioned by the court on the ground of contributory negligence under the Law Reform (Contributory Negligence) Act 1945, this probably does not extend to breach of contract (*Basildon D C v J E Lesser (Properties) Ltd (1985)*). However, the Law Commission have reported that this could be a useful measure for the future. Note also that sometimes apportionment can be achieved via a different route, e.g. in capacity and frustration, by giving the courts discretion in awarding of damages under a statutory provision.

MENTAL DISTRESS

For some time the situation has been that damages in contract could not be recovered as a general principle for mental distress (something more tangible had to be shown, such as pain and suffering from personal injury, or physical inconvenience). However, where the very nature of the contract indicates that the benefit is of a less tangible nature, and the loss ensuing will be non-pecuniary (i.e. not a direct financial loss), such as enjoyment of a holiday, damages can be recovered for disappointment, vexation and mental distress (see *Jackson v Horizon Holidays (1975)* and *Jarvis v Swann Tours (1973)* both concerning compensation for holidays, and *Thake v Maurice (1986)* concerning compensation for a pregnancy and birth following a vasectomy operation).

However, regarding contracts of employment, damages will not be awarded for injury to feelings for wrongful dismissal. This was the decision of the House of Lords in *Addis v Gramophone Co Ltd (1909)* and after some uncertainty was confirmed by the Court of Appeal in *Bliss v S E Thames Regional Health Authority (1985)*.

EXAMINATION QUESTIONS

1 As a general rule contracting parties must perform their obligations completely and exactly. Discuss the ways in which the courts have both applied and avoided this principle. (NEAB)

2 Is the doctrine of frustration merely an excuse for people to escape from a contract simply because things have not turned out as they expected? (UODLE)

3 Critically explain what is meant by 'discharge by breach'. If one party to a contract purports to repudiate his or her obligations, what option does the injured party have?
(UODLE)

4 Dawn and June are keen birdwatchers. They decide to spend two weeks' holiday watching birds in a famous wildfowl reserve. They arrange to rent a cottage owned by Twitcher, which is two miles from the reserve. The rent is £150 per week, £50 of which is payable in advance with the remainder payable on arrival at the cottage. When booking the cottage Dawn and June tell Twitcher that they intend to spend most of their time visiting the wildfowl reserve.

Two weeks before they are due to go on holiday, there is a fire at the reserve which destroys the habitat and kills most of the birds. Dawn and June write to Twitcher cancelling the holiday and requesting the return of the £50 deposit. Twitcher refuses to return the deposit and claims an additional £75 which he has spent on decorating the cottage in preparation for their stay.

Advise Dawn and June. (UODLE)

5 Zena buys a fruit farm and agrees to supply William with a specified quantity of various fruits per year over a three-year period. William owns a processing plant and produces jams and other products from the fruit which he expects from Zena. During the first year the summer is extremely hot, and most of Zena's crop is destroyed by a very bad fire. She makes no effort to find an alternative source of fruit, and after two weeks it becomes apparent that she will not be able to keep to her part of the agreement. William is unable at this stage to obtain another supplier of fruit.

Advise William as to whether the contract will be frustrated. (UODLE)

ANSWERS TO QUESTIONS

OUTLINE ANSWERS TO SELECTED QUESTIONS

Question 1

Introduce with a very brief reference to the four methods of discharging a contract, emphasising that performance as the primary aim of the contracting parties, as this is why the contract is created.

Explain that performance must be:

- exact – *Re Moore and Landauer*; and
- complete – *Cutter v Powell*.

These are examples of the way in which the courts have **applied** the principle. Comment on the harshness of the rule (it may now be mitigated somewhat by the doctrine of frustration), and show how modifications have arisen through case law (thus showing how the courts have **avoided** the principle):

- severable contracts – *Vlierboom v Chapman* compared with *Ritchie v Atkinson*;
- substantial performance – *Boone v Eyre* and *Hoenig v Isaacs* and explain how payment takes place;
- acceptance of partial performance – *Christy v Row* and *Sumpter v Hedges* and explain payment on a *quantum meruit* basis;
- prevention of performance – *Planche v Colburn*;
- tender of performance – *Startup v Macdonald*;
- time of performance – Sale of Goods Act 1979;
- vicarious performance – *Edwards v Newlands*.

Discuss in conclusion (and in response to the question) the general aim of the courts to uphold contracts where possible, and therefore the need for the modifications to the general principles as a way of 'avoiding' their strict application.

Question 2

Introduce with a very brief reference to the four methods of discharge, and explain in general terms the circumstances when frustration will operate. Define frustration accurately. Show how it operates – compare *Paradine v Jane* with *Taylor v Caldwell*. Respond to the question – frustration is aimed at sharing loss in a fair and equitable way between parties. The courts therefore will not allow the doctrine to be used in an unfair or inequitable way, simply as an escape route for an inconvenient contract. They have placed restrictions on its wide interpretation in various ways:

- radically different circumstances – compare *Krell v Henry* with *Herne Bay Steam Boat Co v Hutton*;
- more onerous contract – *Tsakiroglou v Noblee Thorl*;
- self induced frustration – *Maritime National Fish v Ocean Trawlers*;
- express provision – *Metropolitan Water Board v Dick, Kerr and Co*;
- event foreseen – *Walton Harvey v Walker and Homfrays*;
- the Law Reform (Frustrated Contracts) Act 1943 – this itself is a limit to the abuse of the doctrine, as it leaves the final balancing of loss to the courts, and presumably they would not allow a party to profit from the abuse of the doctrine. This being so, the doctrine is unlikely to be used in this way.

TUTOR'S ANSWER

Question 4

Dawn and June have a contract with Twitcher to rent a holiday cottage for £300. The purpose of this contract, from the point of view of Dawn and June, is to have a holiday and watch birds at a reserve. As the reserve is now presumably out of action, or at least not in the state which they imagined it to be, the contract in the eyes of Dawn and June has lost much of its purpose. They have already written to Twitcher and cancelled their holiday, so will wish to know whether the contract is frustrated.

In these circumstances the law would have at one time taken a strict view, and held Dawn and June liable, as seen in *Paradine v Jane*, where rent was due on accommodation even though it was not available. However, the leading case of *Taylor v Caldwell* modified this strict approach, by allowing a contract to be discharged by frustration where a fire destroyed a concert hall which was to be hired for a show. It can be seen from *Taylor v Caldwell* that this contract was totally impossible to complete, as the hall was destroyed. Similarly, in *Morgan v Manser* a contract to perform as a compere was impossible because the performer was called away for war service. However, something less than total impossibility may still amount to frustration.

Frustration, then, is where, during the life of a contract, an event occurs, which is not caused by the fault of either party, which makes performance impossible, illegal, or radically different from that envisaged by the parties.

Illegality is not relevant here, and it can be seen that although the use of the wildfowl reserve is probably impossible (and this was made a point of the contract, in negotiations with Twitcher), the contract for the hire of the cottage can continue, and Dawn and June could still obtain some benefit from it. So the only reason for frustration would be if the contract was now radically different from that intended, to the extent of being pointless.

This type of situation arose in a series of cases which arose in 1903 concerning the cancellation of a coronation procession. In *Krell v Henry* a room had been hired overlooking the procession route in London, and when the procession was cancelled, the contract was held to be frustrated, as it was now completely pointless.

On the other hand, in the case of *Herne Bay Steam Boat Co v Hutton* a boat had been hired to take a party for a pleasure cruise and to watch the king's naval review. When the review was cancelled, the contract was held not to be frustrated because there was still some purpose to it, in the form of the pleasure cruise.

This is the basis on which the court would need to decide whether the contract for the holiday cottage would be frustrated, i.e. is the contract now pointless? The court certainly will not allow parties to avoid a contract merely because it is not now wanted, e.g. because it has become more onerous, as in *Noblee Thorl's* case.

If it is decided that the contract has been breached by Dawn and June, then they would be required to pay full compensation to Twitcher. However, if the contract is held frustrated, then the Law Reform (Frustrated Contracts) Act 1943 will apply. At one time the common law let the loss in a frustrated contract 'lie where it fell', but this resulted at times in hardship or injustice to individuals. Now legislation gives the courts discretion to attempt to share loss where the ending of a contract is not the fault of one party.

Under the Law Reform (Frustrated Contracts) Act 1943 the following provisions apply:

1 Any money paid may be recovered.
2 Any money due is no longer due.
3 The court may order a reasonable sum to be paid for any expenses incurred.
4 The court may order a just sum to be paid for any valuable benefit obtained.

According to these provisions, should the contract be frustrated, then the £50 would be returned to Dawn and June. The remainder of the £300 would not be payable. The money spent on decorating could be seen as a necessary expense, if it was specifically for Dawn and June's visit, and then the court could order payment. However, this could also be seen as a benefit to Twitcher, as his cottage is now improved to the value of £75. It is therefore satisfactory that this final 'balancing' of the sharing of the loss is left in the hands of the court, as they would be in full knowledge of what exactly had taken place, and order payment accordingly.

Dawn and June, therefore, would be advised, as they do not wish to continue with the holiday, to claim that the contract is frustrated. If the court did not feel that the contract had enough purpose to it, following *Krell v Henry*, then the Law Reform (Frustrated Contracts) Act 1943 will apply, and the loss be shared according to its provisions.

STUDENT'S ANSWER WITH TUTOR'S COMMENTS

Question 3

> Discharge of a contract could be defined as bringing the contract to an end and could take various forms. Contracts could be discharged under the doctrine of frustration, or by agreement, or performance or breach.
>
> A breach of contract could arise where one of the parties failed to perform one or more of the obligations on him or her under the contract, and this is called an actual breach, i.e. where something is happening at the moment such as non-performance, defective performance or an untrue statement.
>
> A breach may also occur before performance is due to take place, i.e. where one party informs the other of their intention not to perform his part of the contract. In such a case, the breach is described as an anticipatory breach. It may be explicit, as in *Hochster v De La Tour*, where the defendant agreed in April to employ the plaintiff as a courier commencing in

66 Good introduction, explaining breach 99

June. In May the defendant informed the plaintiff that he would not require his services. The plaintiff claimed damages and succeeded.

It is important to stress that it is the promise to perform which is binding. Therefore if someone indicates their intention not to perform, the other party can sue immediately. However, the right to sue could be lost, as in *Avery v Bowden*, where the plaintiff lost his right to sue by choosing to keep the contract alive, and it later became frustrated because of an outbreak of war.

Alternatively, a breach may be implicit, where the defendant's conduct indicates that he will not complete performance. In *Frost v Knight* the defendant, having agreed to marry the plaintiff on his father's death, broke off the engagement during the father's lifetime. It was held that the plaintiff was at that point entitled to damages.

In order to establish that a breach of contract amounts to a repudiation, it must be shown that the party at fault has beyond reasonable doubt indicated that he has no longer any intention to fulfil his part of the contract (*Woodar Investment v Wimpey*).

The consequences of breach depend on the type of term that is breached, i.e. was the term fundamental to the contract or was it a less important one? A breach of a less important term, also known as a warranty, entitles the innocent party to sue for damages only. A breach of others which are more serious to the contract, i.e. conditions, entitles the innocent party to choose between claiming damages or treating himself as discharged from the contract. Serious breaches of this nature are generally described as repudiatory breaches.

In *Poussard v Spiers and Pond* the plaintiff was entitled to repudiate for breach of condition. Blackburn J said 'failure on the plaintiff's part went to the root of the matter and discharged the defendant'. Unlike in *Bettini v Gye* where the plaintiff could only be compensated by damages since it was a breach of warranty and did not 'go to the root of the matter'.

Discharge by breach can only occur where one of the parties either fails to perform one or more of the obligations on him under the contract or indicates that he does not intend to perform. Once a repudiatory breach has been established, then the innocent party can decide to end the contract or to affirm and claim damages.

66 Brief details of the case would be useful here as an example 99

66 Good – consequence of breach of different terms outlined 99

66 This could be fuller, with more detail on the consequences of breach of different terms 99

66 Reasonable conclusion 99

Tutor's Comments

This answer is clear and explains the basis of breach very well. The material is obviously understood, and arranged in a logical sequence. More detail would be welcome on the significance of the court finding a particular term to be a condition or warranty, and on the uncertainty, on breach, of an innominate term (see Chapter 16 for this – the two topics are closely linked). It is also important to remember the first word of the question, '**critically** explain …'. In view of this some further link could be made between breach and other forms of discharge, along the lines of: '… the courts aim to uphold contracts if possible, so will consider whether substantial or partial performance has taken place, or if an agreement has been formed, or whether frustration is appropriate. If none of these apply, then non-performance will amount to breach.'

On the whole the legal knowledge is good, and the answer is of a grade B standard.

A review sheet for this chapter can be found on p. 219.

19

GENERAL PRINCIPLES OF TORT

AIMS AND PRINCIPLES

VICARIOUS LIABILITY

GENERAL DEFENCES

GETTING STARTED

Tort is an area of law which deals with civil wrongs. It covers wrongs between individuals, which do not generally amount to crimes, but for which a remedy is needed. Tortious liability will arise when a wrong is done which amounts to a breach of a duty of care, towards a person whom the law considers to need protection – a 'neighbour'. So various questions must be asked:

- What rights and duties exist? (or – what must I do or be careful not to do?)
- To whom are these duties owed? (or – who is my neighbour?)
- Has there been a breach of a duty of some kind?
- What damage has been caused?
- How can this be remedied?

Justification for vicarious liability –

- no clear a convincing rationale for v.l.
- deviates from prevalent fault based liability
- perhaps employer in control of behaviour of employee –
  but many employees perform v. skilled tasks.
- perhaps employer careless in selecting employee?
  but liability not based on this premise
  a even competent employee can be negligent once.
- social convenience a rough justice
- employers greater ability to pay damages
- employers can pass costs of insurance premiums down to public through higher prices
- moral justification – employee inflicts loss on plaintiff while carrying out employers business. As employer gains benefit from employees work, he should also bear costs arising from accidents.

ESSENTIAL PRINCIPLES

AIMS AND PRINCIPLES

The word 'tort' generally means a wrong of some kind, and in English law is where a wrong has been done for which a legal remedy will be provided. Of course, a number of other areas of law could fall within that very broad definition, as in both criminal law and the law of contract a wrong could exist for which the law provides a remedy, so a somewhat narrower working definition is needed, and a comparison with other areas of law.

The general idea of tortious liability is a breach of a legal duty for which a remedy is provided in compensation. Professor Winfield defined tort as follows:

'Tortious liability arises from the breach of a duty primarily fixed by law; this duty is towards persons generally and its breach is repressible by an action for unliquidated damages.'

This definition shows the basis on which a remedy is given, in that the court compensates the plaintiff for the breach of duty. The aim of the remedy of damages in tort, then, is to restore the plaintiff, as far as money can do so, to the position in which they would have been had the wrong not happened.

COMPARISONS

The general aims of tort are therefore quite different from the aims of the law of contract, which are to support contracts and to put the plaintiff into the position which they would have been in had the contract been fulfilled. They are even further removed from the general aims of the criminal law, which are to punish the offender and prevent further offences.

Comparison with criminal law

There is therefore considerable overlap with the criminal law, for example in assault and battery, and comparisons can be made between these areas of law, including:

- In tort an individual brings an action against another, whereas in criminal law the state takes action against the defendant.
- In tort a wrong is against an individual, rather than against the state, as in criminal law.
- In tort an individual found liable pays compensation to the other, whereas in criminal law a defendant found guilty is punished.

Comparison with the law of contract

The law of tort is also close in nature to the law of contract, for example in fraudulent misrepresentation and in assessing the remoteness of damage, but between these areas, too, differences arise and comparisons may be made, including:

- Tort protects rights and compensates for wrongs suffered, whereas the law of contract supports and enforces contracts.
- In tort rights and duties are imposed by law between an individual and somebody often unknown to them, whereas in contracts rights and duties are largely agreed by the parties.
- Damages in tort restore the individual to the position they were in before the wrong occurred, whereas damages in contract compensate for loss of contractual rights.

THE CONCEPT OF FAULT

One area of present debate is the concept of finding of **fault**. This is an integral part of some torts, notably negligence, and it is argued by some that it would be better to compensate obvious victims without the need to prove fault. It has been suggested that our society should reconsider the way in which we deal with life's emergencies, either publicly, on large scale, such as a plane crash or ferry disaster, or individually, such as a road accident. This is an attractive proposition, but carries problems of defining boundaries and paying the cost of compensation.

VICARIOUS LIABILITY

Liability may arise in tort not just for a person's own actions, but also for the actions of another. For this to arise there must be a special relationship between the person who did the wrong act and the one who is now liable for it. This liability most often arises in employer-employee (traditionally referred to as 'master and servant') situations, this being justified for a number of reasons:

- The employer is in a better position to pay than the employee (a plaintiff will come to 'the end of the road' in a claim if the person being sued has no money) and, as the employer has profits from the business, they should deal with such problems.

- Today the employer is likely to be insured, the cost of insurance being passed on in the unit price of goods or services.

- The responsibility is likely to act as an encouragement to the employer to ensure high standards in the organisation.

- The employer has the responsibility of choosing competent employees.

For this liability to arise the relationship of employer and employee must be established (see Chapter 23).

Having established such a relationship, the employee must then be seen to be acting in the **course of employment**. Most everyday claims will fall clearly within this requirement, such as a builder's labourer who carelessly splashes concrete on to a customer's car, but some cases are much less clear. Some guidelines exist from existing decisions:

❝May be liable …❞

- An employer may be liable if the employee is performing a lawful task in an unauthorised way (see _Limpus v London General Omnibus Co (1862)_ concerning racing bus drivers, and _Rose v Plenty (1976)_ involving a milkman who allowed a 13 year old to help with deliveries. The employer was liable for injury to the boy even though the milkman should not have had the help).

- An employer may be liable if the employee is benefiting personally during the course of employment (see _Lloyd v Grace Smith (1912)_ where a firm of solicitors was liable for the actions of a clerk in a mortgage fraud).

- An employer may be liable for an employee's action in the course of employment even if it was carried out in a negligent or foolish way (see _Century Insurance v Northern Ireland Road Transport Board (1942)_ regarding an employer who was liable for damage caused by an employee who threw down a lighted match whilst petrol was being transferred from his tanker into a fuel tank at a garage).

❝Will not be liable …❞

The employer will not, on the other hand, be liable if the employee is not acting in the course of employment. Examples include:

- Where the employee is merely travelling to or from work. However, some such journeys may be part of the employment, as in _Smith v Stages (1989)_ where the employees were paid for a journey to Wales and overnight stay, in order to carry out some work for the employer.

- Where the employee does something which he is not entitled to do, as in _Beard v London General Omnibus (1900)_ when a bus conductor tried driving a bus.

- Where the employee is 'on a frolic of his own', as in _Hilton v Thomas Burton (1961)_ where some workmen took an unauthorised break to visit a café and on the way back one of the men was killed in an accident resulting from negligent driving.

PRIMARY LIABILITY

An employer is not liable vicariously for the actions of an independent contractor, but in certain circumstances may be liable directly. This is known as **primary liability**. An employer must choose a contractor of reasonable competence, and if the employer condones a tortious act by a contractor, then the employer may become liable.

❝Non-delegable duties❞

In addition some duties are considered to be **non-delegable**, that is too important to delegate to another. Then it is the task of the employer to see that care is taken. These may arise in a number of ways:

- by law, mainly statute but also sometimes at common law;
- where an activity is extremely hazardous;
- where activity is on or adjoins a highway, e.g. repairing a street lamp.

GENERAL DEFENCES

It may be that when an allegation is made against a person, there is a lawful excuse for behaviour which would amount to the tort. Some defences are available for specific torts, but some are available for more than one tort, and are known as general defences. The more important ones are as follows.

Handwritten margin notes:

Rose v Plenty compared to Twine v Beauis Express Ltd (1946)

T v B - sign on side of vehicle stating who could be carried ∴ plaintiff was trespasser and owed no duty of care. Also lift was not given for purpose beneficial to employer.

R v P - defines scope of employment in wide terms.

The cases seem irreconcilable

DETOURS – when not part of employment - No vicarious liability. (Storey v Ashton 1869).
When going about employers business, then company liable (Williams v Hemphill Ltd 1966 Bus driver detoured for children passengers pleasure).

Volenti as a defence

Consent, or what is more formally known as *volenti*, from the Latin phrase *volenti non fit injuria*. This arises where a plaintiff has consented to taking a risk and cannot then claim damages for injury. The courts appear to be using this less, reluctant to deny a plaintiff a remedy altogether, and relying much more on the use of contributory negligence to achieve similar results.

Sporting events

Sporting events often raise the issue of *volenti*, and it is common for a sportsman willingly to accept the risks of the game. However, the risk must be within reasonable bounds according to the rules of the game, and a player could sue if behaviour went well beyond those bounds – see *Condon v Basi (1985)* concerning a tackle well beyond expectations. Similar principles can also apply to spectators, depending on their own actions, and on whether the organisers have taken reasonable precautions (see *Wilks v Cheltenham Home Guard Motor Cycle and Light Car Club (1971)*).

Rescuers

In rescue cases, where a person goes to the rescue of another and is hurt, *volenti* will not normally apply. In *Haynes v Harwood (1935)* a policeman was compensated for injury received in attempting to stop two bolting horses and trying to prevent injury to others. He acted out of a moral duty, not a willing acceptance of risk of injury.

Employees

Similarly, employees will not be assumed to have willingly accepted risk where work is carried on working in relatively dangerous situations, as there is an unequal relationship (see *Smith v Baker (1891)* where an employee claimed for injury for rocks falling from a crane).

Drunk drivers

Lifts with drunk drivers have caused some difficulty, but are now largely covered by legislation. However, in *Morris v Murray (1990)* volenti was held to apply since the plaintiff knew that the pilot had consumed a huge amount of alcohol and still agreed to go for a ride in his aircraft.

Contributory negligence

Since the Law Reform (Contributory Negligence) Act 1945 the courts now have a useful way of apportioning loss (see *Sayers v Harlow UDC (1958)* where an elderly woman stood on a toilet roll holder to get out of a toilet. See also Chapter 20).

Act of God

An 'act of God' is a naturally occurring event out of the control of people, such as a flash of lightning or a flash flood. This will be a defence in appropriate cases (see *Nicholls v Marsland (1876)* concerning a storm 'greater and more violent than any within the memory of witnesses').

Novus actus interveniens

A new act may come between the defendant and the eventual harm caused, and break what is known as the **chain of causation**. However, if the eventual harm was foreseen then the defence will not apply (*Scott v Sheppard (1773)* where a lighted squib was thrown on to a market stall, and it was picked up and thrown on twice before it exploded and caused harm).

Necessity

Where a person acts out of necessity in preventing further harm this may be a defence (see *Cope v Sharpe* where there was a defence to trespass over land where this took place to prevent harm to the plaintiff's pheasants. See further *Rigby v Chief Constable of Northamptonshire (1985)* where necessity was a defence to trespass and for police use of CS gas to force out a dangerous psychopath).

Inevitable accident

Where nothing could have been done to avoid the harm, then accident will be a defence (see *Stanley v Powell (1891)* where a shot at a pheasant hit a tree and bounced back hitting the plaintiff).

EXAMINATION QUESTIONS

1 Critically examine the circumstances in which the law of torts determines that employers are vicariously liable for the acts of their staff. (UODLE)

2 Adrian has been employed for five years by Daily Deliveries Ltd as a deliveryman. It is a term of Adrian's employment that he may not carry any person other than employees of Daily Deliveries Ltd on his van. In fact, since his employment started, Adrian has been helped on Saturdays, and during school and college holidays, by his son James who is aged 19. James has never been employed by Daily Deliveries Ltd and is aware of the restriction in Adrian's contract of employment. Last month James was helping Adrian as usual when, owing to Adrian's negligent driving of the delivery van on their lunch break, there was an accident in which James was seriously injured.

Daily Deliveries Ltd has now told James that the company has no liability to pay damages to him.

Advise James. (UODLE)

3 George recently had a swimming pool installed in land at the back of his house. The pool was designed by Harris Associates and the construction work was carried out by Truebuild Ltd. Because of unforeseen problems with the land, the work took much longer than originally anticipated and there was noise, dust and obstruction of the rather narrow lane which gave access both to George's land and to that of four of his neighbours.

When the pool was completed, it soon became obvious that the filter mechanism did not operate efficiently and the water was frequently very cloudy. In one part of the pool, the design created a shallow ledge in an otherwise deep area. While visiting for the first time since the pool was ready, George's brother, Frank, dived into this area and severely damaged his neck and back.

The incident was witnessed only by John, George's neighbour, with whom he was on very bad terms. John rushed over to the pool, jumped in and dragged Frank out. In doing so, John cut his arm on a sharp edge on the tiles of the pool and injured his knee which was still weak from a recent operation.

a) Explain what rights George's neighbours may have had in connection with the disturbance caused by the construction work. (10 marks)

b) Consider whether Frank could succeed in an action against Harris Associates and against Truebuild Ltd to recover damages for his injuries. (10 marks)

c) Consider whether John could bring any action to recover damages for the injuries he suffered in going to Frank's aid. (15 marks)

d) Of what legal significance is the fact that Harris Associates is a partnership whilst Truebuild Ltd. is a company? (5 marks)

e) How far do you consider that the law would have ensured a just solution in each of the cases above? (10 marks)

(AEB)

ANSWERS TO QUESTIONS

OUTLINE ANSWER

Question 1

- Introduce the topic of vicarious liability, explaining that it applies generally to employers.
- Explain why it operates in this context, e.g. employees may not have the resources to meet claims; they may have been directed to work in a certain way.
- Consider briefly the scope of employment and the tests to determine who is an employee.
- Outline the situations in which an employer may be liable, e.g. carrying out a lawful task in an unlawful way.

- Outline situations where the employer will not be liable, e.g. travelling to and from work, or where the employee is on a 'frolic of his own'.
- Very briefly refer to primary liability.
- Consider very briefly the defences.
- Conclude with some assessment of the worth of vicarious liability in the employment situation.

STUDENT'S ANSWER WITH TUTOR'S COMMENTS

Question 2

> 66 Forms a conclusion here, which would be better left to the end of the answer 99

> 66 Brief details of the cases should be included, if relevant 99

Negligence is based on the case of *Donoghue v Stevenson*. The neighbour principle is that a duty of care is owed to anyone if it is reasonably foreseeable that they would be affected by an act or omission. Daily Deliveries might not have known that James went in the van but Adrian did, and he was an employee of the firm so that makes them vicariously liable.

Vicarious liability is when an employer is liable for the actions of his employee while in the course of his employment. He does not have to endorse the actions, and may have forbidden them, as in *Limpus v London General Omnibus*, or, more relevantly, *Rose v Plenty*, but the actions must be done during the course of employment.

Not surprisingly, in *Warren v Henley* an employee who attacked a customer was held not to be acting as part of his employment. However a porter who dragged a passenger off the wrong train was held to be acting in the course of employment, even though his actions were not really approved of.

The actions must be done during the time of employment. In *Smith v Sturges* the employers were liable because they paid travel expenses.

To be in the course of employment the employees must not be 'on a frolic of their own', a phrase used in a case where they went out in an employer's car during a break. The employer could still be liable for things happening in break time, if they are reasonable and therefore in the course of employment.

In *Lister v Ronston Ice and Cold Storage* an accident was caused by a son to a father. The father sued the company and the company sued the son and got its money back.

So Daily Deliveries is not liable as James' employer but through Adrian, who caused the accident.

Daily Deliveries could claim the defence of *volenti non fit injuria* or contributory negligence to lessen the claim. *Volenti* is a term which means that a person comes willingly to a risk and therefore cannot claim compensation. They have to be aware of all the facts. In *Morris v Murray* the plaintiff was aware that the defendant was drunk but agreed to go up in his plane anyway. James was aware that Adrian was driving during work time, but did not know that he was going to drive negligently, so a defence of *volenti* might not work.

> 66 A little wider than the question requires 99

James was aware of his father's restriction in the contract of employment and at 19 is old enough to apply for a job with Daily Deliveries himself. Daily Deliveries may also use the defence of contributory negligence which would reduce his compensation if he contributed to the accident. In *Froom v Butcher* compensation was reduced by 20% for not wearing a seat belt. It is possible to be 100% to blame, as in *Pitts v Hunt* where the plaintiff drank with the defendant and encouraged him to ride fast and negligently on his motorbike.

> 66 This is not very relevant to the question 99

The protection claimed by an employee cannot apply to James. In the multiple test in *The Ready Mix Concrete* case it is stated that if a person is able to decide his own work, who to employ and holidays, then he is not an employee but an independent contractor. He would also fail the 'control' test in *Mersey Docks and Harbour Board v Coggins and Grilleth* which held that he would be employed by the persons controlling his actions. However in *O'Kelly v Trusthouse Forte* it was said that a person was more likely to be an employee for the purposes of negligence than for the purposes of the Employment Protection Act 1989.

In conclusion, it is possible that the driving during the lunch break is in the course of employment, and then Daily Deliveries will be liable. James must bring the action within three years under the Limitation Act 1990. There must be a duty of care and a breach of that duty, and a higher standard is owed to the young or disabled, but we do not know of James being either of these. If Daily Deliveries is not liable it may still be possible to obtain compensation from Adrian, for example if the van belonged to him, through insurance.

Tutor's Comments

The answer addresses the main issues, and is good in parts. However, it goes outside the question and becomes irrelevant in places. In others it is relevant, but lacks depth. Better use could be made of case law, comparing facts from decided cases with the situation in the problem. Overall an answer of a good grade C standard.

A review sheet for this chapter can be found on p. 220.

NEGLIGENCE AND OCCUPIERS' LIABILITY

NEGLIGENCE

NERVOUS SHOCK CASES

ECONOMIC LOSS

OCCUPIERS' LIABILITY

GETTING STARTED

The law of negligence has been developed by the judges during the twentieth century. The basic concept is that where the plaintiff or their property is damaged through the careless act or omission of another, the plaintiff should be able to claim compensation. It covers a wide variety of situations including car accidents and medical negligence. To succeed in a negligence claim, a plaintiff needs to prove three things:

■ the defendant owed them a **duty of care**;

■ the defendant broke that duty of care; and

■ as a result of that breach the plaintiff suffered damage.

The concept of owing a duty of care has been through many changes with the judges opening up new areas where a duty is held to exist. However, in some cases, particularly nervous shock and economic loss, the courts have retreated somewhat and put firmer boundaries on what is needed to succeed in such a case.

   Parliament has not played any major role in the development of the tort of negligence, except in the area of occupiers' liability, where there is a duty owed by the occupier of premises to visitors. The other main statutory intervention in the tort of negligence has been in the health and safety rules in employment, although it is still possible for employees to rely on the tort of negligence when claiming compensation for injuries suffered at work.

   Examination questions involve:

■ either a discussion of the development of the law and how satisfactory it is; or

■ a problem situation in which the rules of negligence need to be applied.

ESSENTIAL PRINCIPLES

The modern law of negligence may be said to date from the case of *Donoghue v Stevenson (1932)*. In that case Mrs Donoghue became ill after drinking ginger beer from a bottle which had a decomposing snail in it. She had not bought the drink herself, so she was unable to rely on a breach of contract. Instead she sued the manufacturers of the ginger beer under the tort of negligence, claiming that they owed her a duty of care. The House of Lords decided the case in her favour and the importance of the case lies in the wide *ratio decidendi* given by Lord Atkin. He said that: 'You must take care to avoid acts or omissions which you can reasonably foresee would be likely to injure your neighbour.'

DUTY OF CARE

The basis of negligence is that the defendant owes the plaintiff a duty of care. There are four factors which need to be considered when deciding whether there is a duty of care, though not necessarily all will be referred to in any particular case. These are:

- **foresight** – is it reasonably foreseeable that the plaintiff will be injured by the defendant's acts or omissions? (*Bourhill v Young (1943)*);
- **proximity** – the parties must be sufficiently proximate (close) for the duty to exist;
- **whether the imposition of a duty of care** would be 'fair, just and reasonable' (*Marc Rich & Co v Bishop Rock Marine Co Ltd (1995)*);
- **public policy considerations** – would the recognition of a duty open the 'floodgates'?

'Egg shell skull' cases

If it is reasonably foreseeable that a primary victim may be injured, then the fact that the plaintiff is particularly vulnerable in some way is irrelevant. This means that a plaintiff who has a very thin skull and is therefore more seriously injured than a 'normal' person may claim for all the injuries suffered. This is true even if the precise type of injury is unforeseeable, as in *Page v Smith (1995)*, where the plaintiff was involved in a road accident caused by the defendant's negligence. The plaintiff was physically unhurt but claimed that the accident had worsened the ME from which he suffered.

BREACH OF DUTY

Even if the plaintiff succeeds in showing that the defendant owes a duty of care, this is not enough. There must be a breach of that duty. Deciding whether the defendant has acted negligently is based on an objective test of what the 'reasonable' man would do. The courts will consider:

- **the magnitude of the risk** – if there is only a small risk of the happening, then there is no liability (*Bolton v Stone (1951)*);
- **practicality of precautions** – if the cost of taking precautions is out of all proportion to the risk involved the courts are unlikely to impose liability (*Latimer v AEC Ltd (1953)*);
- **any special skill possessed by the defendant** – a professional will be judged by the standard of the reasonable man with those skills; this means that doctors will be judged by accepted medical standards (*Bolam v Friern Hospital Management Committee (1957)*), but a learner driver will be judged by normal driving standards and the inexperience discounted (*Nettleship v Weston (1971)*).

RESULTING DAMAGE

The damage must result from the breach of duty. This is usually a question of fact and is illustrated by the case of *Barnett v Chelsea and Kensington Hospital Management Committee (1968)*. In this unusual case the plaintiff's husband was one of three nightwatchmen who had called at a hospital because they felt ill after drinking tea at work. The doctor on duty did not examine the men but sent a message, via a nurse, that they should go home and see their own doctors. They did so, but the plaintiff's husband died a few hours later from arsenic poisoning. There was a clear breach of duty by the hospital doctor when he failed to examine the men, but this breach did not cause the death as the medical evidence showed that the quantity of arsenic in the man's system meant it was already too late to save his life when he called at the hospital. As a result the plaintiff lost her claim.

REMOTENESS OF DAMAGE

If the damage is too far removed from the defendant's act or omission, then the plaintiff will not be able to claim. This was established by *The Wagon Mound (1961)* where fuel oil had been negligently spilled in a harbour. Two days later the oil caught fire because of welding operations on another ship with the result that the plaintiff's wharf burnt down. It was held that such damage was not foreseeable and was too remote for the plaintiff to be able to claim.

However, if the type of injury is foreseeable, then the defendant will be liable even if that injury occurs in an unexpected way (*Hughes v Lord Advocate (1963)*)

Intervening act

If there is a *novus actus interveniens* this may relieve the defendant of liablility as in the case of *Topp v London Country Bus (South West) Ltd (1993)*. However, if the new act is reasonably foreseeable then the defendant will remain liable.

RES IPSA LOQUITUR

This Latin phrase means 'things speak for themselves'. It is a rule of evidence designed to make it easier for a plaintiff to succeed in situations where it is obvious that someone has been negligent, but the plaintiff cannot say exactly how. The plaintiff has to show that:

- the defendant was in control of the situation which caused the plaintiff's injuries; and
- the injury was more likely to have been caused by negligence than not.

If the plaintiff proves these, then the burden of proof moves to the defendant who must try to prove that he or she was not negligent. The rule has been used where:

- the plaintiff was struck by six bags of sugar which fell from the defendant's warehouse (*Scott v London & St Katherine Docks (1865)*);
- a swab was left inside a patient during an operation (*Mahon v Osborne (1939)*).

CONTRIBUTORY NEGLIGENCE

This is where the plaintiff has been partly to blame for the incident, but may still claim damages from the defendant. The damages will be reduced by the percentage that the plaintiff was to blame (*Sayers v Harlow UDC (1957)*) or failed to take care for their own safety, for example by not wearing a seat belt (*Owens v Brimmell (1976)*).

NERVOUS SHOCK CASES

One of the more difficult areas of negligence are cases where someone other than the primary victim suffers from nervous shock as a result of the incident. Although the defendant is liable to the primary victim, should the defendant also be liable to other persons? The law in this area has changed more than once. Initially it was held that there could be no claim for such a situation, but in *McLoughlin v O'Brien (1982)* a mother who suffered nervous shock on learning of a serious accident to her family and seeing them severely hurt was able to claim.

The leading cases now are those arising from the Hillsborough disaster. In order to succeed with such a claim the plaintiff must prove:

1   that the defendant's negligence caused an identifiable psychiatric condition, mere 'ordinary human emotion' being insufficient to claim for nervous shock (*Reilly v Merseyside Regional Health Authority (1994)*);

2   that there was a close relationship between the primary victim and the plaintiff; workmates do not necessarily come into this category, so seeing workmates injured or killed will not give rise to a claim (*McFarlane v EE Caledonian Ltd (1994), Robertson v Forth Bridge Joint Board (1995)*);

3   that the plaintiff was present at the scene of the accident or its immediate aftermath; the phrase 'immediate aftermath' has been interpreted very narrowly, with decisions that:

- identifying a body in a mortuary a few hours after the incident was held not to be the 'immediate aftermath';
- being informed that a 14 year old son had been crushed by a reversing vehicle soon after the incident, following the ambulance when the boy was transferred to another hospital, seeing him on the evening of that day and then remaining with him for two days while he was on a life support machine until he died, was insufficient to claim (*Taylor v Shieldness Produce (1994)*).

ECONOMIC LOSS

Cases where the plaintiff has suffered financial loss are approached in a different way from other cases of negligence. This is shown by the statement of Lord Bridge in *Caparo Industries plc v Dickman (1990)* when he said:

> 'One of the law's most important distinctions always to be observed lies in the law's essentially different approach to the different kinds of damage which one party may have suffered in the consequence of the acts and omissions of another. It is quite one thing to owe a duty of care to avoid causing injury to the person or property of others. It is quite another to avoid causing others to suffer purely economic loss.'

The general rule is, therefore, that a plaintiff cannot claim for economic loss caused by the defendant's negligent acts or omissions. This was made clear in the cases of *D & F Estates Ltd v Church Commissioners for England (1989)* and *Murphy v Brentwood District Council (1990)*.

An exception to the general rule is shown by *White v Jones (1995)* where a solicitor who failed to alter the will of a client was held to be liable to the disappointed beneficiaries.

ECONOMIC LOSS CAUSED BY A NEGLIGENT MISSTATEMENT

The major exception under which a plaintiff can claim for economic loss stems from the decision in *Hedley Byrne v Heller & Partners (1964)* where the House of Lords held that it was possible to claim for economic loss which had been caused by a negligent misstatement, but only where there was a special relationship between the parties. In *Caparo Industries plc v Dickman (1990)* Lord Oliver set out a list of criteria from which a sufficiently proximate relationship might be established. This list was extended in *James McNaughton Paper Group v Hicks Anderson & Co (1991)* so that the following factors are considered:

- the purpose for which which the statement was made;
- the purpose for which the statement was communicated;
- the relationship between advisor, advisee and the relevant third party;
- the size of any class to which the advisee belongs;
- the state of knowledge of the advisor;
- reliance by the advisee.

OCCUPIERS' LIABILITY

The concept of a duty of care to visitors to premises was formulated as part of the general common law of negligence. However, this area of the law is now governed by the Occupiers' Liability Act 1957 and the Occupiers' Liability Act 1984. The 1957 Act states that there are two categories of visitor:

- lawful visitors; and
- persons who are not lawful visitors.

The 1957 Act also sets out that an occupier of premises has:

> 'a duty to take such care as in all the circumstances of the case is reasonable to see that the visitor will be reasonably safe in using the premises for the purposes for which he is invited to be there.'

It must be stressed that this duty is only owed to **lawful visitors**.

Such care as is reasonable in all the circumstances

66 Child visitors 99

This phrase means that the facts of each case must be considered. A major point is that an occupier must take greater care where there are **child visitors**. In *Glasgow Corporation v Taylor (1922)* a seven year old boy died after eating poisonous berries from a park and it was held that the corporation had failed to exercise reasonable care towards child visitors, as they had no warning notices and no fences to prevent children from reaching the berries. Where the visitors are older, a warning notice may be sufficient.

Independent contractors

An occupier is not normally liable for any danger created by the work of independent contractors on the plaintiff's land (*O'Connor v Swan and Edgar (1963)*).

NON-VISITORS

The Occupiers' Liability Act 1957 applies only to lawful visitors, but the common law extended the situations where a duty was owed, to include **child trespassers** (*British Railways Board v Herrington (1972)*). Subsequently, Parliament passed the Occupiers' Liability Act 1984 which states that an occupier owes a duty of care to 'non-visitors' if the occupier:

- is aware of the danger or has reasonable grounds to believe that it exists; and

- knows or has reasonable grounds to believe that there are non-visitors in the vicinity of the danger or that non-visitors may come into the vicinity; and

- the risk is one from which, in all the circumstances, he may be reasonably expected to offer the non-visitors some protection.

EXAMINATION QUESTIONS

1   How satisfactory is the present system whereby compensation for personal injuries arising from a negligent action depends on proof of fault? Are there any alternatives?
(UODLE)

2   In relation to the concept of nervous shock, Lord Oliver has stated that he could not 'regard the present state of the law as entirely satisfactory or as logically defensible' and concluded that only 'considerations of policy' made it explicable. Is Lord Oliver's view justified?
(UODLE)

3   Mr King and his son, Augustus, are both injured when their car is involved in collision with a bus. The collision is caused by the bus driver's negligence. Augustus's hip is badly jarred. Mr King suffers severe spinal injuries. Both are rushed to St Crisp's Hospital where Mr King is left unattended for many hours. The staff X-rayed Augustus's head but fail to examine his hip. As a result Augustus is in much pain for several days before his hip is finally X-rayed and a fracture identified. Subsequently, Augustus develops a weakness in his hip. The medical evidence indicates that such a weakness would occur in 80% of patients injured in this way, but that the delay in treatment for the fracture made it virtually certain that the weakness would develop. As a result of the accident Mr King is paralysed from the waist down. The medical evidence indicates that this would have occurred even if he had been treated immediately for the injuries he had sustained. When Mrs King is told by a consultant at St Crisp's Hospital of the permanent injuries to her husband and son, she suffers from severe depression.

Advise Mr King, Augustus and Mrs King as to any potential claims they may have.
(UODLE)

4   About two years ago, Daisy decided to buy a piece of land and to have a house built on it. She found a site she liked and, while at a party, told her friends about it. Tom, a surveyor, who was also a guest at the party, told her that he knew the area well, so Daisy asked him if the land would be suitable for her purpose. He said that it would, but did not tell her that special foundations would be needed because of the type of subsoil in the area. Relying on Tom's statement, Daisy did not have a survey done but employed Shoddy Builders Ltd to get on with the work. The building was inspected at various times by a building inspector working for Newtown Borough Council. The building inspector did not notice that Shoddy Builders Ltd had not used the special foundations.

After Daisy moved in, she noticed cracks in the plasterwork which rapidly got worse. She instructed a surveyor to carry out a full survey. The surveyor's report stated that, because the house did not have the special foundation it was subsiding and in need of urgent repair. As Shoddy Builders Ltd had gone out of business, Daisy could not sue the company for the cost of necessary remedial work.

Consider whether Daisy has any claim in tort against Tom and/or Newtown Borough Council.
(UODLE)

ANSWERS TO QUESTIONS

OUTLINE ANSWER

Question 3

Consider each potential plaintiff separately.

1   Mr King – the question says that the accident was caused by the bus driver's negligence (a duty of care to other road users is well established) – so the bus driver owes Mr King a duty of care and has broken that duty; the key factor is whether the wait for attention at the hospital has broken the chain of causation; note what the question says – 'medical evidence indicates that this would have occurred even if he had been treated immediately' – this makes it clear that the bus driver is liable for the injury and that the negligence of the hospital has had no effect.

2   Augustus – again the starting point is the negligence of the bus driver, but the issue of causation is important; there is a delay of several days; does this mean that the bus driver is no longer liable? probably not; can Augustus sue the hospital? did the doctor exercise the skill expected (*Bolam*)? is the 20% increase enough to hold that the hospital caused the weak hip? probably not.

3   Mrs King – this is a nervous shock situation and she must establish that she suffered a recognisable illness (depression); that she is sufficiently close to the primary victims (as wife and mother this should cause no problem); finally that she saw the 'immediate aftermath' – this seems to rule out her claim.

TUTOR'S ANSWER

Question 2

In order to sue for nervous shock it has long been established that it is necessary for the plaintiff to show that they have suffered an identifiable psychiatric illness as a result of the defendant's action. Liability under the rule in nervous shock has never been allowed for the ordinary shock, grief or surprise a person may suffer, for the simple reason that the court system would become overburdened and, in addition, it may be argued that it would be unfair on any possible defendant.

Nervous shock is dealt with differently by the court with regard to the duty of care aspect of a negligence claim. There are many reasons for this; the fear of fraudulent cases for such a non-tangible illness and problems over the long term medical prognosis being two such reasons. However, possibly the most important reason that the courts treat nervous shock cases differently is on the grounds of public policy. Nervous shock may affect a large and intermediate group following any major tragedy and this would result in vast amounts of litigation. On this basis the courts have always rejected the concept of reasonable foreseeability of damage alone. Instead they have always imposed a number of artificial limitations on claims for nervous shock based purely on the policy reasons highlighted by Lord Oliver.

The historical development shows how the rules relating to nervous shock have undergone gradual development followed by retraction. Traditionally, a claim for nervous shock could not succeed unless it could be shown that the defendant deliberately inflicted the nervous shock upon the plaintiff. This is illustrated by the case of *Wilkinson v Downton* which created a sub-strand of the law of nervous shock that still exists. In the case of *Victorian Railway Commission v Coultas,* the plaintiff could not recover for nervous shock as the court held that there had been no deliberate infliction. A major change in the law came about in the case of *Dulieu v White and Sons* in which the first claim for nervous shock without intention was allowed on the basis of fear of one's own safety. This was extended further in the case of *Hambrook v Stokes Bros* when the mother of a young child was allowed to claim for the nervous shock she suffered as the result of fearing that her daughter was hurt. However, in this case a policy consideration was enforced to restrict the law. This was that the plaintiff had to witness the accident with her own 'unaided senses' in order to recover damages.

The law regarding nervous shock after this case became somewhat confused, as can be shown through the case of *Bourhill v Young* in which it was stated that the plaintiff could not recover because she was outside the geographical area of foresight. It seemed that two principles were important in the law at this time, one relating to the closeness of the plaintiff to the action and whether the harm was reasonably foreseeable, and the second relating to the relationship between the person suffering nervous shock and the person placed in danger. Although normally only close relations could claim there were cases in which the category who could claim, was extended, for example, to workmates in the case of *Dooley v Cammel Laird*.

This was how the law stood when the case of *McLoughlin v O'Brien* came to the House of Lords in 1983. The facts in this case were that the plaintiff's family were involved in an accident and badly injured. At the time the plaintiff was several miles away, but was informed of the accident and went to the hospital to identify her family and suffered nervous shock as a result. Although the plaintiff was not in the proximity of the accident her case was allowed, but the judgment of their Lordships varied. The majority said that policy reasons should restrict the law, and Lord Wilberforce laid down several guidelines as to when nervous shock cases should be allowed. However, two judges, Lord Bridge and Lord Scarman, decided the case on the grounds of foreseeability of damage alone. They said that policy reasons should not restrict this area of the law. The importance of this case lies in its subsequent interpretation because, although it did not have a majority ruling, the broad and expansive test of reasonable foreseeability was adopted. This led to a major expansion of the law of nervous shock. Cases which demonstrate this are *Attia v Britsh Gas* in which it was held that someone could recover for property, and *Hevican v Ruane* in which it was held that the parents of a child could claim after being told about her death by a third party. Neither of these cases fulfilled both of the requirements set out by Lord Wilberforce in *McLoughlin* and it was thought that a 'floodgate' situation in the law of nervous shock was occurring.

The courts became very concerned about this, fearing that the tort would become out of control. There was a significant shift in judicial opinion relating to nervous shock in the late 1980s which was in accordance with the court's general wish to limit the tort of negligence after a 'litigation happy' period. The courts have since gradually retracted from the rules and imposed more restrictions.

The question of the imposition of duty of care returned to the House of Lords in the case of *Alcock v Chief Constable of South Yorkshire* following the Hillsborough disaster. The court had to consider many delicate areas of the tort with regard to these claims. One of the most significant of these was the relationship aspect; was it possible for brothers and grandparents to recover for the death of their relatives after suffering nervous shock? The court also had to consider whether those who watched the event on television were owed a duty of care. The House of Lords unanimously dismissed the approach and strongly rejected the test of reasonable foreseeability of damage in such cases. This represents the turn in the tide of judicial opinion with regard to nervous shock. The Lords stated that there were two main requirements of a claim for nervous shock that needed to be satisfied.

The first of these was relationship. It was stated that there needed to be a sufficiently close relationship of love and affection between the primary victim and the plaintiff so that it would be reasonably foreseeable that the plaintiff would suffer nervous shock in the event of the death or injury of the primary victim. This did not restrict the relationship to a set one such as parent/child, however, but where there is such a close relationship there seems to be a rebuttable presumption of liability created. The Lords stated that other relationships could lead to a claim but the plaintiff would have to show evidence to prove such a close relationship. The Lords held that normally no duty would be owed to a bystander, but would continue to be extended to a rescuer.

Secondly, the Lords held that the plaintiff had to be proximate in terms of time and space to the accident or come upon its immediate aftermath. Suffering nervous shock as a result of being told by a third party was not sufficient, nor was there a duty normally owed to those who saw the incident on television. Although the Law Lords refrained from laying down a clear test as to what amounted to immediate aftermath, subsequent cases have taken a very strict view of what constitutes immediate aftermath.

Therefore it has been shown that in recent years the Lords have redefined the law of nervous shock and, taking into consideration policy reasons, have considerably restricted the law. Many, like Lord Oliver, have argued that this is not fair or defensible. The requirement that people may have to show a close relationship of love and affection may bring to the law a very distasteful practice of defendants trying to produce evidence to the contrary. Also, it seems that the concept of proximity to the accident is purely a legal one, as medical evidence has shown that regardless of whether someone sees the accident or hears about it later they may suffer equally. Furthermore, it could be argued that the somewhat bizarre situation may arise where one is now more likely to be able to claim for nervous shock caused by seeing one's property burnt down than by seeing a relation injured in an accident. This is because the Lords failed to overrule the decision in *Attia v British Gas*.

One area where the courts had prevously not imposed policy restrictions is that of cases involving rescuers. It is thought that people when rescuing are not expressly concerned with their own welfare and so should not be restricted from claiming. However, in recent litigation brought by police officers involved in rescue at the Hillsborough disaster, the courts have imposed policy restrictions on this area of the law. It was stated that a claim in nervous shock is now limited to rescuers in the front line and not to those who may see dead bodies later. Once again policy reasons have led to limitations in the law on nervous shock.

In conclusion it has been shown that many policy reasons have been imposed on the law with an aim of restricting it and this has produced somewhat illogical rules that have no other basis.

STUDENT'S ANSWER WITH TUTOR'S COMMENTS

Question 4

> **Negligent mis-statement needs to be explained**

> **Again there is a need for more depth – the correct points are being identified but there is no development**

> **A good distinction between physical damage and economic loss**

Daisy could try to sue Tom for negligent mis-statement as per *Hedley Byrne v Heller*, as she was relying on his statement and he was in a position of expertise.

Her problem is that she met him at a party and not in the course of business. Tom may claim that he could not reasonably have expected her to rely upon his statement, and in cases of economic loss the plaintiff must show a strong proximate relationship to the defendant if he is to succeed. This was emphasised in *Caparo Industries v Dickman*.

In several decided cases it has been found that a duty of care was owed by surveyors acting for the bank or building society in respect of assessing the property for mortgage purposes. This was despite the fact that they had warned purchasers not to rely on their findings as it was found that people rarely bothered with a second inspection. The rule, however, is different for local authorities; they will only have a liability if there is physical damage; they are not liable for pure economic loss. This was decided in *Murphy v Brentwood District Council*.

In Daisy's case the cost of remedial work is considered economic loss and she cannot claim this from Newtown Borough Council. If she suffered physical damage as a result of the subsidence then she could claim from the Council as they owe her a duty of care in accordance with the decision in *Dutton v Bognor Regis UDC*.

Unfortunately for Daisy, it appears that she is unable to claim from either Tom or Newtown Borough Council.

Tutor's Comments

This essay has identified the points that need to be discussed, but there is not enough depth. The decision in *Hedley Byrne v Heller* should be discussed, and more importantly the criteria given in *Caparo Industries v Dickman* (and extended by the case of *James McNaughten Paper Group v Hicks Anderson & Co*) should be given fully. The student states correctly that there is a problem because Tom's advice was given at a party; again this could be developed and the case of *Chaudry v Prabhaker*, which involved just such a situation, could be used.
This essay would be awarded a grade D.

A review sheet for this chapter can be found on p. 220.

CHAPTER 21

TRESPASS, NUISANCE AND DEFAMATION

GETTING STARTED

This chapter concerns a group of torts which may provide in some cases an alternative to negligence. Being older doctrines, they were at one time the only routes to a remedy. Now many more actions are brought in negligence, but the older torts are still of value on occasions. Also, apart from being interesting, they form the basis of many examination questions. The definitions, principles, particular defences and remedies should be learned for each one.

In problem questions:

- the appropriate tort should be applied, but it should always be considered whether an action in negligence may also be brought (Chapter 20);
- the general defences (Chapter 19) should also be considered.

Remember again that questions could involve more than one incident and more than one issue.

TRESPASS TO THE PERSON

TRESPASS TO GOODS

TRESPASS TO LAND

NUISANCE

DEFAMATION

TRESPASS TO THE PERSON

ESSENTIAL PRINCIPLES

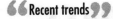

Trespass to the person is a wrong to another person, and can take the form of:

- assault;
- battery;
- false imprisonment.

The tort is actionable *per se*, that is 'in itself', and without having to prove that any damage followed. Two recent trends are that:

❝Recent trends❞

1 It is becoming increasingly likely that where trespass to the person is caused negligently, an action will be brought in negligence rather than trespass (see comments of Lord Denning in *Letang v Cooper (1965)*).

2 There is some debate as to whether the trespass must be intended or negligent (rather than purely accidental) (see *Fowler v Lanning (1959)* and *Wilson v Pringle (1986)*).

RELATIONSHIP WITH CRIMINAL LAW

Assault and battery may also amount to criminal offences, and then compensation may be claimed under the Criminal Injuries Compensation Scheme. However, claims may still be made in tort for substantial compensation, or to make an example of the offender, quite commonly now the police or a store detective.

ASSAULT AND BATTERY

Assault and battery usually go together, but it is possible in unusual circumstances for one to arise without the other.

Assault

The tort of assault is where a person is put in fear of an immediate battery, or unwanted physical force. An example of assault alone is the violent waving of a clenched fist, but impact being prevented by another person, as in *Stephens v Myers (1830)*. It must be possible to carry out the battery – see *Thomas v National Union of Mineworkers (1985)* where violent gestures came from inside vehicles. In addition the words of the defendant may indicate that the battery will not happen, as in *Turberville v Savage (1699)*.

Battery

Battery is the application of physical force to a person. It is accepted that normal social contact, such as a tap on the shoulder or jostling in a crowd, will not amount to a battery, but the 'least touching of another in anger' may be a battery (*Cole v Turner (1704)*). A requirement of hostile touching was suggested in *Wilson v Pringle (1986)*. There must be an intention to apply physical force, but not necessarily the intention to hurt the other person. Some examples of batteries include: a football supporter being hit by a policeman's truncheon (*Connor v Chief Constable of Cambridgeshire (1984)*); throwing water (*Pursell v Horn (1838)*); and punching and kicking by police (*Leon v Metropolitan Police Commissioner (1986)*).

Defences

Some defences may be raised to assault and battery:

- statutory authority, e.g. for breath tests, and lawful arrest using reasonable force;
- reasonable chastisement of a child;
- self-defence using reasonable force;
- consent to medical treatment (but not to negligent treatment).

Note that special rules relate to the police under the Police and Criminal Evidence Act 1984.

FALSE IMPRISONMENT

False imprisonment is unlawfully depriving a person of free movement. It is more than just keeping a person in prison or a room, and can include such things as using handcuffs or keeping someone in a car. If there is a reasonable way of escape there is no false imprisonment (*Bird v Jones (1845)*).

Defences

- lawful arrest;
- custody under a court order;
- holding in a mental hospital under a mental health order;
- reasonable parental control.

Remedies

The usual remedy is damages – either nominal, substantial, or in a few cases exemplary. Very occasionally the order of *habeas corpus* could be available for false imprisonment, and injunction may be available to prevent interference.

TRESPASS TO GOODS

Trespass to goods is the **unlawful interference of goods in the possession of another**. This could involve damage to the goods, but not necessarily. If, however, damage does not occur, then the award of compensation is likely to be nominal. The action does not need to be malicious in any way (see *Kirk v Gregory (1865)* where goods were moved to a cupboard in another room for safekeeping, and subsequently stolen. The person moving them was held liable for trespass).

It is only necessary to show **possession, not ownership**, as seen in *Parker v British Airways Board (1982)* where the proceeds of sale of a bracelet found on the floor at Heathrow airport had to be handed over to the finder in an action in trespass.

REMEDIES

The usual remedy is damages to compensate for the harm caused. The court may order the goods to be returned.

TRESPASS TO LAND

66 Definition of trespass 99

Just as trespass to goods is interfering with another person's possessions, trespass to land is interfering with another person's land. The law considers that being on another person's land without permission is interfering, so trespass can be defined as: **unlawfully entering or remaining on land in the possession of the plaintiff, or placing or projecting any object upon such land.**

Obvious unlawful entry to land, such as walking across land or camping on it is therefore a trespass (although this is not a crime, as signs would have us believe), as is remaining on land without permission, such as refusing to leave a cinema at the end of a performance. In *Gregory v Piper (1829)* leaning on a wall was held to be trespass. A plaintiff must be in possession of the land to sue in trespass.

AIRSPACE

66 Can they fly over me? 99

The space above land raises some difficulty. In *Kelson v Imperial Tobacco (1957)* an advertisement projecting over property was held to be trespass, and so was a large swinging crane in *Woolerton v Costain (1970)*. However, in *Bernstein v Skyviews (1978)*, regarding the taking of aerial photographs, it was said that trespass did not occur unless it was at such a height that it interfered with the other party's use of the land.

Airspace could not be protected to an unlimited height as aircraft, satellites, etc. need to pass by. The Civil Aviation Act 1982 allows passing of aircraft 'over any property at a height above the ground which having regard to wind, weather and all the circumstances of the case is reasonable'.

DEFENCES

66 Do they have permission? 99

- A person may have a lawful reason to be on the land, such as a police officer with rights to search the property, an electricity board official, or a neighbour with a court order to enter to repair adjoining property. Such people must not exceed the lawful reason for their entry.

- Licence or permission from the person in possession of the land may be express or implied, for example to attend a sporting event or to deliver goods. Where a person repeatedly trespasses without objection from the person in possession, an implied licence could arise, making the former trespasser a lawful visitor for the purposes of occupier's liability (with the greater protection of the 1957 Act rather than the 1984 Act – see Chapter 20).

- The defendant may have entered the land to recover goods put there by the plaintiff.

- The trespass may be necessary to prevent some other event, such as danger to life or a nuisance.

REMEDIES

Trespass is actionable *per se*, so the plaintiff may sue for the trespass itself, without there having been any damage caused. In limited circumstances, such as under the Criminal Justice and Public Order Act 1994, or on railways, the trespass may amount to a crime.

In a civil action the remedies available are:

- **damages** – however, if there is no harm caused the damages awarded will be nominal;
- **injunction** – to prevent further action;
- **recovery of land** – an order may be given, for example for the plaintiff to regain possession of a house.

In requesting a trespasser to leave land, only reasonable force may be used should the trespasser refuse. Unreasonable force may amount to assault and battery. The use of wheel clamps is also now considered reasonable, provided the fine is not excessive.

NUISANCE

A nuisance in tort may be one of two types: private or public nuisance. In addition, statute has made provision to protect the environment, for example in the Clean Air Act 1956 and the Control of Pollution Act 1974.

PRIVATE NUISANCE

Private nuisance is something which **unreasonably interferes with a person's use and enjoyment of land**. Some examples of actions held to be nuisances include tree roots growing under a neighbour's land (*Butler v Standard Telephone and Cable (1940)*) and smells from a pig farm (*Bone v Seal (1975)*).

Continuance

There must normally be some continuing act, but sometimes what appears to be a single act is held to be the culmination of a state of affairs, as in *Midwood v Mayor of Manchester (1905)* where an explosion occurred after a build-up of gas over a period of time. More than one occurrence will not necessarily amount to continuance, as it must be generally ongoing (see *Bolton v Stone (1951)*) where evidence was given that the ball from a cricket ground had been hit over into the road only six times in 35 years).

Unreasonableness

Lord Denning said, in *Miller v Jackson (1977)*, that the essence of private nuisance is 'the **unreasonable use** by a man of his land to the detriment of his neighbour'. Various factors could amount to unreasonable use:

- **extent of the interference** – generally the interference must be more substantial than 'normal' social inconvenience;
- **time of day** when the interference takes place;
- **sensitivity of the plaintiff** – the standard is generally that of the 'normal' neighbour, so damage to unusually sensitive brown paper was not nuisance in *Robinson v Kilvert (1889)*, but damage to a crop of orchids was, in *McKinnon v Walker (1951)*, because more 'normally' grown plants would have suffered in a similar way;
- **locality** – the general nature of the area is taken into account – 'what would be a nuisance in Belgravia Square would not necessarily be so in Bermondsey' (*Sturges v Bridgman (1879)*);
- **malice** is not normally a factor in itself, but may add to the unreasonableness of the action, as did the deliberate noise during music lessons in *Christie v Davey (1893)*;
- **social utility** may be of relevance, but will not prevent an action in nuisance – in *Adams v Ursell (1913)* the smell from a fish and chip shop was held to be a nuisance.

Who can sue?

Only a person with a **legal interest** in the land can sue, usually the person being in possession or occupation of the land. It is usual to sue the occupier of the land, but the creator of the nuisance may also be sued. In some circumstances the occupier could be sued vicariously for the nuisances of others on the land occupied.

DEFENCES

- **statutory authority** – in *Allen v Gulf Oil Refining (1981)* statute authorised the operation of an oil refinery;

- **prescription** – after 20 years there may be a prescriptive right to continue the act which would otherwise form a nuisance, but the time begins from when the plaintiff becomes aware of the nuisance (*Sturges v Bridgman (1879)*);
- **coming to the nuisance** – it was argued by Lord Denning in *Miller v Jackson (1977)* that in moving near to a cricket ground the plaintiff knew the area and 'came to the nuisance', but this was rejected as a defence.

REMEDIES

- **damages** may be appropriate if harm has been caused;
- **injunction** is a common remedy, to prevent the nuisance from continuing;
- **abatement of the nuisance** – a self-help remedy which allows the plaintiff to remove the nuisance if this can be done without trespassing, e.g. cutting off overhanging branches, and giving them back to the neighbour.

PUBLIC NUISANCE

❝Where the public is affected❞

Public nuisance is an act or omission which affects the comfort and convenience of a class of people. Because of its public nature it is considered a crime and could involve prosecution by the Attorney-General. Examples include smoke, fumes, obstructing the highway and pop festivals. In *Castle v St Augustine's Links (1922)* a golf course was considered a nuisance, interfering regularly with the highway, and in *R v Shorrock (1993)* an occupier of land was found guilty of public nuisance for allowing an acid house party on his land.

PRIVATE ACTION IN PUBLIC NUISANCE

❝Where an individual particularly suffers❞

Sometimes an individual may be able to show that particular damage was caused over and above that suffered by other members of the group, such as the taxi driver who lost the sight of one eye because of a golf ball straying from St Augustine's Links (see *Castle v St Augustine's Links* (above)).

STRICT LIABILITY IN *RYLANDS AND FLETCHER*

Various liabilities exist in tort, such as liability for harm to one's 'neighbour' in negligence, vicarious liability and occupier's liability. Sometimes liability arises without any bad intention on the part of the tortfeasor. It may arise just from owning something which causes harm, irrespective of any intention or otherwise of the owner.

❝The rule in *Rylands v Fletcher*❞

The rule in *Rylands v Fletcher (1868)* arose where the defendant had a reservoir built without having sealed up some old mine shafts. The reservoir water leaked along them and flooded the plaintiff's mine. The defendant had not intended this, but was nevertheless liable. The rule is, then, that when a person brings on to land anything non-natural which is likely to do mischief and it escapes and causes damage, the owner is liable. The rule does not apply to natural things like rock-fall due to natural erosion or thistle seed blown by the wind.

❝Strict liability or negligence?❞

The importance of the rule in *Rylands v Fletcher* has now diminished somewhat with the development of the ordinary rules of negligence and nuisance, and in particular with the decision of the House of Lords in *Cambridge Water v Eastern Counties Leather (1994)*, concerning the leaking of solvent into the public water supply. It was held that there must be foreseeability of damage of the particular kind caused for liability to exist. This brings the rule much closer to negligence (see Chapter 20). This trend is not totally new (see *Mason v Levy Auto Parts (1967)* where McKenna J suggested that a standard of duty of care was involved, and thus liability, found here under the rule in *Rylands v Fletcher* could have more easily been found in negligence).

DEFAMATION

Where a **defamatory statement** is published which harms the reputation of an individual an action may arise in libel or slander.

A defamatory statement is one which tends to lower a person in the estimation of right thinking people generally, or to cause them to shun or avoid the person.

LIBEL

❝Written down❞

Libel is where the publication is in a permanent form, and can also amount to a crime. A large number of notorious cases arise in newspaper and magazine articles, such as that of Telly Savalas, the Kojak actor, who was described in a newspaper as a 'big amiable beast of a man who cannot cope with superstardom', and Cosmos holidays whose holidays were impliedly criticised on television and portrayed against music evoking Colditz, a prisoner of war camp.

Publication could also take the form of paintings, statues and musical recordings, and in *Monson v Tussauds (1894),* a waxwork model in the 'Chamber of Horrors'.

SLANDER

 "Spoken"

Slander is where the publication is not in a permanent form, and is mostly found in speech. It is not a crime, perhaps being regarded as morally less serious than libel.

IDENTIFICATION OF THE PLAINTIFF

The plaintiff must be clearly identified in the defamatory statement for an action to succeed. This may not necessarily be the plaintiff's actual name – for example the reference by some nickname to a well-known target of a satirical paper or programme.

DEFENCES

The statement may prove to be justified or may be protected by privilege, such as in the Houses of Parliament or in court. Alternatively, the statements could be considered **fair comment**, that is, a believed opinion, not made maliciously, on a matter of public interest. The Defamation Act 1952 provides a defence by publication of a correction and apology, with a payment into court.

Other arguments may be raised by way of defence. **Justification** may arise where the defendant is able to show the substantial truth of the statement. The Defamation Act in addition provides that where more than one statement is made, the defence may still be allowed even if all statements are not proved to be true, but the reputation of the plaintiff is not affected.

Absolute privilege will be a defence to statements made, regardless of whether they were malicious, in certain circumstances, including those made in parliamentary proceedings; in judicial proceedings, e.g. court hearings, by judge, jury, lawyers or witnesses; in state communications at ministerial level and in interviews between solicitors and clients.

Qualified privilege may be raised in the protection of the public interest, or of a private interest, where statements are shown to be made without malice, and not published more widely than is necessary.

It is also important to consider whether statements are really defamatory. Some statements are made innocently, in genuine good faith, whilst others could be made which do not, on the surface, appear defamatory, but which contain an **innuendo** which has a derogatory meaning. This may be well understood by those who know the person about whom the statement is made, and evidence would be brought to court on the meaning of the words.

Remedies

An important and useful remedy are injunction (both permanent and interlocutory). However once the statement has been published damages are commonly awarded, although the level of damages has been the subject of much criticism, on occasions being excessively high.

EXAMINATION QUESTIONS

1 Analyse the elements of the tort of false imprisonment. (UODLE)

2 Consider the elements of the tort created by *Rylands v Fletcher (1868)*. Illustrate your answer with cases and/or examples of situations in which an action based on this principle may arise. (UODLE)

3 For the past 12 months, a local store, Bargain Buys, has suffered a lot of theft. The store detective, Mr Plod, has had his suspicions that a group of young people who come into the store regularly are to blame. About a month ago Mr Plod identified Mohammed and Jeremy as members of the group. They were asked to go to the manager's office, where they were told that they would not in future be allowed into the shop.

Two weeks later Mohammed and Jeremy went into the shop where they met some friends. As they stood chatting Mr Plod spotted them and, going up to them, grabbed each of them by one arm, saying he would take them to the manager's office. Jeremy managed to free himself by punching Mr Plod but, as he ran away through the store, he slipped and fell. Mr Plod again grabbed him and took both young men to the manager's office, where he locked the door, telling them that they would stay there until the police arrived.

About three hours later Mohammed and Jeremy were released, the manager and the police agreeing that there was no evidence at all that they had been involved in the thefts.

Consider what, if any, rights of action Bargain Buys, Mr Plod, Mohammed and Jeremy may have in tort.

(UODLE)

ANSWERS TO QUESTIONS

OUTLINE ANSWER

Question 2

Outline the principles of the rule in *Rylands v Fletcher* and, as it is the key case in the answer, relate the material facts in some detail (but do not be tempted to spend the bulk of the essay in long narration):

- explain the strict nature of the liability – no intention needed;
- examine the scope of 'things brought on to the land' – must be things which are not naturally found there – and 'for the defendant's own purposes';
- consider the meaning of 'likely to do mischief';
- indicate the need for an 'escape';
- there must be a non-natural use;
- status of the defendant – one who owns or occupies the land or who has control of the thing causing the problem;
- status of the plaintiff – may be an occupier, or merely suffering from an escape on to the land of a third party.

Consider how recent case law may be turning the rule into more of a fault-based principle, culminating in *Cambridge Water v Eastern Counties Leather*, involving assessment of the standard of duty of care, and foreseeability.

This is about the elements of the rule, rather than the remedies, but it is appropriate to mention that in damages, also, it appears that the difference between the rule and the tort of negligence is decreasing.

Ensure that the answer contains relevant cases to illustrate the points made.

Conclude by summarising the elements of the rule and assessing whether they are changing.

STUDENT'S ANSWER WITH TUTOR'S COMMENTS

Question 3

> **Deals with trespass to land and remedies**

> **Could comment on Bargain Buys' right to withdraw licence to be in the shop**

> **Assault and battery by Mr Plod**

> **Considers requirements carefully**

The following rights of action may result from the situation.

Bargain Buys could sue both Mohammed and Jeremy in trespass to land. This is because they have possession of the land and have expressly told the boys not to enter the premises. It is not necessary that they show any harm as a result of the trespass, as it is actionable *per se*. The boys would be trespassing by wrongful entry and thus would be liable. The remedy the store would probably seek would be an injunction, as damages would be available but would be trivial.

Both Mohammed and Jeremy could sue Mr Plod for assault, battery and false imprisonment. An assault is an action which causes another person to fear the direct infliction of physical damage. The assault would be committed when Mr Plod went to grab the boys. The boys could also sue him for battery. Battery is the infliction of direct physical force upon another person. The requirements for battery are unclear. In the case of *Wilson v Pringle* it was stated that the act had to be hostile for it to amount to a battery. It is unclear whether this still remains after the case of *F v West Berkshire Health Authority*. However, if the court decided that hostility was not a necessary element it would be clear that a battery had been committed. If hostility is thought to be a necessary requirement then the court will have to assess whether the store detective was acting with hostility.

The boys may also have an action in false imprisonment. In order for it to be an unlawful

"Deals with false imprisonment"

imprisonment, the restraint must be complete as shown through the case of *Bird v Jones*. In this case the door was locked and the boys had no way of escaping, thus the restraint was complete. It is no longer, under the rule in *Meering v Graham White Aviation*, necessary to show knowledge of the imprisonment, but this on the facts of the case is established anyway.

The third aspect of any unlawful imprisonment action is for the plaintiffs to show that the restraint was unlawful. Even though the boys were trespassers it is very unlikely that the restraint would be found to be lawful. There would be no defence available to the store detective as he has no powers of arrest. In making a citizen's arrest on the boys the detective must have reasonable suspicion, which we are told that he has. However, mistaken suspicion is no defence, therefore it seems likely that there has been an unlawful imprisonment made against the two boys.

"Vicarious liability considered"

Instead of suing Mr Plod the boys may wish to sue Bargain Buys for their vicarious liability for their employee's actions. It seems clear that Mr Plod is an employee. However, the court would have to consider whether the assault, battery and false imprisonment would take Mr Plod outside the course of his employment. This seems unlikely unless he uses unreasonable force as it is his job to apprehend those he believes to have either trespassed or stolen.

"Occupiers' liability"

Jeremy could also sue Bargain Buys under the statutory provision of the Occupiers' Liability Act 1984. This states that a limited duty is owed to a trespasser. It is not clear whether Jeremy slipped on something in the store but if he did he could sue under this provision. He may also sue in negligence if there has been a spill on the floor but he will have to show that a duty was owed, that it has been breached and that this breach caused his harm.

"Assault and battery by Jeremy, and defences"

Mr Plod could sue Jeremy for assault and battery and the same rules as stated above would apply. However, Jeremy may be able to plead the defence of self-defence. In such a situation the court will assess whether the defendant acted in proportion to the risk and whether they used reasonable force. This seems somewhat debatable on the facts of this case as we are not told the harm caused by the punch. However, Jeremy may also propose the defence of *ex turpi causi*. This means that the other person should not benefit from their own wrongdoing. As it seems likely that Mr Plod or his employer will be found to be liable in trespass to the person, this defence may operate.

Tutor's Comments

An answer of a very high standard which covers the various torts raised by the question and considers the defences which may be appropriate. The legal knowledge is good and is applied to the problem methodically and intelligently, with comment on the state of the law where appropriate. An answer of grade A standard.

A review sheet for this chapter can be found on p. 221.

CONSUMER LAW

GETTING STARTED

Consumer protection is concerned with ensuring that the law works well in helping individuals who may lack bargaining power, and not just form a framework for trading. This has been accomplished in two main ways:

1   over a long period through the common law, as cases of difficulties have been taken to court;

2   recognising that this was not enough, and that the consumer needed clearer rights which were more easily enforceable, through Parliament, with a large amount of legislation in this field.

This chapter looks at the contractual basis which forms the legal relationship in consumer dealing, and then goes on to examine the provisions of the main statutes affecting the consumer. Questions set are likely to concentrate on:

- the contract between the consumer and the retailer (see chapters on contract, especially Chapter 15);
- the immediate liability on the retailer for defective products supplied under the Sale of Goods Act 1979;
- the extension of liability for goods supplied other than under a sale and for services;
- the liability on the producer under the Consumer Protection Act 1987 and possibly in tort (see chapters on tort, especially Chapter 20)

Remember that more than one area may be involved, particularly in general essay questions on the protection of the consumer, and in problem questions where there is more than one route to a remedy.

THE CONTRACTUAL BASIS AND THE CONSUMER

THE SALE OF GOODS ACT 1979

THE SALE AND SUPPLY OF GOODS ACT 1994

THE SUPPLY OF GOODS AND SERVICES ACT 1982

THE CONSUMER PROTECTION ACT 1987

THE UNFAIR CONTRACT TERMS ACT 1977

THE CONSUMER CREDIT ACT 1974

ESSENTIAL PRINCIPLES

THE CONTRACTUAL BASIS AND THE CONSUMER

THE CONTRACT

Many commercial deals take place between large organisations, who trade with each other in the supply of goods and services, and it is assumed that, on the whole, they have the resources to make fair bargains. However, a huge number of deals take place every day, which form contracts between ordinary people and those in commerce in some way. All of these 'deals' involving the exchange of money for goods or services form contracts, so to recap on the formation of a contract see Chapter 15. If there is no contract, less protection is available, and in many cases, there is no protection. So if, for example, a person is given a hairdryer by a friend for a present, the contract of sale is between the buyer and seller. If the hairdryer does not work, the legal remedy is for the buyer to return it to the shop, not the friend (although in practice a shop will normally give an exchange or refund to maintain good customer relations). Of course, there may also be other remedies. For example, if the hairdryer not only malfunctioned, but also injured the user, there would be remedy not only in contract but also in the tort of negligence, in addition to any statutory protection. However, the contractual basis of such deals remains very important.

> **Recap on forming a contract**

> **Additional remedy in tort**

THE CONSUMER

> **Inequality of bargaining power**

An individual in such a situation often has little bargaining power and is less able to negotiate freely than is a person in a business situation. Recognising this, the courts have in many cases tried to protect individuals, but the great bulk of protection has come from Acts of Parliament, in an attempt to remedy the imbalance of power in consumer contracts.

> **Who is a consumer?**

Some of the protection given by legislation only applies to consumer contracts. The basis of a consumer contract is where a person buys as an individual from someone who is in business.

Where this protection does *not* apply, then the principle of **caveat emptor** applies, that is, 'let the buyer beware'. Of course, an individual could be in business as a seller of goods, but at some times, e.g. at the weekend, be a consumer in shopping for the family or pursuing a hobby.

THE SALE OF GOODS ACT 1979 AS AMENDED BY THE SALE AND SUPPLY OF GOODS ACT 1994

THE SALE OF GOODS

The Sale of Goods Act 1979 was a major step forward for the consumer, updating an Act passed in 1893. It applies to the sale of goods, defined in s. 2(1) as a 'contract by which the seller transfers or agrees to transfer the property in goods to the buyer for a money consideration, called the price'. So some money, at least, must be given, and an exchange of goods for goods is excluded.

THE PASSING OF PROPERTY

> **When does ownership begin?**

The moment at which ownership of property transfers to the other party is very important in determining whether certain liability arises. The point at which property passes can be determined by the parties, providing the goods have been 'ascertained', or identified. If the point at which property passes has not been specified, then certain rules apply from ss. 16 to 18 of the Act:

- **goods deliverable** – property passes on contract;
- **specific goods not yet deliverable** – property passes when the seller has them ready and tells the buyer;
- **goods on approval** – property passes on acceptance by buyer or lapse of time;
- **unascertained or future goods** – property passes when goods are 'unconditionally appropriated' to the contract.

RISK

The risk of some kind of damage to goods, or their loss, may be arranged specifically by the parties, but otherwise will normally pass when the property passes.

TERMS IMPLIED BY SECTIONS 12 TO 15

> **Consumer rights under the Act**

The Sale of Goods Act 1979 implies five basic, but important, terms into contracts for the sale of goods in ss. 12 to 15:

1 **Title** – s. 12 implies a condition that the seller has a right to sell the goods (*Rowland v Divall (1923)*) concerning the sale of a stolen car).

2 **Description** – s. 13 implies a condition that the goods will be as described (*Beale v Taylor (1967)* concerning two 'half cars' joined together). There must be reliance on the description – (*Harlingdon and Leinster v Christopher Hill Fine Art (1991)* regarding a painting bought at 'own risk'). This is increasingly important in self-service shopping, with reliance on signs and packets.

3 **Satisfactory quality** – s. 14(2) of the Sale of Goods Act 1979 implied a condition that goods will be of 'merchantable' quality. From 3 January 1995 the Sale and Supply of Goods Act 1994 has changed this to 'satisfactory' quality. (Regarding the sale of cars see *Bernstein v Pamsons Motors (1987)* and *Rogers v Parish (1987)*.) The new Act states that the quality of goods includes their state and condition, and covers the following aspects: fitness for all purposes for which these goods are commonly supplied; appearance and finish; freedom from minor defects; safety; and durability.

4 **Fitness for a particular purpose** – s. 14(3) implies a condition that goods will be fit for a purpose made known to the seller (*Griffiths v Peter Conway (1939)*). Sometimes the purpose is implied because there is only one obvious purpose (*Priest v Last (1903)* regarding a hole in a hot water bottle).

5 **Sale by sample** – s. 15 implies a condition that the sample will correspond with the whole of the goods in quality (*Drummond v Van Ingen (1887)* states that the purpose of a sample is to 'present to the eye the real meaning and intention of the parties').

The case of *Rogers v Parish* (above) would repay reading as the Court of Appeal raised some important points, such as:

- what amounts to acceptance;
- external appearance (the case involved a new Range Rover);
- the effect of a repair being possible;
- manufacturer's warranty;
- use of the vehicle between periods of breakdown.

EXCLUSION

❝Avoiding the Act❞

Section 12 cannot be excluded from any contract. Sections 13 to 15 cannot be excluded from a consumer contract (where a buyer is not 'in the course of a business'), and can only be excluded from other contracts if this is reasonable.

ACCEPTANCE

Accepting the goods will normally mean that they cannot then be rejected by the buyer. However, the buyer should have a chance to examine the goods. Acceptance may be by words or actions, or by lapse of time. See the two 'car' cases above. The new Sale and Supply of Goods Act 1994 has attempted to improve the position of the consumer on acceptance of goods.

THE SUPPLY OF GOODS AND SERVICES ACT 1982

❝Similar rights where there is no sale of goods❞

Where goods are handed over, or services undertaken, but nothing is actually bought over a counter, as in a shop sale, a consumer could still be in need of protection, and yet not fall within the definition of a sale under the Sale of Goods Act 1979. Although preceding this Act, *Samuels v Davis (1943)* highlights the problem, raising the issue of whether the supply of a set of false teeth is a sale of goods.

The Supply of Goods and Services Act 1982 implies similar conditions into contracts as the Sale of Goods Act, where goods are transferred, and also gives similar rights to a consumer in hiring goods. It also protects a consumer by implying conditions into a contract for services, such as one for painting and decorating, or servicing a car. These are as follows:

- the service will be carried out **with reasonable care and skill** (*Wilson v Best Travel (1993)* regarding a holiday in Greece, where the customer fell through a glass door, which although ordinary glass, complied with local requirements, and was therefore held reasonable);
- the service will be carried out **within a reasonable time**, where a time limit is not specified in the contract;
- a **reasonable price** will be paid for the service, where this is not specified in the contract.

LIABILITY ON THE PRODUCER

This Act was passed as a direct result of Britain's membership of the European Union, giving effect to the European Product Liability Directive, and s. 1 provides that the Act should be construed in accordance with the directive. Just as a claim in negligence may be made by a *user* – who is not necessarily the buyer – of a product which causes harm, the Consumer Protection Act 1987 gives protection to this person by legislation. It also creates criminal liability if certain safety procedures are infringed.

THE PRODUCER

Strict liability for a defective product is placed on the producer, without having to prove fault. The producer will normally, but not necessarily, be the manufacturer, and in addition the retailer may be liable for 'own brand' products.

THE DEFECT

A product will be defective if the safety 'is not such as persons generally are entitled to expect'. The product may be defective because of a fault in the manufacturing process, a problem of design, or warning and instructions given to the consumer.

DAMAGE COVERED

The Act covers liability for:

- death;
- personal injury;
- damage to property valued at over £275;

but *not* for damage to the product itself (see *Aswan Engineering Establishment v Lupdine (1987)* regarding a burst tyre causing damage to a car).

DEFENCES

Certain defences are available under the Act, including:

- the producer is not in business (such as the sale of home made products for charity);
- the defect did not exist at the time of manufacture;
- only the component was supplied, whereas the fault lay in the whole product design;
- the state of scientific and technical knowledge was such that the producer would not be expected to have discovered the defect.

The last defence causes the most worrying problems, as it could mean that the manufacturer of a product such as the Thalidomide drug may not be liable for harm caused.

The Act then is not totally satisfactory, but takes consumer protection a further step forward.

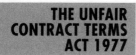

The Unfair Contract Terms Act 1977 stepped in largely to give protection to consumers who found that they were not protected because of either:

- a term in a written contract which they had not noticed or understood; or
- a notice which had become incorporated as a term of a contract.

These terms generally took the form of an exemption clause, that is one which either limits liability (a **limitation clause**) or excludes liability (an **exclusion clause**). Because consumers, with little bargaining power, were not able to negotiate over these terms, they were in an unfair position.

COMMON LAW PROTECTION

The common law restricts the use of them to some extent by requiring:

- incorporation as a term (see Chapter 16) – the term must not come too late (*Olley v Marlborough Court Hotel (1949)*) and it must be brought to the attention of the other party (*Thornton v Shoe Lane Parking (1971)*).
- construction to cover the damage caused (again, see Chapter 16) – the term must not offend the main purpose rule or the *contra proferentem* rule.

Added to these requirements now are the main provisions in the Unfair Contract Terms Act 1977.

- exemption from liability for death or personal injury caused by negligence will not be allowed;
- exemption from other liability caused by negligence will only be allowed if reasonable.

Schedule 2 of the Unfair Contract Terms Act 1977 makes some suggestions regarding reasonableness:

- the bargaining strength of the parties;
- whether any inducement was given to agree to the term;
- whether the customer knew of the term;
- whether the goods were specially manufactured.

See cases from Chapter 16 on reasonableness.

EUROPEAN DIRECTIVE

Again, Britain's membership of the European Union has had an effect on consumer protection, this time via the European Directive on Unfair Terms in Consumer Contracts (93/13) which came into effect at the beginning of July 1995. The directive considers terms which cause a 'significant imbalance' in the rights and duties under a contract, to the detriment of the consumer, 'contrary to the requirement of good faith'. (See Chapter 16.)

The general trend in protecting the consumer can be seen as a still growing area of law, particularly in light of our membership of the European Union.

THE CONSUMER CREDIT ACT 1974

When a consumer purchases goods using a credit card, this Act provides them with further protection, as an action may be brought against the credit card company where the price was between £100 and £30,000.

"Buying on credit"

For hire purchase goods the contract is between the consumer and the finance house, and an action may be brought against the finance house if the price was less than £15,000.

EXAMINATION QUESTIONS

1   'A manufacturer's guarantee provides a consumer with no rights and is therefore a worthless piece of paper.' Discuss.   (WJEC)

2   'The validity of a contract depends upon the relative bargaining strengths of the parties.' Discuss in relation to twentieth-century consumer protection legislation.   (WJEC)

3   Neddy bought an 'Estelle' watch for £200 from Stamwell Jewellery Store. It was advertised as 'being able, on the press of a button, to show the time in all the time zones of the world'. Ruth, the shop manager, had informed Neddy that in making this claim the shop had relied upon Estelle's sales publicity. When Neddy got home and tried out the facility, he found that it did not work.

Advise Neddy.   (WJEC)

4   A Ltd is a manufacturer of fire extinguishers and safety equipment. It has recently developed a new product which it describes as being the most efficient on the market for dealing with electrical fires because of a new chemical compound in the foam which the appliance uses. B, a retailer of safety equipment, buys 50 extinguishers and places them on immediate sale, adopting A's description of the product. C, a customer of B, buys an extinguisher which she finds necessary to use after only one week on a fire which has broken out in the electrical wiring of her car. The extinguisher is slow to act but after some delay the flames are put out. However, the heat from the fire causes the foam to vaporise and produce a toxic gas which seriously injures C.

What are the legal rights of C in this matter, and what are the liabilities of A Ltd and B?   (ULEAC)

5   A, wanting a refrigerator for his small flat, approached a retailer, B, who recommended a particular model priced at £100. Despite B's assurance, the refrigerator was too large to fit into A's kitchen. After a dispute between A and B, A decided to take possession of the

refrigerator, then giving it to his mother, C. C employed an electrician, D, to install a new electrical socket in her house for the refrigerator. D also installed the machine. Three days later the refrigerator ceased to function. C continued to use the new socket but now for her electric kettle. Because the socket had been wired incorrectly by D, an electrical fire was caused which damaged the kitchen.

What are the legal issues which these problems raise: What are the legal rights of the individuals concerned? (ULEAC)

ANSWERS TO QUESTIONS

OUTLINE ANSWERS TO SELECTED QUESTIONS

Question 1

The question is really asking what protection is available to a consumer against faulty manufacture, and suggesting that with the protection available the manufacturer's warranty gives no extra rights. However, this can be challenged to some extent, so say this in your introduction.

Then run through the protection available:

- the contract of sale and the position of the consumer;
- the Sale of Goods Act 1979 and the Sale and Supply of Goods Act 1994 for goods not of 'satisfactory quality' etc.;
- the Consumer Protection Act 1987 where damage is caused as a result of faulty goods;
- a brief mention of the Unfair Contract Terms Act 1977 regarding the exclusion of liability;
- the Consumer Credit Act 1974 regarding goods bought with a credit card.

You can now consider more specifically whether there is any advantage in buying goods with a manufacturer's warranty. You may like to include the following points:

- since the manufacturer uses this as a selling point, he is by implication suggesting that his product is of high quality, and therefore the consumer is entitled to expect a high standard in assessing 'satisfactory quality';
- there may be a faster route to a remedy with a warranty, as the manufacturer may have set a system in motion to deal with defective products more quickly than taking the company to court.

Question 4

The bulk of your answer will be the statutory provisions (see main chapter notes), but it is also relevant to state that common law provisions may be available:

- there may be liability in negligence for the injury to C;
- misrepresentation could be considered, although this is not a very fruitful route to a remedy as B relied on A's information;
- any possible criminal liability will similarly not produce a remedy for C;
- consider the Sale of Goods Act 1979 (as amended by the Sale and Supply of Goods Act 1994) ss. 13 to 15, regarding the terms implied into the contract between B and C;
- consider the Consumer Protection Act 1987 and the liability on A for the injury to C;
- consider the need to recall other extinguishers.

Conclude, responding to the question, on the extent of the protection now given to C as consumer, and the liability on A and B.

TUTOR'S ANSWER

Question 2

The long-established laissez-faire notion of a contract being formed between any two parties, over anything upon which they choose to agree, and with any terms which they negotiate, has been modified over the years by both common law and statute. One major difficulty with total freedom was that the parties often did not have equal bargaining strength, and the weaker party would then be in a 'take it or leave it' situation. This could lead to oppression on the part of the stronger party, and obvious unfairness.

The main inroad into this position has been this century, in the form of legislation designed to protect the consumer. Following the old 1893 Act, the Sale of Goods Act 1979 was a leap forward in aiming to provide built-in protection for the consumer in every contract of sale deemed to be a consumer contract. Now, where an ordinary individual buys from a person in business, in other words, a consumer sale, various conditions are automatically built into the contract, giving the consumer rights which would previously have needed to be negotiated. This does not make the contract as agreed any less valid, but adds terms to it, which protect the consumer, the party with less bargaining strength.

These rights, under sections 12 to 15, are that the seller has the right to sell; the goods will be as described; they will be of merchantable quality and fit for the purpose bought; and that, if a sample is shown, the rest of the goods will correspond with the sample. The new Sale and Supply of Goods Act 1994 has amended the requirement of merchantable quality to satisfactory quality. This gives the buyer automatic protection against faulty goods, and places a burden on the retailer to supply goods of reasonable quality.

Should goods be returned to the retailer, the remedy for the consumer is easy and immediate, compared with the previous position of having to prove breach of contract or find a manufacturer to sue. The retailer then may argue with the manufacturer over the faulty goods, but he is in a better position to do so, as he is in business. The resulting small increase in price passed on to the consumer is perfectly acceptable, in exchange for an assurance that he will obtain satisfactory goods without having to fight for this from a weak starting position.

The Unfair Contract Terms Act 1977 was also a great step forward, this time in protecting the consumer from unfair exemption clauses. The Act provides that a party may not exempt itself from liability for personal injury or death through negligence, and that exemption from other liability will only be allowed if it is reasonable.

This clearly prevents a party with greater bargaining strength relying on a clause which would have previously been used to escape liability towards the weaker party. Statements such as 'We do not accept liability for damage to persons or belongings, however caused' are now of limited effect. On the other hand, there is nothing at all wrong with a freely bargained term which provides for late delivery in return for a lower price.

A further recent development is in the European Directive on Unfair Terms in Consumer Contracts (93/13) which came into effect in 1995. This aims to give protection where there is a 'significant imbalance' in the rights and duties owed, to the detriment of the consumer, 'contrary to the requirements of good faith'. This is a slightly different approach from the present approach in English law, and exactly how it will be implemented remains to be seen.

Further protection is given to the consumer in the Consumer Protection Act 1987 and the Consumer Credit Act 1994, but these do not affect the contract of sale to the same extent as the legislation already discussed.

So to conclude it can be seen that the validity of a contract only depends on the relative bargaining strengths of the parties to the extent that it must be reasonable. The common law in some ways may render a contract invalid in such circumstances, e.g. if undue influence was found to exist. However legislation tends to add terms to a contract, as in the Sale of Goods Act 1979, or prevent terms from operating, as in the Unfair Contract Terms Act 1977, rather than destroy its validity altogether.

A review sheet for this chapter can be found on p. 222.

EMPLOYMENT LAW

THE CONTRACT OF EMPLOYMENT

DUTIES OF EMPLOYER/EMPLOYEE

TERMINATION OF EMPLOYMENT

DISCRIMINATION

GETTING STARTED

There have been many changes to employment law during the 1980s and 1990s. Some of these stem from political motives, as for example when the Conservative government limited the Trade Unions on matters such as secondary picketing. Other changes have come from European law, particularly on sex discrimination and health and safety issues.

There are several areas on which questions can be set, but the common ones are:

- **who is an employee** – distinguishing between independent contractors and employees;
- **duties of employers** – particularly on health and safety;
- **unfair dismissal**;
- **discrimination**.

Many of the problems in employment come from the termination of the contract and here are some key definitions:

- **wrongful dismissal** – this occurs when the employer fails to give any, or sufficient, notice of the termination of the contract;
- **unfair dismissal** – there is no valid reason for the dismissal;
- **constructive dismissal** – the employer treats the employee in such a way that the employee is forced to resign; this may also be wrongful dismissal and unfair dismissal.

THE CONTRACT OF EMPLOYMENT

ESSENTIAL PRINCIPLES

WHO IS AN EMPLOYEE?

The law distinguishes between a **contract of services** under which a person is employed, and a **contract for services**, where the person remains self-employed.

There are four main reasons for making this distinction:

1 An employer is obliged to deduct tax and national insurance contributions from employees' wages.

2 An employee has protection under employment law, especially against unfair dismissal and redundancy.

3 There are certain rights and duties implied into a contract of employment.

4 An employer is vicariously liable for the torts of employees, but is not normally legally responsible for independent contractors.

HOW TO DISTINGUISH BETWEEN AN EMPLOYEE AND AN INDEPENDENT CONTRACTOR

It is not always easy to decide if a person is employed or self-employed. Obviously, a starting point is to see what the parties believe the position to be; however, this is not conclusive. The courts have developed tests for making the decision:

1 **The control test** – this looks at whether the 'employer' is in control of what the alleged employee does at work. If the worker can be told what to do and the manner of doing it, then it is an employment situation.

2 **The integration test** – if the work done is an integral part of the employer's business, then there is a situation of employment; if the work is only an accessory to the business, then the person is self-employed.

3 **The economic reality test or the multiple test** – this is a broader test than the other two and looks at all the circumstances as well as control and integration (*Ready Mixed Concrete (South East) Ltd v Minister of Pensions and National Insurance (1968)*).

FORMATION OF THE CONTRACT

The normal rules of contract apply, so that an employment contract may be made verbally or in writing. The offer must be sufficiently clear so that an acceptance will form a binding contract.

Terms of the contract

The parties may agree specific terms. Obviously, these will include the actual work to be done and the rate of pay, but may also have terms about other matters, for example, geographical mobility of the employee, the length of notice to be given to terminate the contract or a restraint of trade clause which may affect the employee after he leaves that employment. Contracts usually also include implied terms, which may be implied by custom, union agreements, by statute or by the common law.

Written particulars of employment

Under the Employment Protection (Consolidation) Act 1978, an employer must give a written statement of employment to any employee who works at least one month. This statement must be given within two months of the start of the employment. It has to contain key facts:

- the names of the employer and the employee;
- the date when the employment began;
- the job title or brief description of the work;
- place and hours of working;
- rate of pay and when payment is made;
- length of notice.

There must also be information about holiday entitlement, sick pay, pension provisions, grievance procedure and disciplinary rules. However, this statement is *not* the contract of employment.

DUTIES OF EMPLOYER/ EMPLOYEE

THE DUTIES OF AN EMPLOYER

To pay wages

This does not mean that the employer has to provide work. In *Collier v Sunday Referee Publishing Company Ltd (1940)* the judge expressed the general rule by saying: 'Provided I pay my cook her wages regularly, she cannot complain if I choose to take any or all of my meals out.'

This rule does not apply:

- where the **employee's pay** depends on work, e.g. piecework or commission;
- where the **employee will lose skills** or qualifications, as with commercial pilots;
- where the **employee's reputation** may be damaged by not being employed, as with actors.

Health and safety

This is a very important duty of the employer. There are specific obligations set out in Acts of Parliament and regulations, but in addition to this the common law implies the following general obligations:

- a duty to provide a **safe system of work**;
- a duty to provide a **safe place of work**;
- a duty to provide **proper equipment**;
- a duty to provide **competent staff**.

"Common law protection"

Under the common law, an employee who is injured as a result of the employer breaching any of these may take an action for the tort of negligence (see Chapter 20 for fuller information on negligence). In *Paris v Stepney Borough Council (1951)* a motor mechanic was able to sue his employer successfully when the employer failed to provide him with protective goggles, although the employers knew that he was blind in one eye and so any injury to his good eye would be catastrophic. *Hudson v Ridge (1957)* provides an unusual example of a breach of duty to provide competent staff, where a known practical joker injured a fellow employee.

The **Health and Safety at Work etc Act 1974** is the main statutory provision. Section 2 places the employer under a general duty to ensure, so far as is reasonably practical, the health, safety and welfare of all employees.

To treat the employee with respect

An employer must treat employees with respect. This covers situations of bullying, sexual harassment and humiliating employees. If such behaviour forces the employee to leave work, then this is constructive dismissal and the employee may claim for wrongful and unfair dismissal.

To allow time off for public duties

Section 29 of the Employment Protection (Consolidation) Act 1978 states that an employer must allow employees time off, when necessary, to carry out public duties such as:

- sitting as a lay magistrate;
- being a local councillor;
- being a school governor.

The Trade Union and Labour Relations (Consolidation) Act 1992 ensures that trade union officials are allowed time off for their duties.

DUTIES OF THE EMPLOYEE

Obedience

An employee must obey all reasonable lawful instructions in connection with work. A serious breach of this duty may be grounds for instant dismissal, particularly if it is the culmination of several incidents, as in *Pepper v Webb (1969)*. An employee does not have to obey orders to do an illegal act or an order which would place the employee in physical danger.

To act in good faith

An employee must *not*:

- make a secret profit out of his employment; or

■ disclose confidential information or use it for his own gain.

If there is a restraint of trade clause in the contract, an employee may be prevented from using information or skills after he leaves that employer. However, the courts will not allow such clauses to be too wide in scope. The employer must show that there is some genuine interest to protect and that the restraint clause is not wider than needed for that protection. In *Mason v Provident Clothing and Supply Company (1913)* the restraint clause tried to prevent the ex-employee from competing within a 25-mile radius of London, even though she had only come into contact with her employer's customers in one part of London. This clause was held to be too wide and so not valid.

TERMINATION OF EMPLOYMENT

NOTICE

Notice must be given to terminate the contract. This rule applies to both employers and employees. The only exceptions are:

■ fixed term contracts which end automatically on the set date;

■ where there is a serious breach of the employee's duty which justifies instant dismissal;

■ where the employer's behaviour justifies the employee in leaving instantly.

Periods of notice

The contract of employment may include the length of notice to be given by each party. If there is no agreed period the Employment Protection (Consolidation) Act 1978 sets out minimum periods of notice. These are:

■ any *employee* who has worked for at least four weeks must give one week's notice;

■ an *employer* must give:

– one week's notice to any employee who has worked at least four weeks;

– two weeks' notice to an employee who has two years' continuous service;

– an extra week's notice for each years' service thereafter up to a maximum of twelve weeks.

It must be stressed that these are minimum periods and courts may decide that a longer period is justified in certain occupations.

UNFAIR DISMISSAL

The Employment Protection (Consolidation) Act 1978 and Trade Union and Labour Relations (Consolidation) Act 1992 state that the following reasons are considered **automatically unfair**:

■ pregnancy;

■ trade union membership or non-membership;

■ taking action over health and safety matters.

Potential fair reasons for dismissal

These are:

■ **misconduct** – this covers a wide range of misbehaviour including persistent lateness, disobedience or assaulting a fellow employee;

■ **incapacity** – this is assessed by considering the 'skill, aptitude, health or any other physical or mental quality' required for the work;

■ **employment in breach of the law** – this means it would be illegal to continue to employ the person, e.g. a bus driver who is disqualified from driving;

■ **redundancy** – the employer no longer has any work for the employee; the selection for redundancy must also be fair;

■ **some other substantial reason** – this has been held to cover a wide variety of situations, including a reorganisation of work where the employee refuses to co-operate, and a clash of personalities which seriously affects the employer's business.

Protected employees

Only employees who have been employed continuously for at least two years have the right to claim for unfair dismissal. However, where the claim is because of dismissal connected with sex discrimination, the employee is protected even in the first two years (*Webb v Emo Air Cargo (1994)*).

The following employees **cannot claim** for unfair dismissal:

- those over the age of 65 or over the retirement age for the particular job;
- those employed abroad.

Industrial tribunals

Claims for unfair dismissal must be made to an industrial tribunal. If successful the tribunal can order re-instatement or re-engagement (but this is rare) and award compensation.

REDUNDANCY

This is defined in s. 81 of the Employment Protection (Consolidation) Act 1978. Essentially, it means that the employer no longer has work for that particular employee. This may be because of a closure of one place of business or because of a lessening in demand.

Procedure

The employer should notify the Department of Employment and consult with any union involved on:

- ways of avoiding redundancies;
- reducing the number of employees affected;
- explaining the selection criteria.

Redundancy payment

This is calculated by taking the number of continuous years worked for the employer, up to a maximum of twenty, and applying the following:

- service after 41st birthday – one and a half weeks' pay per year;
- service from 22nd birthday to 41st birthday – one week's pay per year;
- service from 18th birthday to 22nd birthday – half a week's pay per year.

There is also a maximum wage which is applied and this is £210 per week, earnings over this figure are disregarded. This means that the statutory redundancy payment is very limited. However, an employer may be prepared to offer more to those who take voluntary redundancy.

DISCRIMINATION

SEX DISCRIMINATION

The **Equal Pay Act 1970** makes it unlawful to discriminate between men and women in terms of payment and other contractual conditions of employment, e.g. overtime or piecework payments. It is not necessary to be doing an identical job in order to claim, it is enough to show that the work is of equal value. A job evaluation study may be used to establish what work is considered as equal value.

The **Sex Discrimination Act 1975** makes other discriminatory practices unlawful. This includes:

- advertising for employees;
- deciding who to interview;
- selecting for employment;
- the terms on which a job is offered;
- benefits such as pension schemes or company cars;
- dismissals and redundancies.

There are **exceptions** when an employer *may* discriminate and these are:

- where the work is abroad;
- where sex is a genuine occupation qualification as in:
  - authenticity – modelling, acting;
  - privacy or decency – lavatory or changing room attendant;
  - personal services or welfare work; e.g. a counsellor to help rape victims.

RACIAL DISCRIMINATION

The **Race Relations Act 1976** makes it unlawful to discriminate against a person on the basis of racial grounds and this includes colour, race, nationality, ethnic or national origin. This applies to any area of employment including pay and all the same matters as in the Sex Discrimination Act 1975.

DIRECT AND INDIRECT DISCRIMINATION

Direct discrimination is where the person is treated less favourably because of their sex or race.

Indirect discrimination occurs when a condition is attached to a job which will exclude one sex or race more than others. To be considered indirect discrimination, the proportion of those who can comply must be considerably smaller; the condition must not be justified and it must be to the person's detriment.

EXAMINATION QUESTIONS

1   'Despite the many radical changes which have taken place in labour law, the distinction between a "contract of service" and a "contract for services" remains crucial.' Discuss.
(WJEC)

2   'It is contrary to both common sense and fairness that the law of the European Union can provide a remedy in sex discrimination cases but not generally in cases of racial discrimination.' Discuss.
(WJEC)

3   P, who is a qualified computer programmer, has been employed by Q for a period of ten years and has received additional specialised training. She recently became pregnant and, four months into her pregnancy, her employer informed her that she was dismissed as she could no longer perform her duties adequately and that she would not be taken back after the baby was born. As a result of these events Q went on to employ another person whom he had to train at considerable expense.

Consequently, Q has made a policy decision that he will only employ men in the future. P is now seriously concerned about her present and future financial position and job prospects.

Consider the validity of Q's actions and the rights of P in these circumstances.   (ULEAC)

4   John Mattas is a highly paid foreign exchange broker with ABC Merchant Bank plc. In his contract of employment, the period of notice stipulated is twenty weeks, but there is also a covenant restricting him from undertaking 'any work involving foreign currency in the United Kingdom for a two-year period upon termination of employment'. John Mattas has given in his notice and wishes to undertake foreign exchange currency work with Tooke Foreign Banking Services plc.

Advise ABC Merchant Bank plc.
(WJEC)

ANSWERS TO QUESTIONS

OUTLINE ANSWER

Question 1

Define what is meant by:

1   contract of service – employed status; and

2   contract for services – self employed status.

Point out the areas in which the distinction is crucial; these should include:

■ tax and national insurance obligations;

■ employer's duties to employees under health and safety legislation;

- protection from unfair dismissal for employees who have worked for two years;
- redundancy rights of employees;
- employer vicariously liable for acts of employees.

Discuss whether changes in the labour laws have materially affected any of these; the main conclusion is that employees now enjoy more protection in most areas and so the distinction remains crucial.

TUTOR'S ANSWER

Question 4

As John's contract included a restraint of trade covenant preventing him from undertaking 'any work involving foreign currency in the United Kingdom for a two-year period' after he leaves his employment with ABC Merchant Bank, it is clear that the bank will hope that this covenant can be enforced.

The courts are not very keen on enforcing such covenants and will usually only do so if it is reasonable in the circumstances. In order to decide this, two main points are considered. First, has the employer a genuine proprietary interest to protect? This can be clientele, confidential information or trade connections. Secondly, is the covenant drafted in such a way that it is no wider than is necessary to protect those interests?

Looking at the first point the courts are not prepared to allow such covenants to prevent what is considered to be merely healthy competition. This can be seen from the case of *Strange v Mann (1965)*, in which the manager of a bookmakers had agreed not to engage in similar business to his former employer within a twelve-mile radius. The court held that there was no genuine proprietary interest to be protected as the manager did not have any infuence over his former employer's clientele since he had mainly dealt with them over the phone. It is difficult to advise ABC Merchant Bank that they have a genuine proprietary interest to protect. A foreign exchange broker is unlikely to have any effect on clientele.

However, it may be possible to argue that John has acquired trade secrets or knowledge through his work with them and in such circumstances the courts may uphold the covenant as they did in *Forster and Sons v Suggett*, where the employee had knowledge of a secret glass-making process.

Even if the courts decide that there is a genuine proprietary interest to protect, ABC must be aware that the extent of the covenant can still be challenged as being unnecessarily wide. The actual clause needs to be considered in detail. There are three restrictions involved: first, the type of work ('any work involving foreign currency'); second, the area (which is the whole of the United Kingdom); and third, the length of time (which is two years). Taking this last point, two years is clearly not excessive and the courts would probably uphold this.

There are, however, problems with both the other two points. The requirement not to engage in any work involving foreign currency is effectively preventing John from earning his living in his normal occupation of foreign exchange broker and the courts may decide that this is unreasonable. In *Fellows & Sons v Fisher (1976)* a firm of solicitors sought to enforce a restraint clause under which a conveyancing clerk had agreed not to be employed or concerned in the legal profession. This attempt to exclude any work in the legal profession was thought to be unreasonable and declared void. This decision may well be followed in John's case and so ABC Merchant Bank would not be able to enforce the covenant.

The final point is the area involved. This is given as the whole of the United Kingdom and such clauses have been allowed where there was a need for such wide protection. However, ABC will have to persuade the court that there is such a need.

Overall, it is unlikely that ABC will succeed in enforcing the covenant.

STUDENT'S ANSWER WITH TUTOR'S COMMENTS

Question 3

❝A good starting point❞

The first point to realise in looking at Q's actions is that dismissing an employee because they are pregnant is one of the reasons that is considered automatically unfair under the Employment Protection (Consolidation) Act 1978.

Q claims that P is no longer able to perform her duties adequately. Even if this is true, it is not a fair reason for dismissing her, although before the Trade Union Reform and

Employment Rights Act 1993 (TURERA) it was possible for an employer to dismiss a pregnant employee if she was incapable of doing her job because of the pregnancy or there was a risk in relation to her health and safety. TURERA amended the Employment Protection (Consolidation) Act 1978 so that dismissal through pregnancy is automatically unfair. If there is a code of practice which recommends that pregnant women should not continue in that particular employment, then P can be suspended from work on maternity grounds if there is no other suitable employment for her to do. During any period of suspension P should be paid her normal wages.

It is also law that employees are entitled to maternity leave of 14 weeks, though this will not usually start until eleven weeks before the expected date of birth. Since P has been employed for more than two years she qualifies for maternity absence, which can be up to 40 weeks. She should also have the right to return to work at the end of her maternity absence.

Since P has been unfairly dismissed, she may make a claim to an industrial tribunal and is likely to receive a significant amount in compensation. Following the Marshall case, there is no limit on the amount the tribunal can award, and in cases brought against the Ministry of Defence for dismissing pregnant women from the forces, there have been some very high awards. P will have no problem in bringing a claim before a tribunal as she has been continuously employed by Q for ten years. Employees must be continuously employed for a minimum of two years to become protected employees and so able to claim for unfair dismissal.

Q's policy decision to employ only men in the future is also invalid. This is under the Sex Discrimination Act 1975 which makes it illegal to discriminate on the grounds of sex in advertising jobs, deciding who to interview and in selecting someone for a job. Q's policy decision is direct discrimination against women and may well lead to further claims against him.

> 66 Sensible application of up to date law 99

> 66 The two year rule does not apply to dismissals on the grounds of pregnancy 99

Tutor's Comments

A good understanding of most of the rights of pregnant employees. The only error is the failure to realise that a claim can be made for dismissal on the grounds of pregnancy at any time during employment as decided in *Webb v EMO Air Cargo 1994*, since unfavourable treatment on the grounds of pregnancy is automatically discrimination on the grounds of sex. The other point which could have been discussed is whether P has the right to be re-instated in her job. The powers of tribunals to order re-instatement or re-engagement are relevant.

Just worth a grade B.

A review sheet for this chapter can be found on p. 222.

24

RIGHTS AND FREEDOMS

THE EUROPEAN CONVENTION ON HUMAN RIGHTS

PROTECTION OF RIGHTS AND FREEDOMS IN ENGLISH LAW

GETTING STARTED

This chapter looks briefly at the protection of the rights and freedoms of the individual by the state and by the general law. Of course, many rights are protected by other areas of law, and these should be remembered, such as the right not to be hurt, the right to enjoy peaceful occupation of one's property, the freedom to contract, and the right not to have goods taken away.

The European Convention on Human Rights is a protection of an area of rights generally known as civil liberties, and this is examined in some detail in the chapter, together with the various English laws which stand along with the convention to protect the individual.

In answering examination questions, look for examples from areas of law with which you are familiar, and from real life, besides citing cases where appropriate. Remember that this is a topic which covers a wide range of legal principles, and these may be needed in answering examination questions.

ESSENTIAL PRINCIPLES

In this country a lot of our behaviour is based on the assumption that we have certain rights and freedoms in our actions and in our private lives, such as freedom of speech, religion and from discrimination. We often take these for granted, at least until something goes wrong, but they are, in many cases, protected by law. Some of these are longstanding and stem from old laws, such as the freedom given in the Magna Carta in 1215.

In Britain, unlike America and some other countries, we do not have a written constitution or a formal Bill of Rights, and many of our freedoms are not as formal as in other societies.

EUROPEAN CONVENTION ON HUMAN RIGHTS

The European Convention on Human Rights, formed after World War II, in 1950, consists of 32 members, including the United Kingdom. It was adopted by the Council of Europe, which is not part of the European Union, but is a larger organisation with wider membership. The European Court of Human Rights in Strasbourg was established in 1959 to protect the rights given in the convention. Individuals may apply directly to this, and member states may be reported by other member states. If necessary, and if no settlement is reached, the court will hear a case in full in order to give judgement.

FREEDOMS GIVEN UNDER THE EUROPEAN CONVENTION ON HUMAN RIGHTS

- **Article 1** provides that states which are parties to the convention (which includes the United Kingdom) 'shall secure to everyone within their jurisdiction' the rights and freedoms defined in Article 2 onwards.

The convention then lists various rights and freedoms which are deemed to be fundamental to members. Included are:

- **Article 2** – the right to life.
- **Article 3** – freedom from torture and inhuman or degrading treatment or punishment.
- **Article 4** – freedom from slavery.
- **Article 5** – the right to liberty of person, apart from lawful arrest or detention.
- **Article 6** – the right to a fair trial.
- **Article 7** – freedom from retroactive penal law.
- **Article 8** – the right to respect for private and family life, home and correspondence.
- **Article 9** – freedom of thought, conscience and religion.
- **Article 10** – freedom of expression.
- **Article 11** – freedom of peaceful assembly and association.
- **Article 12** – the right to marry.
- **Article 13** – the right to an effective remedy before a national authority if rights are violated.
- **Article 14** – freedom from discrimination in the exercise of the above rights.

PROTECTION OF RIGHTS AND FREEDOMS IN ENGLISH LAW

Many of these rights are now protected quite well in English law. For example:

- **The right to liberty** (Article 5) has been protected to some extent in English law from as far back as the Magna Carta, and today under legislation such as the Police and Criminal Evidence Act 1984 (see chapter 6).
- **Freedom of association** (Article 11) is mainly covered by trade union law, although there is not quite total freedom in this country (see the *GCHQ case (1984)* and the Prevention of Terrorism Act 1989).
- **Peaceful assembly** comes within the same Article and there is generally total freedom to meet in private in English law. However, there are some restrictions on meetings in public, for example where such meetings cause a breach of the peace, an obstruction of the highway (Highways Act 1980), where there is riot or disorder (Public Order Act 1986), and under the Criminal Justice and Public Order Act 1994 regarding measures aimed at 'rave' parties, 'New Age' travellers and hunt protesters.
- Statute law goes a long way to protecting **freedom from discrimination** under the Sex Discrimination Acts 1975 and 1986 and the Race Relations Act 1976. In addition, there is the

opportunity to bring cases to the Race Relations Tribunal, and both the Commission for Racial Equality and the Equal Opportunities Commission help to promote the intention of the legislation. Direct European law has also had a large impact on this area, cases being taken to the European Court of Justice.

- **Freedom of expression**, or speech (Article 11) exists to a large extent, and certainly more than in some countries, but is subject to limitations. One of these limitations is the law of defamation (see Chapter 21) which limits freedom to publish (in permanent or spoken form) untrue or derogatory statements about another person. The criminal law also limits the publication of material considered to be obscene, such as pornographic material. In addition, the law relating to contempt of court may prevent publication of material which is the subject of court proceedings (the *sub judice* rule) and information concerning children in court is only available with the permission of the court. State security may also, on occasions, limit freedom of speech.

❝Not every right fully protected❞

❝The balancing of conflicting rights❞

Not every right, then, is fully protected. The difficulty is often that the protection of one person's right may involve the limit of another person's freedom, and the law must balance the two. For example, we have seen already that the protection of privacy through defamation may lead to restriction in freedom of speech. The rights of an unborn child may conflict with the rights of a mother to treat her own body as she wishes. The right that some would claim to smoke cigarettes may conflict with the right that others would claim to a clean environment.

Some would argue that there should be a Bill of Rights that would formulate our national rights more clearly, rather than leave it to lawyers to 'find' them amongst the existing law. Others would prefer to adopt more positively the European Convention on Human Rights into European and national law. Whatever measures are taken, however, it can be seen that an absolute state of freedom cannot exist if an orderly society is to continue, and some restriction on a person's total liberty is sometimes necessary. The issue to decide is how far this should be allowed to go.

EXAMINATION QUESTIONS

1 By what means, and to what extent, does the European Convention on Human Rights protect the liberty of the individual? (WJEC)

2 By what means, and to what extent, does the law provide for the protection of an individual's privacy and reputation against intrusion by the newspapers and broadcasting media? (WJEC)

3 Last Saturday H, a member of a religious group, set up a platform of wooden boxes in the town centre and began to preach through a public address sound system to the passersby. Some of the crowd which gathered began to shout abuse at H. I, a policeman, observed and reported the incident and, as a result, twelve policemen arrived. H was asked to stop, but refused, and eventually the police had to carry him away. In the struggle which he put up H caused a policeman to fall and break a leg. Some of the onlookers took advantage of the confusion and, in a gang of twenty or so, began to run down the street frightening many shoppers and breaking some shop windows. The members of this gang have been identified by the police. H has informed the senior police officer in the town that in three days his religious group plans to hold another meeting in the town centre in a school hall after a procession through the town from the group's headquarters.

What actions might be taken by the police or by private individuals in respect of the events of last Saturday and the forthcoming meeting? (ULEAC)

ANSWERS TO QUESTIONS

OUTLINE ANSWERS TO SELECTED QUESTIONS

Question 1

- Introduce the European Convention on Human Rights and explain very briefly its origins and aims.

- Describe how its provisions may be enforced through the European Court of Human Rights, and consider the impact of this on individual states (UK being in breach, access by individuals).

- Discuss in detail the main protections given under the convention and examine the extent to which these are protected in English law.

- Consider whether there is a better method of providing this protection.

- Examine the balancing of rights and freedoms between individuals and between an indivual and the state.

Question 2

Introduce by explaining that there is no direct right to privacy in English law, but that the general notion of privacy is protected in a variety of ways. This may be an area that you could develop as a need for reform.

Outline the protections which exist:

- The law of defamation will prevent the media from publishing untrue or derogatory statements about a person, either in spoken form, i.e. slander, or written form, i.e. libel. See chapter 21. However this does not prevent in any way the publication of true statements which the individual does not wish to be known.

- The criminal law prevents the publication of material which is considered to be obscene or pornographic. However the views of individuals vary greatly on what is acceptable in this area, so material which a person may not wish to be published may not come within this law.

- Material which is the subject of legal proceedings may come within the *sub judice* rule, publication being prevented. In addition information concerning children is only available with the permission of the court.

- The right to respect for private and family life, home and correspondence is protected under the European Convention on Human Rights. This is good protection, but more difficult to access.

This 'package' of rights gives reasonable protection, but is not found in one comprehensive set of laws. It could be argued that this is an area in need of reform and codification.

In addition, the right to privacy must be balanced against the right to free expression and publication of information to the public. The right to free expression is also protected under the European Convention on Human Rights. Obviously a reasonable balance must be sought between these competing rights.

A review sheet for this chapter can be found on p. 223.

REVIEW SHEETS

Chapter 3

1   Explain the meaning of the phrase 'common law'?

_____

_____

_____

2   What is meant by the following?
   a)   *Ratio decidendi*

_____

_____

   b)   *Obiter dicta*

_____

_____

   c)   Binding precedent

_____

_____

   d)   Persuasive precedent

_____

_____

3   Explain the effect of the Practice Statement.

_____

_____

_____

4   What are the rules regarding the Court of Appeal:
   a)   following decisions of the House of Lords?

_____

_____

   b)   following its own previous decisions?

_____

_____

5   Outline the advantages and disadvantages of judicial precedent.

_____

_____

_____

_____

6   Why was there a conflict between equity and the common law?

_____

_____

_____

7 Describe four equitable remedies

_____

_____

_____

_____

Chapter 4

1 Briefly explain the stages a Bill goes through before it becomes an Act of Parliament.

_____

_____

_____

_____

2 What is meant by 'Parliamentary sovereignty'?

_____

_____

_____

_____

3 What is delegated legislation and who has the power to make it?

_____

_____

_____

_____

4 How does Parliament keep control over delegated legislation?

_____

_____

_____

_____

5 Give a brief explanation of:
   a) the literal rule

_____

_____

   b) the golden rule

_____

_____

   c) the mischief rule

_____

_____

6 Explain the conflict between the literal and the purposive approach.

_____

_____

_____

_____

7   What is meant in European law by vertical effect and horizontal effect?

_____

_____

_____

_____

Chapter 5

1   Explain in which court the following cases would be tried.
a)   A personal injury case in which the plaintiff is claiming £100,000.

_____

_____

b)   A case where the plaintiff is claiming damages of £1,500 for faulty goods.

_____

_____

2   What advantages are there in using the small claims procedure?

_____

_____

_____

_____

3   What appeals are possible in civil cases?

_____

_____

_____

_____

4   Consider the advantages and disadvantages of tribunals.

_____

_____

_____

_____

5   How are tribunals controlled?

_____

_____

_____

_____

6   When will arbitration be used?

_____

_____

_____

_____

7   What is meant by ADR?

_____

_____

_____

Chapter 6

1   Explain in which court the following cases would be tried:
    a)   A charge of drunk driving.

_____

_____

    b)   A case of theft.

_____

_____

    c)   A case of murder.

_____

_____

2   Explain the police powers under PACE to:
    a)   stop and search a person

_____

_____

    b)   search premises

_____

_____

    c)   arrest a suspect

_____

_____

3   What safeguards are there for a person who is detained for questioning in a police station?

_____

_____

_____

_____

4   What factors will the magistrates consider when deciding whether or not to grant bail?

_____

_____

_____

_____

5   Outline the types of cases heard in the Magistrates' Court.

_____

_____

_____

_____

6   What are the implications of choosing trial by jury?

_____

_____

_____

_____

7   What appeals are possible after a trial in the Magistrates' Court?

_____

_____

_____

_____

8   What protection is there against miscarriages of justice?

_____

_____

_____

_____

Chapter 7

1   Explain the difference between the work of barristers and solicitors.

_____

_____

2   What would be the advantages and disadvantages of fusing the two professions?

_____

_____

_____

_____

3   What distinctions are there between superior judges and inferior judges?

_____

_____

_____

4   What comments can be made about the composition of the judiciary?

_____

_____

_____

_____

5   How is the independence of the judiciary protected?

_____

_____

_____

_____

Chapter 8

1   How can a citizen obtain advice on a legal problem?

_____

_____

_____

_____

2   What are the means and merits tests in *civil* legal aid cases?

_____

_____

_____

_____

3   What is meant by the statutory charge?

_____

_____

_____

4   Explain the means and merits tests in *criminal* legal aid cases.

_____

_____

_____

_____

_____

5   What are the main criticisms of the legal aid schemes?

_____

_____

_____

_____

Chapter 9

1   Give the name for *qualified* magistrates.

_____

_____

2   How are *lay* magistrates appointed and what training do they receive?

_____

_____

_____

_____

3   What are the main problems of using *lay* magistrates?

_____

_____

_____

_____

4   Explain what is meant by:
    a)   disqualified from jury service

_____

_____

    b)   ineligible for jury service

_____

_____

c)   excusable as of right from jury service

5   Outline the main advantages and disadvantages of using juries in *criminal* cases.

6   In which types of *civil* cases can a jury be used?

7   What are the special problems of the use of juries in *civil* cases?

Chapter 10

1   Explain what is meant by *actus reus*?

2   When can an omission be suffiicent for the *actus reus* of a crime?

3   What are the main rules on intervening acts and their effect on the causation of a crime?

4   What is meant by *mens rea*?

5   Describe the approach of the courts to the concept of foresight of consequences in specific intent crimes.

_____

_____

_____

6   Explain what is meant by:
  a)   subjective recklessness

_____

_____

  b)   objective recklessness

_____

_____

7   What is transferred malice?

_____

_____

_____

8   When will the courts decide that a crime is one of strict liability?

_____

_____

_____

9   What justification is there for having crimes of strict liability?

_____

_____

_____

10 In what four ways can a secondary party be liable under the Accessories and Abettors Act 1861?

_____

_____

_____

11 What does the prosecution have to prove for a defendant to be guilty of an attempt?

_____

_____

_____

_____

Chapter 11

1   What is the legal definition of insanity?

_____

_____

_____

2   Explain the difference between insane automatism and non-insane automatism.

_____

_____

_____

_____

3   When will voluntary intoxication negate the *mens rea* of a crime and provide the defendant with a defence?

_____

_____

_____

_____

4   For which crimes is duress *not* a defence?

_____

_____

_____

_____

5   What factors are considered in the defence of duress?

_____

_____

_____

_____

Chapter 12

1   Give the definition of murder and explain the meaning of the phrase 'malice aforethought'.

_____

_____

_____

_____

2   When will diminished responsibility be a defence to a charge of murder?

_____

_____

_____

_____

3   Why is timing important in the defence of provocation?

_____

_____

_____

_____

4   What characteristics will the court consider for the defence of provocation?

_____

_____

_____

_____

5   What elements must be proved for constructive manslaughter?

_____

_____

_____

_____

6   Explain when a defendant will be guilty of manslaughter by gross negligence.

_____

_____

_____

_____

7   What is the *mens rea* required for a defendant to be guilty of assault or battery?

_____

_____

_____

_____

8   What is the difference between the *mens rea* required for the offences under s. 18 and s. 20 of the Offences Against the Person Act 1861?

_____

_____

_____

_____

Chapter 13

1   Give the definition of theft.

_____

_____

_____

_____

2   What does s. 2 of the Theft Act 1968 say about the meaning of 'dishonest'?

_____

_____

_____

_____

3   Define robbery and explain what makes it different to theft.

_____

_____

_____

_____

4   Explain the differences between committing burglary under s. 9(1)a and (1)b of the Theft Act 1968.

_____

_____

_____

5 Define the offence of obtaining property by deception.

_____

_____

_____

_____

6 What has to be proved for the offence of taking a conveyance without consent?

_____

_____

_____

_____

Chapter 14

1 What is the key difference between the retributive and utilitarian approaches to sentencing?

_____

_____

_____

_____

2 What are the four main principles in the utilitarian theory of sentencing?

_____

_____

_____

_____

3 What background factors might a court consider when sentencing an offender?

_____

_____

_____

_____

4 List the main types of sentences available for adult offenders.

_____

_____

_____

_____

Chapter 15

1 Identify three situations where goods for sale have been held to be an invitation to treat rather than an offer.

_____

_____

_____

_____

_____

2　List six ways in which an offer may be terminated.

_____

_____

_____

3　What is the postal rule and on which case is it based?

_____

_____

_____

_____

4　Give an example from case law to illustrate the point that past consideration is not valid. Why was payment enforced in *Lampleigh v Braithwait*?

_____

_____

_____

_____

_____

_____

5　What are the two presumptions applied by the courts in deciding whether legal intent is present?

_____

_____

_____

_____

6　Give an example, from case law, of the following :
　a)　Goods supplied to a minor which were not necessaries.

_____

_____

_____

　b)　A service provided to a minor which was a necessary.

_____

_____

_____

7　Outline the two important provisions of the Minors' Contracts Act 1987 which have helped remedy the imbalance which was felt to exist between minors and adults.

_____

_____

_____

Chapter 16

1   Identify four factors that the courts will take into account when deciding whether a statement is a term or a representation.

_____

_____

_____

_____

2   Which two questions, arising from the case of _Parker v S E Railway_, will the courts ask when deciding if a term is incorporated into a contract?

_____

_____

_____

_____

3   Which two tests do the courts use when implying terms into a contract?

_____

_____

_____

_____

4   Differentiate between a condition and a warranty.

_____

_____

_____

_____

5   Explain the use of an innominate term when a contract is breached.

_____

_____

_____

_____

6   What are the two main provisions of the Unfair Contract Terms Act 1977 in relation to exemption clauses?

_____

_____

_____

_____

7   Identify five established exceptions to the doctrine of privity.

_____

_____

_____

_____

8   Explain three situations where attempts have been made to avoid the strict doctrine of privity.

_____

_____

_____

_____

_____

_____

Chapter 17

1   List the four vitiating factors which could make an otherwise well formed contract invalid.

_____

_____

_____

_____

2   Define misrepresentation.

_____

_____

3   Is silence normally a misrepresentation?

_____

_____

4   Explain four ways in which rescission could be barred following a misrepresentation.

_____

_____

_____

_____

_____

_____

5   What is meant by *res extincta* in connection with the law of mistake in contract?

_____

_____

_____

_____

6   Why was an old lady's agreement held void in *Cumming v Ince*?

_____

_____

_____

7   Why was economic duress found to exist in *Atlas Express v Kafco*?

_____

_____

_____

8 When is undue influence presumed to exist?

_____

_____

_____

_____

9 How may this presumption be rebutted?

_____

_____

_____

_____

10 Why was the transaction set aside in *Barclays v O'Brien?*

_____

_____

_____

_____

Chapter 18

1 List four ways in which a contract may be discharged.

_____

_____

_____

_____

2 What is a severable contract?

_____

_____

_____

_____

3 How may a contract become frustrated?

_____

_____

_____

_____

4 Outline the main provisions of the Law Reform (Frustrated Contracts) Act 1943

_____

_____

_____

_____

_____

5　Differentiate between the loss of bargain basis and the reliance basis of assessing damages for breach of contract.

_____

_____

_____

_____

_____

_____

Chapter 19

1　How did Professor Winfield define tort?

_____

_____

_____

_____

2　Make one point of comparison between tort and criminal law, and one point of comparison between tort and the law of contract.

_____

_____

_____

_____

3　What is meant by vicarious liability?

_____

_____

4　Explain the meaning of the defence _volenti non fit injuria_.

_____

_____

_____

_____

5　What is an Act of God?

_____

_____

Chapter 20

1　What factors will the courts consider when deciding whether a duty of care is owed?

_____

_____

_____

_____

2　What points will be considered in deciding whether there has been a breach of duty?

_____

_____

_____

_____

3   Explain what is meant by:
   a)   *res ipsa loquitur*?

_____

_____

   b)   contributory negligence?

_____

_____

4   In nervous shock cases what three points must be proved?

_____

_____

_____

5   What differences are there in the duty owed to 'visitors' and 'non-visitors'?

_____

_____

_____

_____

Chapter 21

1   Explain the meaning of:
   a)   assault

_____

_____

   b)   battery

_____

_____

2   Explain the meaning of trespass to land.

_____

_____

_____

_____

3   What is meant by private nuisance?

_____

_____

_____

_____

4   Suggest some factors which the courts will consider when deciding whether behaviour is unreasonable enough to amount to private nuisance.

_____

_____

_____

_____

5   Differentiate between libel and slander.

_____

_____

_____

_____

_____

_____

Chapter 22

1   Why can a person who receives a gift from a friend not insist on a refund if a fault is discovered in the product?

_____

_____

_____

_____

2   a)   Who in law is a consumer?

_____

_____

b)   Why should a consumer need particular protection?

_____

_____

3   Which five terms are implied into all consumer contracts under sections 12 to 15 of the Sale of Goods Act 1979?

_____

_____

_____

_____

_____

4   What was the aim of the Supply of Goods and Services Act 1982?

_____

_____

_____

_____

5   What additional protection is provided for the consumer by the Consumer Protection Act 1987?

_____

_____

_____

_____

Chapter 23

1   How do the courts distinguish between an employee and an independent contractor?

_____

_____

_____

_____

2   What are the common law duties regarding an employer's observance of health and safety of his employees?

_____

_____

_____

_____

3   Explain what is meant by:
a)   unfair dismissal

_____

_____

b)   wrongful dismissal

_____

_____

c)   constructive dismissal

_____

_____

4   When may a dismissal be 'potentially fair'?

_____

_____

_____

_____

5   Explain how a redundancy payment is calculated.

_____

_____

_____

_____

Chapter 24

1   When was the European Convention on Human Rights formed, and where is the European Court of Human Rights situated?

_____

_____

2   Who may apply to the European Court of Human Rights?

_____

_____

_____

3   Name five rights and freedoms protected by the European Convention on Human Rights.

_____

_____

_____

_____

4   Identify three ways in which rights and freedoms are protected by English law.

_____

_____

_____

5   Identify two areas where a balance must be struck between conflicting rights and interests.

_____

_____

_____

_____

INDEX